THE SPIRITUALITY OF WESTERN CHRISTENDOM

The

Western

CISTERCIAN PUBLICATIONS, INC.

Spirituality of

Christendom

Introduction by JEAN LECLERCQ

Edited by E. ROZANNE ELDER

Kalamazoo, Michigan 49008 | *1976*

© Cistercian Publications Inc. 1976

Published for
The Medieval Institute &
The Institute of Cistercian Studies,
Western Michigan University

Cistercian Studies Series Nbr. 30

A Special Volume of the Series:

Studies in Medieval Culture

Available in Europe and The Commonwealth through
A. R., Mowbray & Co. Ltd.
Osney Mead, Oxford OX2 OEG

Set and printed in the United States of America by
Printing Services, Western Michigan University

Library of Congress Cataloging in Publication Nbr. 76-22615
ISBN 0 87907 987 8

To

JEAN LECLERCQ

Doctor egregius et praeclarus

Personal rebirth is the work of the divine Spirit, but it is also the fulfilling and perfecting of the basically spiritual constitution of man, the 'existent' being who has a freedom and a creativity that makes him more than just another item in the inventory of created things. Man 'stands out' from all other creatures on earth and has the possibility of exience, of going out and transcending himself into a fuller form of life. This possibility was his from the moment that breath or spirit was breathed into him by God, bestowing on him the divine image and the possibility of closeness to God and participation in the divine life. Already then we have gone far toward establishing the thesis . . . that spirituality is, in simple terms, the process of becoming a person in the fullest sense.

John Macquarrie
Paths in Spirituality

Paths in Spirituality (New York: Harper and Row, 1972) pp. 46-7. Quoted by permission.

Preface

Technology characterizes western civilization today. By rational analysis and objectivity, western man provides for his comfort, his longevity, and therefore, he hopes, his happiness. Fifty years ago few voices could be heard to dissent from this creed. Today we are hearing new cries—most vociferously from the young—cries expressing serious doubts that happiness lies in better tooth-paste and faster rockets. Instead of proclaiming a better world in greater comfort and efficiency, some westerners have renewed the search for intellectual and spiritual values which, they argue, have been cast aside in our battle to conquer the microbe and tame the environment. Instead of demanding happiness through material conveniences, they desire a happiness based not on greater comfort, but on a knowledge of humanity's place in the world of plants and other animals. A knowledge of each man's deepest self, unmasked from the *persona* behind which he hides, even from himself. A knowledge about life and intelligence which may surpass man's finite limitations and the foibles of his domination. A knowledge of what is and of our response to what is.

Many of these anti-materialist malcontents are turning to psychology and the scientific tools it gives to the inner search. Many are turning to the eastern traditions of Zen and Yoga. Many, through ignorance or despair, have not even considered the tradition on which the rapidly-vanishing spiritual values of their own culture is based.

The pursuit of happiness is not new. All persons at all times and in all cultures have sought it. In the western world, Christianity provided the foundations for this search for fifteen hundred years—without serious rival until the industrial, scientific, and political revolutions nudged aside spiritual values and replaced them with ideologies.

Successive generations lived their culture, borrowed from their predecessors, and bequeathed to their progeny a synthesis which in the course of two millenia created western civilization. Roman practicality drew on hellenistic intellectualism. Christianity fused both practicality and philosophical inquiry to its faith in the revelation of God. The germanic tribesmen who overran Europe at the end of antiquity assimilated what they could understand and, through the very few literate men who remained, kept tucked away what they could not. Western art, institutions, literature, philosophy, theology, and even superstitions all reflect the interweaving of these cultural strands in the tapestry of a uniquely western spirituality. It is a spirituality which expressed itself most articulately in the Middle Ages, but it endures today in being affirmed or rejected in every aspect of western civilization.

It is this western christian spirituality, this peculiarly occidental approach to the realities of man and nature and God, which this volume explores. The articles here were originally presented as lectures during a three-week workshop at which scholars from several academic disciplines explored the roots and expressions of western spirituality by analysing specific persons within the tradition. There is a wide variation in the manner of presentation and in the methodology, and therefore in the presuppositions, of the speakers.

Scholar-in-residence during the workshop was Jean Leclercq, perhaps our generation's best known student of medieval spirituality, a man with an encyclopaedic command of his subject and an infectious enthusiasm for sharing it. Each evening he and the day's lecturer held colloquium, inviting questions from members for the workshop and casting new light not only on the past but on the present.

We regret that not all the papers read during the three weeks could be included in this volume. They were all stimulating and each contributed a unique insight. Robert

M. Grant of the University of Chicago began the workshop
with an examination of the foundation documents of
christian spirituality, the writings of John and Paul—texts
to which other speakers continually referred back. John
Eudes Bamberger of the Cistercian Abbey of the Genesee
spoke on the teachings of Evagrius Ponticus, a fourth century monk who set the course of western asceticism. Edmund Colledge of the Pontifical Institute of Mediaeval
Studies, Toronto, reported on the critical edition which he
and James Walsh have made of Julian of Norwich's
*Revelations of Divine Love.** Cornelius J. Dyck of the
Associated Mennonite Biblical Seminaries, Elkhart, In-
diana, traced the intensely scriptural spiritualities of sixteenth-century Anabaptism.

Supplementary lectures illuminated other expressions
of western spirituality. John Cook of Yale University, who
was spending the summer as visiting lecturer at neigh-
boring Kalamazoo College, was prevailed upon to deliver
an illustrated lecture on *Gothic Art: Medieval Spirituality
in Stone.* Thomas Seiler of Western Michigan University
took on the formidable task of preparing two lectures: one
on the Grail legends of the High Middle Ages, and a second
on the spirituality of Dante.

One paper is included here which was presented not at
the seminar itself, but at the Conference on Medieval
Studies the preceeding May. Keith J. Egan's study of the
theology of the monastic life was pirated shamelessly from
the 'mother-journal' of this volume, *Studies in Medieval
Culture,* because it articulated so succinctly the monastic
spirituality of the west. Because the monks dominated the
spiritual life of the medieval church, thereby providing the
approach to God most violently reacted against at the
Reformation, Professor Egan's study provides invaluable
insights to several other papers.

Some fifty persons took part in the workshop. Members
included practising scholars, professors of literature and
history, protestant and catholic pastors, graduate and un-
dergraduate students. In addition to attending and
discussing the sweeping array of lectures for three weeks

and coping with a Kalamazoo July, they spent untold hours reading pertinent texts—whenever possible in the original Latin.

The Spirituality of Western Christendom workshop was an experiment for the Medieval Institute and the Institute of Cistercian Studies. We are grateful to the National Endowment for the Humanities for the grant which made it possible and to all those who worked for it and participated in it. We owe a special debt of gratitude to Jean Leclercq for his generosity in sharing three weeks from his busy life with us and by his insights unifying disparate lectures into a cohesive whole. The enthusiasm of the members—lecturers and auditors—made the workshop a heady experience and one which we are eager to repeat. For we are convinced that without a knowledge of his own past, western man cannot discern the direction in which he moves. He can only frustrate himself by groping in circles, neither affirming nor rejecting the influences which have made him what he is and his world what it is. He can be only an outsider, envying the traditions of others yet blind to his own, and therefore to himself.

E.R.E.

* This paper will appear in the journal *Mediaeval Studies* (1976).

TABLE OF CONTENTS

INTRODUCTION

By Jean Leclercq

The present volume deals with the spiritual tradition of Western Christendom and studies it for its sake, without separating it from other traditions and without reference to those spiritualities which reject or ignore Jesus Christ. In this respect, the text's approach is distinctive. That other traditions are also studied is a matter of rejoicing. In the past, and in particular during the last several decades, Far Eastern spiritualities have been under consideration in the West and Christian scholars have studied the Near Eastern tradition known as Islam. For several years, such diverse circumstances as powerful material support and in some instances competent scholarly activity—motives not always religious in nature—have led to increased writings on Islam. It is not always easy to dismiss the impression that if this process continues, the Christian tradition which made the Western world what it is will survive only in popular piety, where it is alive, deeply rooted, but not fully developed. Therefore it was important to strive to reveal it, to reflect upon it, to live with the joy it can bring.

Such a goal was attempted during the 1975 Summer Program of the Institute for Cistercian Studies and The Medieval Institute at Western Michigan University. For several weeks, some fifty researchers, students and professors of various backgrounds, shared their time, dividing their interests between study and personal and communal reflection and, if they wished, engaging in various forms of prayer. All of these activities can justly be called contemplative. A written account cannot fully express the joy, the calm enthusiasm, the happy weeks shared by the participants. Before presenting some of the papers which were delivered, then discussed, it is necessary to recall that they take their full meaning, especially in this instance, only in the context of the shared experience. It is hoped that these topics may also lead the reader to a similar experience.

Let us state here the program's intention: the study of Christian spirituality in the Western world from an interdisciplinary point of view. First, a clarification of *spirituality:* further review of the term will be in order, but at this point we must assert that the study of the reality it encompasses implies history and theology. History, because the living experience was and remains a fact or, more precisely, a comprehensive whole, an extended series of facts, which can and must undergo an objective scrutiny based upon the identification of manifestations of the spiritual life, of the influences exerted on them, of the sources from which they derive and of the expressions they have been given in various areas, such as literature, art, and institutions. These facts, once known, verified, and organized, must be subjected to an analysis made possible by theology, in the traditional sense, that is, theology which includes confrontation with faith, enlightenment by reason, and the effort of comprehension from any human being seeking God and therefore already found by him. There is in any theology worthy of the name a meeting and a dialogue of love. In turn, theological reflection activates psychology, sociology, linguistics: disciplines known to help man to know himself better. An experience of our relationship to God took place before us, continues within us and, we are assured, will remain after us. Theological effort places us at the very center of the great current of life, brings us close to its source, and compels us to share it with others, unable as we are to keep to ourselves alone the joy of knowing we are loved.

Western as it is, this Christian spirituality does not exclude other spiritual currents springing forth from Jesus Christ's message. On the contrary, it can only be understood in relation to the entire Eastern Christian heritage from which it gained so much. Western Christianity, with its explicit connection to the Incarnation of God in Jesus Christ, sets itself apart, however, from the great and rich traditions of Africa, Oceania and pre-Columbian America as well as from those studied most frequently today: the religious traditions of Far Eastern Asia, and Judaism and Islam in the Near East. Christian tradition will be able to integrate all the values God placed in all traditions to the extent that it preserves its own identity, without merging, without leaning towards a syncretism in which all the traditions would deteriorate. The very necessity of remaining faithful to Christianity, particularly as it was lived in this western part of Christendom, assumes that we must know first our own heritage's distinctive values. If that condition is fulfilled, then, without losing our values in the context of a larger religious background, we will be able to situate them, to enrich them with the values of non-Western Christian traditions as well as with those of non-Christian religions.

One of the joys experienced during the 1975 Summer Program was to observe the representatives of various Christian churches trying to share their own traditions, to empathize with others, to see—beyond what still separates them—something of greater importance, what unites them. The successive chapters in this volume reflect this idea: they do not present a summary of everything that could have been said, nor do they offer a premature synthesis of all that is common to the periods and movements represented. Instead they present a spectrum of typical examples, each having its riches and its limitations.

Following this Introduction, a brief overview of the principle themes discussed will be given, recalling in particular the discussions which followed the presentation. Then some general conclusions will be drawn concerning the notion of 'spirituality' and finally a few remarks of the state of its study today.

A Beginning: Augustine

Because the lectures given are easily available for reading, there is no need to summarize here. Nevertheless, it will be useful to reiterate a basic element which emerged in the course of all the discussions: to realize the importance of vocabulary. Ever since the Word became man and spoke the language of his own culture, and his witnesses transmitted and interpreted his message in the language of their own culture, human words have received a new dignity. They have become a way to express the divine. The richness and the nuances unique to each of them must be respected and scrutinized. There is a sacred philology, and the history and the theology of spirituality doubtlessly constitute the area where it is most important.[1]

This was apparent from the very beginning in Vernon J. Bourke's lecture on St Augustine, whose experience, thought, and language were to exercise a decisive influence on subsequent evolution down to our time. Before becoming a thinker, and in the process of becoming one, Augustine was first a man, a unique and concrete person: an African, a student in a large Roman city in Italy; struggling with a long and painful inner crisis, meeting a man named Ambrose, reading Bishop Athanasius' account of the life of Anthony; a convert from Manicheism to Christianity, the founder of communities for clerics, monks, and religious, the local bishop of Hippo, a universal teacher, a dialectician using his skills to engage in the fight against sometimes conflicting heresies. It is in the midst of all these daily experiences and because of them that he reflected upon the Christian mystery, and primarily as he experienced it himself. His entire philosophy and theology would always be based on a metaphysic of conversion, a particular conversion: his own. Augustine knew that the Universal could only be reached through the personal. 'Oh fool, who believes I am not thee!' exclaimed a nineteenth-century French poet.

Professor Bourke was indeed inspired in presenting Augustine's teachings not in the guise of an abstract syn-

thesis done once and for all. Instead he presented it according to a chronological order, allowing us to witness the
saint's progressive formation, which resembled a large
river not so much calmly crossing vast plains along which it
enriched itself with new deposits as meandering, being
diverted, cascading downwards, being interrupted. When,
towards the end of his life, the Bishop of Hippo decided to
consider again everything he had ever written, he did not
remember in his *Retractations* all of his works, the dates or
the conditions under which he had written them, so active
had his life been. And yet his life had not been unsettled.
He maintained a peace, a mastery of self which allowed him
to reconcile opposing aspects of the Christian mystery. The
contrast in emphasis which Augustine put on one or
another aspect of Christianity is disconcerting to a few contemporary historians. One must be a skillful master to
manage all of Augustine's teachings, a task successfully accomplished by Etienne Gilson and Vernon J. Bourke.
Against the Pelagians who attributed too much power to
nature in the acquisition of salvation, it was necessary to affirm that in this order everything comes from God and, in
this sense, to affirm that nature is not enough. But against
the Manicheans, who disparaged nature to an extreme, he
had to prove that everything in nature is not bad. The body
itself has great dignity, to be manifested at the time of the
resurrection, a subject treated in a memorable lecture by H.
I. Marrou.[2]

In the same way, Professor Bourke has us witnessing
the progression by which Augustine's personality
developed: the first period when his dual activity as a
pastor, preaching and catechizing, and a polemicist,
engaging in controversy, gave him the opportunity of perceiving and explaining the successive levels by which he
moved from a psychological experience of things religious
to a theological reflexion on its content. Next came the
period of full activity during which everything was transformed more explicitly than ever before into an act of love.
This was the time of the great works of mystical theology,
the *Confessions* and *On the Trinity*. Affective fervor and

speculative analysis grew simultaneously. They led eventually to the works of the third period of complete spiritual maturity, when love recognized increasingly clearly that all is grace, that all comes from God, and that man's principle duty is to be in a state of grace, i.e., expectant, receptive, welcoming, grateful. Augustine's great works on grace, faith, hope and charity, freedom and predestination were written at this time, all of them finding perfect conciliation in the extraordinary historical-sociological synthesis known as *The City of God*.

During the long inner evolution and outer activity marking his career, Augustine remained completely a pastor and a monk. Even as bishop, he never lost the interest in monks which he had shown at the time of his conversion and of his return to Africa. His work as a bishop and battler against everything divisive in Christianity had reinforced in him a conviction and, in the best sense of the word, an obsession with the common good, the unity of the Church, the active communion among Christians. He reminded the monks of Africa, the 'hippies' of the fifth century, that their duty was to work for this and not to divide the Church over their too abundant hair, which disconcerted the faithful. He believed that keeping a certain distance from the world, and for monks a real separation from the world, was prerequisite to an authentic presence in the world, just as he reacted negatively to any aberrant form of counter culture.

It is against this socio-psychological and cultural backdrop that the vocabulary of the text presented by Professor Bourke takes on its full significance. Growth of an experience? What is more significant in this regard than Augustine's own words in the *Confessions* (from chapter 16 to 18 of l.7): 'And I saw *(et vidi)* . . . and I felt through experience *(et sensi expertus)* . . . I admired *(et miratar)* . . . I became certain *(eramque artissimus)* . . . I had found *(inveneram)* . . . I rose up to the intelligence *(erexit se ad intelligentiam suam)* . . . And I succeeded in seeing, as in a flash *(ictus trepidantis aspectus)* . . . and contemplating what I had understood *(intellecta comperi)*. But I was not able to maintain my gaze at this level of splendor (*sed aciem figere non evalui*), and I fell, as if struck by my own weakness (*repercussa infirmitate*).'

How many decisive elements there are in such a page for the entire spiritual evolution of the West: the theory of the Fall, as if struck by a blow (the *reverberatio* expressed by St Gregory the Great); degrees of mystical experience expressed in similar terms and perhaps inspired by the same source in Bernard's works; intuition of God as that which can be conceived as the greatest, will say St Anselm, the best, will echo Bernard. Much of it is highlighted and enriched by allusions to weight *(pondere meo)*, one of St Gregory's favorite themes, to true self-knowledge (*me esse*), a theme common to St Bernard, William of Saint Thierry, and Luther. All of these are presented in a tone of 'confession,' a style eventually adopted by John of Fécamp and many others. Another text, chapter 24 of 1.22 in *The Trinity* was also discussed and completed the evocation of the spiritual experience by recalling the reconciliation possible and necessary between man's consciousness of his misery and the faith he has in his own importance and dignity because he has been created in God's image. As to the importance of the Epistle to the Romans as a privileged source of any theology of sin, grace, and regained freedom to choose God, it was to become the foundation of the theology of St Bernard, of Luther and of many others just as it had been for St Augustine. St Bernard was to rewrite for his time, but under the same title, Augustine's *De gratia et libero arbitrio*. Luther, as we know, would modify the statement, but the problem and the key words used in its formulation—even if leading to different conclusions—had been brought to the attention of the Western world by Augustine of Hippo.

THE ORIENTAL CONTRIBUTION

Because of his influence, Augustine deserves to have special attention paid to his teachings. Very early, however, a new current from the Orient came to enrich the Western tradition, which already owed much to the Christianized platonism of the first centuries. This is the contribution made by the East first through its ancient monasticism and then through the thinker Dionysius.

During the Summer Program, Abbot John Eudes Bamberger spoke of Evagrius and Cassian. Although his lectures are not included in this volume, they must be given a place in this Introduction, for without the monasticism of the Orient, as without Augustine, nothing which follows can be explained. J. E. Bamberger is at the same time both a psychologist by professional training and an Orientalist. In the latter capacity he has specialized in Evagrius Ponticus, a fourth century writer whose works offer ample material for reflection by historians, psychologists, and theologians. A theorist of what was for most Eastern Christian monks a *praxis* lived but not explained, Evagrius himself had learned much from Origen, that genial third century innovator, outstanding poet, and fervent lover of the Word of God. Like Augustine and like Western spiritual writers, especially within the monastic tradition, Evagrius chooses experience as his point of departure. He devotes major importance to the psychological analysis of states of mind such as *acedia,* a sort of religious 'spleen' whose meaning is quite complex and rather ambiguous. He examines also the temptations to instability, the need to move. In all these spiritual situations, judgment must come from a sound theology and the judicious use of psychological methods. In the course of his presentation and during the discussion, Father Bamberger suggested enlightening parallels, at times similarities and at others differences, with the Far Eastern traditions, Zen in particular, and with the problems raised by modern psychologists since Freud. It was encouraging to observe that certain neurasthenic states, often benign but still sources of conflict, were already realities to the monks of antiquity whom we so easily tend to idealize.

'Just in case you think you are normal!' was the provocative title of a lecture in a psychology program. If we today reject the notion that 'normal people' do exist (how

boring it would be to live with them!), then it becomes
necessary to complement the means of resolving conflicts
laid out by antiquity with those gained through the newer
psychological discoveries of recent times. In the past, there
was a casual tendency to classify each individual in some
very general categories. Today we know that 'everybody is a
case.' The fundamental criteria for discerning spirits
remain the same as in antiquity, from St Paul to Evagrius
to Ignatius of Loyola: purification of the heart, which
means, of intentions and motivations; obedience to the
Word of God; the need to study theology in a climate of
prayer, but even more, to make theology a prayer and
prayer a theology, as we hear in the Ignatian maxim: 'El
estudio hecho oracion,' study become prayer. This
teaching, so rich and nuanced that we can only summarize
by simplifying it, has exercised an influence on all subsequent Western traditions, either directly, thanks to early
Latin translations of Evagrius, or through intermediate
writers who had assimilated this doctrine and expressed it
in florilegia or personal syntheses.

J. E. Bamberger chose Cassian's writings as a case in
point, and for his demonstration distributed copies of
chapters 3 through 14 of *The Ninth Conference,* one of
Cassian's major texts, in which he recounts Abbot Isaac's
views on prayer. In this important text Augustinian
language is obvious, as is a vocabulary which would eventually become part of St Benedict's rule. It is also a very
coherent theology of 'perpetual prayer.' This formula,
derived from several passages in the New Testament, inspired the monks' centuries-old practices. The central idea
always remains 'purity of heart,' and consequently the
prayer rising from it has a specific goal: contemplation.
Conditions leading to this are humility, obedience, humble
service to the brothers. The results can be summarized in a
litany of terms, each bringing to mind an aspect of the unspeakable peace the sinner can achieve through God's
grace: tranquility, serenity, stability, solidity, firmness,
rest, leisure, sabbath, free spiritual breath. Temptations,
tensions, and difficulties are not lacking, but they have

ceased to be obstacles; they have instead become means to
inner peace. They do not separate man from God, they are
the opportunities of reaffirming unity with him. The common goal is realized by each man according to his own
limits, in conformity with his own nature and the grace he
receives. Anticipating a word which will begin each chapter
of the third part of St Gregory's *Rule for Pastors,* Cassian
repeats a dozen times *aliter.* Each person stands in the
presence of God 'in a different way,' yet it is always the
presence of a forgiven sinner before God. Each person
shares the same attitude, the same expectancy, the same
desire for God, the same obscure and veiled yet sure and
joyous beginning of what is to be the boundless joy of
heaven. Personal history and eschatology, self-renunciation
and allegiance to him who can fill us with his being and
happiness, simplicity surpassing any duplicity, any com-
plicity, and multiplicity, any complexity, and an inner unity
which we today call 'psychic integration,' are not utopian
gifts. Those who have experienced this unity can attest to it;
each of them in expressing it bears the mark of his cultural
limitations. Still, these two great witnesses, Evagrius and
Cassian, give confidence in a tradition which reconciles
lofty aspiration with a sense of reality.

It fell to Guntram Bischoff to illustrate the contribution
of another great witness from Eastern Christianity,
Dionysius, who, to inner experience acquired through
monasticism, was able to add a vast systematization in
which the liturgical rites appear as a means first to prepare
the experience, and then to express it. The lecturer was
careful to define thoroughly some of the words he
used—words sometimes grossly abused by others—in particular, the terms *mythical* and *gnostic.* Each has its own
history and neither should be used without consideration of
its entire literary and cultural context. This task was accomplished with elaborate finesse by Professor Bischoff.
Without summarizing, I think it sufficient to indicate that
here again the basic problem was a unity waiting to be
rediscovered, a reintegration remedying disintegration, a
fulfillment beginning in this life waiting for full

eschatological realization. As this level of transcendent and universal realities, it is legitimate to suggest a few similarities with some basic principles of Hinduism and other non-Christian traditions. All converge toward an absolute unity but they must be led there through humble channels and it is our duty to recognize the limits and the necessity of the voyage.

A GREAT CENTURY

The history of religious, or other, culture—and we can almost say, religious and other culture—is a rich terrain, the result of successive and superimposed geological layers: the fertile surface would not exist if the lower strata did not make possible the appearance of life. From time to time during the great transformations known in sociology and geology as mutations, new species arise. From hidden depths sources spring forth, and their waters, on contact with each level, carry new elements, acquire chemical and radioactive properties, giving these thermal things healthful properties that defy analysis or explanation. And so it is that after eleven hundred years of successive enrichment, the twelfth century is the first of the great periods which, while maintaining continuity with the past, bore new fruit: new religious institutions, new types of men and women living an intense spiritual life, new political, social, psychological problems, new solutions, new and abundant writings. In this golden century many representatives could have been chosen, among them, Abelard, John of Salisbury, Chrétien de Troyes, Hildegard, Elizabeth of Schönau—the list is endless. Three names were singled out during the Summer Program, and were presented by scholars whose scientific competence matched the enthusiasm they brought to the subject.

To speak of St Bernard of Clairvaux is no easy task after everything that has already been said and written about this attractive and disconcerting personality, a charming and irritating man with whom it is difficult to remain objective and detached. The 'solidity' of John R. Sommerfeldt was needed. His long-time acquaintance with the Abbot of Clairvaux, his contained enthusiasm, well measured and motivated, made him the ideal candidate to pick up the challenge and to dare to situate, in a sociolgical context, the historical monument, the force of nature and of grace that was Bernard, in the midst of his contemporaries, most of whom were far from being equal to this giant. How was this powerful personality going to react among so many ordinary and often mediocre people? Professor Sommerfeldt's masterful presentation was complemented by a minute analysis of texts in which every element was taken into consideration: the beauty emanating from the quality of the images and the musicality of the style, the doctrinal density enhanced by a vocabulary extremely rich in traditional echoes and new nuances.

As did Augustine and many others after him, Bernard found himself confronted, within as well as without, with a double reality: the misery of man, born of a race marred by sin, and man's nobility, rooted in the fact that he has been created and recreated in God's image. Of great importance—as with Augustine—is the theme of passage, the phenomenon of continual conversion leading from 'infancy' (*anima puerilis*) to the maturity of 'adulthood' (*ad perfectam aetatem*). Bernard mentioned in the *First Sermon on the Canticle,* and again expresses it in the *Fourth Sermon* as moving from the beginning first steps *(primordia)* to achievement *(perfectio).* The condition for the process and the ever present guide on this itinerary is the humility solemnly taught in *Sermon 34,* and expressed with exhuberant humor at the end of *Epistle 87,* in which Bernard compares himself to an *ioculator* who, reversing all balance of values, walks on his hands, feet in the air. In all the texts presented—the seventh and ninth chapters of *Degrees of Humility,* the fortieth chapter of *Sermons,* Letter 142—we witness real scenes of juggling in which Bernard was playing with words, their sounds, prefixes and endings, and also tossing about ideas as a poet of genius throws in all directions, without apparent order, suggestive images and enchanting sonorities. Profound and powerful order does exist: it is born of love seemingly ignoring dialectic reasoning because its own 'weight'—to use St Augustine's and St Gregory's word—brings it back to its center. There at last, man finds his unity; he reconciles all his instinctive and anarchic pulsations, all the spiritual and sublime aspirations which make him a mystery to himself. He attains stability, that is, faithfulness to God, in his perseverance in serving him. He finally discovers the universality of love: *ad latitudinem transeam caritatis.* But it all began in the experience of the self, and it is this humility once accepted, interpreted, and understood which leads to joy, a sort of flight—'who will give me the wings of a dove?'—a wish to be fully satisfied in the eschatology totally revealed, but already partly fulfilled in an eschatology begun. These basic intuitions common to all men who have received God's light had been formulated previously by St Paul, St Augustine, Cassian and many others. Bernard gave them a rejuvenated expression and, after him, Luther and others also expressed them. Interpretations given, consequences drawn may vary, but the fact remains that at a time of great spiritual awakening, an exceptional man of God had given the 'start' signal for a new probe into the mystery of man.

At the beginning of this mutation in the history of spirituality, William of Saint Thierry, a friend of Bernard, played a role almost as important as did Bernard himself. Among William's works his masterpiece, *The Letter to the Brothers of Mont Dieu,* written for Carthusian monks, stands out. E. Rozanne Elder presented William of Saint Thierry with a wealth of precise scientific information combined with that great psychological depth in which women excel. The task was not easy, given the refined subtleties of the language, vocabulary and thought of William, the aristocrat of theology. He, at least more often than Bernard, had taken the trouble to elaborate his teachings in synthetic form. Because William had done this several times at various stages in his spiritual evolution, a great deal of patience and precision was needed to show how these superimposed schemes coincided. There is an admirable coherence between them, but one must discern it and then clarify it. There is no need to summarize here the lecturer's successful elucidation of William's work, for it can be read in its entirety. It is enough to underline once more the elements of play, spiritual freedom, charm and beauty contained in the stylistic expression of these great poets who were much more and better than professors.

William's goal was to realize man's union with God by unifying within himself, indeed by identifying, his total capacity for knowledge and for love. The image of God is completely oriented, bent, towards a full realization to be achieved in the end, *ibi.* Now we are here, *hic.* In the interval between these two small words and the realities they symbolize lies an intermediary space—*interim*—which is also a period of expectation, *donec.* It is a time when man feels the 'weight' of the flesh, a time when he is exposed to temptations of all kinds. For thinkers like William, and for many of his contemporaries, these were not temptations against faith but rather temptations within the faith: they were tests and trials. Everywhere around the cloisters, theology was opening up new roads. The confusion of some contemporary Christians when confronted by renewed theologies helps us perceive the distress experienced by many of the faithful and by the monks at the beginning of the twelfth century, when scholasticism blossomed forth in the cities' schools. Against this backdrop Abelard is silhouetted: the vigorous teacher seldom named but distrusted by William, who thought he might cause damage to minds less strong and less well-equipped than his.

In the midst of this controversy, for William and for those for whom he felt responsible, as for Augustine, Evagrius and others of the same tradition, the remedy was to be found in a desire for a real knowledge of self. Worthy of notice in his vocabulary is the importance of such words as examination, motivation, 'debate with self,' 'consideration of truth in all its aspects,' 'discipline' and 'exercises' meant to pacify the inner man, 'study' in its context of *studium,* that is, engagement of the whole being in the search: Then a passage from 'simple faith' to 'reasoned faith' becomes possible. The result is *affectus,* which is more than affection or affectivity, but is the fact that one is touched, 'affected' in the depths of one's being by the truth glimpsed. Then, faith, reason, and love are reconciled, in a different way than Abelard did, but in a way that answers the ever present needs and the existential problems of Christians. Only a few specialists in the history of doctrine during the first half of the twelfth century still find reasons to read Abelard's works, some of which have not yet been edited, while William of St Thierry's writings are constantly being published, translated and analyzed. Anxious by nature, but calmed by grace and asceticism, William helps his reader to participate in a sort of anticipation of the definitive *ibi* offered by contemplative knowledge, the monastic approach to theology.

There were conflicts, controversies and sometimes violence at the level of doctrine, but these existed as well in politics, whether secular or religious, the two having been so often and so dangerously associated. Hence the interest of Guntram Bischoff in *Praemonstratensian Eschatology.* In action as in contemplation, man is strained between an *ibi* to come and a *hic* already present. However, on the means of passing from the one to the other there may be hesitations, temptations to hope as well as to faith. One of the witnesses who was scrutinized and whose texts were commented on was Anselm of Havelberg, who in the first book of his *Dialogues,* chapters eight to ten, spoke of his concern for the Church of his time and also of his conviction that God's wisdom would win over men's egoism and brutality. In a manner very similar to Bernard's and possibly derived from him, Anselm describes the successive trials the Church undergoes and the appearance of new forms of fervor which demonstrate the Church's continued 'youth.' Among recent institutions he praises the Templars, true monks and soldiers. The account is very close to Bernard's description and no doubt inspired by him. Anselm of Havelberg was a good writer and a good theologian, but everything confirms that the point of departure for renewal is to be sought in the giant who dominated the first half of the century and who guided the second: St Bernard of Clairvaux.

History never stands still. The twelfth century—particularly its first half—is a summit, but it is still a part of a range of mountains with heights and depths, peaks and valleys, the journey or rather the pilgrimage of human existence through which is never completely the same for each pilgrim. After the golden age of the great theologians of the contemplation of God and love of neighbor, scholasticism enriched Christian thought in ways less sublime but still necessary to progress. Then, at the end of the century, two unexpected figures emerged, God's presents to his Church and to the human community; the unpredictable St Francis and St Dominic, whose spiritual insight and virtue were equalled by his innate gift for organization. St Dominic and the Order of Preaching Brothers would give birth to a line of theologians and mystics, at times both at once. The mystics would be wonderfully represented by women; the theologians led by Thomas Aquinas. Because a program limited to a few weeks cannot devote equal attention to everything and everyone, St Francis was chosen as the 'representative man.' Instead of elaborating on theories about him, Duane V. Lapanski strove to show the real man, a man personally visited by God: a man to whom 'something happened,' or better yet, 'somebody happened to speak and asked for an answer.' The reader will be able to read further on the evocation of Francis' adventures and his dialogue of love, drawn with fervor and enthusiasm by a faithful disciple. The lecture did not pretend to resolve all the critical problems relating to the 'true story' of Francis, problems due in part to legends and other tales we have heard about him. It is almost impossible for a man of such exceptional stature to avoid the embellishment that a collective consciousness projects on what is beyond understanding.

Many erudite people, not only among St Francis' sons,

strive today to reach the real Francis through literary reconstructions of what he should have been according to the norms of his society. Father Lapsanski's purpose was to arouse in us an experience of 'St Francis' mystery,' to share with us what he felt, to create in us an empathy for a man who was so human and yet so penetrated by the divine. The ensuing discussion turned to the psychosomatic considerations without which no experience of God can be realized: St Francis' conflict with his father, with the society of his class and time, with accepted values he found wanting; the development of an illness that plagued him and was to lead him to ecstatic pains during his mature years, an inexplicable combination of incomprehension and suffering on the one hand and on the other of the serene and expansive joy of his final years. Spirituality can be the object of a theory but with Francis as with the great witnesses previously discussed, it is first and remains fundamentally an experience.

It is more to this tradition of Franciscan devotion than to Bernardine piety that all the 'dramatization' of the Christian mystery in the liturgy of the Late Middle Ages is due. Clifford Davidson acted judiciously by treating his subject not in a general way, but in connection with a concrete example, York in the fifteenth century. Augustine, Dionysius, Bernard, and William of Saint Thierry had all insisted less on Christ's passion than on his glorification, his passage from 'life in the days of his flesh' to the Resurrection-Ascension through which he entered once and forever a new way of being, while remaining the same Jesus. Beginning with the thirteenth century, however, pseudo-Bernards, keeping only one side of the diptic, then pseudo-Bonaventures, also fascinated by only one aspect of 'St Francis' mystery,' resolved to present the most humble aspects of the Lord's life: his birth and death. This development marked the start of 'stagings' calling on tender devotion, sensitive performance, use of 'audio-visual' aids, music and the theater, iconographic representations: It marked new synthesis of all the possibilities for human expression and was enhanced by recent advances in technology which made possible the written texts and melodies, the instruments capable of performing them, and new techniques of painting or carving works which reached not only the princely elite able to acquire precious illuminated manuscripts, but also a wide public. It was not, of course, like television, but it was already a non-mystical, a psychological vision, a participation through sight in the invisible and intimate presence of Christ in man's heart, a popular teaching method reaching not only a cloistered elite, but also the crowds assembled in a cathedral or around its close. An astounding anticipation of what is today the mass media, but without commercialism and without a break with the doctrinal roots, and from it sprang luxuriant vegetation, the medieval theater. Once more, collaboration between experts in theology, literature, art history and musicology was necessary. Once more one of the striking lessons to emerge from the Summer Program was that no specialist today can work in isolation. Professor Davidson showed us all the joy that can result from the discovery, accomplished in common, of various levels of religious experience, from the depth of faith to the outer level where it is expressed by acting it, enjoying it, praying under its influence, with emotion, compassion and a legitimate satisfaction of all the senses.

Humanity grows and evolution continues. Suddenly in the sixteenth century an unforeseeable man emerged. Without him, what happened in the following years would not have occurred. Martin Luther had sunk deep roots into medieval monastic devotion, but he was to add riches born from his own experience. The special interest of Darrell R. Reinke and his audience lay in reconstituting what might have been the drama lived by the young Luther during his years as an Augustinian friar at Erfurt and at Wittenberg, then in examining the linguistic expression Luther used to try to formulate, to judge, his experience and to pursue the search for God in his own manner away from the cloister. The textual similarities of terms and themes between Luther and St Bernard are quite evident: *imitatio, effectus-affectus,* experience and so on. Bernard's experience as it affected Luther and the Lutheran tradition has often been studied, by J. Lortz and others, from the standpoint of comparative literature; they compared formulations—*Quellenforschung* is the process—and it had to be done. Reinke's effort, however, is much more original because he reached beyond sentences to what was common to Luther's experience and the preceding monastic tradition.

The last article in this volume reveals a similar trend. In it Otto Gründler studies John Calvin's spirituality and what he has to say on the subject touches on a larger problem requiring immediate attention.

RELIGION, MYSTICISM, SPIRITUALITY

What is, in fact, this 'spirituality' examined by eight scholars extending their research over more than ten centuries? Are there common elements to be organized under the same headings, to be studied from so many different viewpoints? One guarantee of the seriousness of these articles lies in the fact that the authors, either in their texts or in the ensuing discussions, had the opportunity of defining the exact meaning of the terms they used. It is so easy, nowadays, to confuse everything in a vocabulary which is so esoteric at times that the realities it is meant to represent are lost.

For St Paul and the early fathers of the Church, the word 'spiritual' was opposed not to 'corporal' but to 'carnal,' in the equally pauline sense of the word: the whole man, body and soul, under the law of sin but capable of grace. The first Latin writers from North Africa coined the word *spiritualitas* to designate all of the activities of life according to the Holy Spirit, and this tradition remained unchanged up to and through the monastic middle ages. Later, under the influence of scholasticism and the sharp dichotomy between spirit and matter, the word spiritual started to be distinguished not from what is carnal, in the pauline context, but from what is corporal matter. At that time, it disappeared from the vocabulary of 'spiritual writers,' till it was rescued from oblivion by come French scholars who, in the first third of the twentieth century, founded the *Dictionnaire de la Spiritualité,* still being published.[3] In the interval, other words had to be used, 'mysticism' in particular. This term also had its origins in participation in the Christian 'mystery' through faith and worship. Over the years, however, it put on a significant psychological overtone which, although legitimate, could lead to exacerbated forms of emotionalism and in the process trigger defensive reactions or opposition. Therefore it was important in each case, for each period and author, to define which reality was understood by the word. J. Sommerfeldt did this for St Bernard, R. Elder for William, G. Bischoff as he defined the 'gnosticism' of Dionysius and 'myth' among the Premonstratensians. In all instances it was a complex blend of knowledge, reasoning, wisdom, love, intuition, poetry, contemplation of divine truth, and engagement in its service among men.

That clarification takes on importance in Otto Gründler's final synthesis concerning Calvin. I do not intend to summarize here—which would be to simplify and thereby falsify—the distinctions Professor Gründler introduces between the religious man, the Christian man, the spiritual man, and the mystical man. There is a gradation which goes from obscure faith common to all to the 'illumination,' its very name implying light. Both of these experiences are found in all Christian spiritual tradition. There are variations in its perception and expression and in the reasoned elaboration it is given, but there is unity and continuity as to the realities themselves. Had it only demonstrated that fact, the Summer Program of 1975, the essential points of which are included in this volume, would have served extremely well the historians, theorists, and practitioners of Christian spirituality.

THE STATE OF CONTEMPORARY STUDY

The time has come to formulate a general impression of what was revealed by the 1975 Summer Program and is reflected, partly at least, in this volume. Without a doubt, the lived experience, the sharing of ideas, and friendship, added a great deal to the lectures. However, the experience as well as the book raises two kinds of problems and begins to shed light upon them: first, the problem of complexity, of the potential for intense spiritual study; second, the question of the relevance of this study today especially in the United States.

All during the weeks which led to this volume and its articles, spirituality appeared as a convergence of all the disciplines known to man, that is, the disciplines whose subject is not what humans have said or done, but what they have been. History, with its demands for chronology, paleography and other auxiliary sciences; philology, with its rigorous method for grasping vocabulary; linguistics, allowing textual analysis and in turn knowledge of the authors; codicology as a tool for organizing and disseminating manuscripts, and in so doing providing contact between them and their readers; philosophy, as it developed in the course of the centuries; psychology in its many guises, calling at times on psychiatry and medicine; sociology, knowledge of laws and institutions, disciplines of economic and political changes; liturgy, iconography, musicology and at last, crowning, integrating, unifying, interpreting all of these disciplines while respecting their methods, theology.

From the Old Testament to modern theology, across all Christian confessions, a continuous current, flowing from God and passing through a constantly growing humanity, has made possible for us an accumulation of treasures of beauty, opportunities of joy, love, commitment, and service, whose resources are far from being exhausted. One of the wonderful things about our time is that we insist more on convergences than divergences. This profound unity springs from the part of truth inherent in the historic realization of the Christian message; knowledge of this truth is a result of science, the science of research, which assumes the existence of tools for such work, in particular, editions, translations, publications. In this area, Western Michigan University possesses a very promising program.

Across such a vast domain, it is already possible to build bridges, to bring close together and establish connections, for example, between Guigo II the Carthusian at the end of the twelfth century and St John of the Cross in the sixteenth century, or many others the reader will find mentioned or elaborated in the pages of this volume. There are human and religious constants, religious because human, in a faith that has as its fundamental principle the Incarnation of God in a man, Jesus Christ. Through time and space, what allows access to Jesus in a way satisfying to the aspirations of men of all times is the spiritual approach or, to state it in the technical manner authorized by tradition and still accepted, contemplative study. While one of the temptations of our time would be to seek a vague religious 'experience,' either in emotionalism or esoterism or syncretism, a reconciliation of faith and reason opens up a way less easy but surer and leading further. We need study which is completely serious and demanding in its methodology, and in its results satisfying to the whole human being. A purely critical science could only be sterile, a purely sentimental devotion would not be nourishing, not sufficient to prepare for the challenges that life in the Christian faith must include. That is the meaning and the goal of a program of contemplative studies.

It is admirable that such an aspiration is being voiced today and is beginning to receive an answer. Our generation is not the first to feel such needs, and it is encouraging for us to recall how many similar crises have caused reactions and brought about similar remedies. The difference now is that we are better equipped scientifically than ever before. Several of the articles included in this volume lead us to think that great minds, whether Augustine, Bernard, Francis, Luther, or Calvin, have often been victims of their disciples. During the last third of the eighteenth century in particular, desiccative thinking, a by-product of the scientism and rationalism of the time known as the 'enlightenment' or *Aufklärung,* a way of knowing and reasoning that left little room for esthetics, poetry, or the role of the 'heart' in human experience, provoked in

England, Germany, France and finally everywhere in
Europe and the United States, a revival called 'roman-
ticism,' a rich and complex movement not analyzed in this
volume.[4] Hans W. Frei, in a basic book, has shown how the
dissolution of the biblical story under the influence of a
disintegrating criticism had led a return to symbolism,
poetry, esthetics, and total experience.[5] Men felt anew the
need for a certain empathy into something that is beyond
the deliberate reasoning prevalent in a given past-area, empathy into its unitive, internal source of thinking, feeling,
imagining and acting in both the collective group and the
particular individual.[6]

Today, after magnificent yet unsatisfying progress in
technology, the same aspiration is felt. Father Yves Congar
formulated it admirably when he spoke of the immense
spiritual experience of the second Vatican Council for the
Roman Catholic Church and for observers from other
denominations:

What soon emerged at the Council, in the name of a vision and of a
pastoral approach was, at root, what St Bernard had claimed against
Abelard, Pascal against the apologetics of baroque theology, and M.
Blondel against the heirs to these same apologetics. It had to do with the
truly religious character of the knowledge of God, against a takeover and
a treatment derived exclusively from rationalism.[7]

Today, particularly in the United States, an astonishing
renewal of interest in the Middle Ages has been
manifested—as attested by the some thousand professors
and students, all relatively young, assembling each year
during the Medieval Studies Conference at Western
Michigan University. Someone has even noted that the film
industry in these past few years has portrayed the Middle
Ages as it was seen by nineteenth century romanticists.[8]
How are we to interpret these phenomena? It is not enough
to see in them a sort of escapism from the demands of contemporary existence, a sort of retrospective dream. More
likely it is a search for spiritual values capable of completing or at least counterbalancing the increased material
affluence created by modern technology. Still, the Middle

Ages must be perceived and interpreted correctly, that is, objectively. Schleiermacher used to say that the interpreter must understand an author better than he understands himself.[9] In succession, for almost two centuries—this time the historical cycle coincides with the American bicentennial—the Middle Ages have been disregarded and then rediscovered, only to be forgotten again or viewed with suspicion. The time has come to know that period, to appreciate it for what it was, in truth, with its limitations but also with its greatness and its richness. The foreigner present at this re-evaluation is tempted to express his admiration and gratitude toward the country hosting this revival by a play on words which St Bernard and his medieval contemporaries would have appreciated—the juxtaposition of the names of friendship and the United States: *Amica-America.*

A promising future is opening up in contemplative studies, especially in the area of medieval Christian spirituality and the periods which prepared it or were born from it. The 1975 Summer Program is not a utopia, it was a reality. The present volume reaffirms the values of truth and Christian experience esteemed and communicated by all the participants. This book is an act of faith.

Smith College
April 24, 1976

Translated by Monique Coyne

NOTES

[1] It is easy to understand why the program's organizers saw to it that those who wished to could devote each morning to the study of Latin.

[2] H. I. Marrou, *The Resurrection and St Augustine's Theology of Human Values* (Villanova, Pa.: Villanova Press, 1966).

[3] I have traced the history of the word and concept 'spirituality' under the title 'Spiritualitas,' in *Studi Medievali,* 3 (1962) p. 279-296.

[4] I have done so under the title 'Le renouveau monastique de D. Guéranger,' in 'Le renouveau religieux du XIX siècle,' *Studia monastica* 18 (1976).

[5] Hans W. Frei, *Hermeneutics* (New Haven and London: Yale University Press, 1974).

[6] Frei, p. 242.

[7] 'Bloc Notes du P. Congar,' in *Information Catholiques International* (December 1, 1965) p. 5.

[8] According to Joy Gould Boyern, 'The "Gothic" Vogue Hits the Movies,' in *The Wall Street Journal,* July 21, 1975.

[9] Frei, p. 243.

AUGUSTINE OF HIPPO:
THE APPROACH OF THE SOUL TO GOD

Augustine (354-430) was born and died in North Africa, under Roman rule a stronghold of Christianity. Despite his mother's urgings, he converted to Christianity only after a long struggle and experiments with Manichaeanism and the philosophy of Neo-Platonism, which greatly influenced his theology. After teaching rhetoric for a time at Rome, he moved to Milan, the learned and gentle bishop of which, Ambrose, deeply impressed him both by his erudition and by his way of life.

After hesitating at the ethical demands of Christianity, Augustine was finally moved to put away his mistress of fifteen years and seek baptism. Returning to North Africa, he lived an austere common life with some friends at a 'monastery' at Tagaste. He was ordained priest in 391, and four years later became the bishop of Hippo Regius. A prodigious writer, Augustine composed polemical works and apologetics, sermons and philosophical treatises. His influence on all subsequent Western theology, protestant and catholic, has been immeasurable. As he lay dying, the barbarian Vandals were besieging his see city; the so-called Dark Ages were about to descend on the West and to extinguish forever the Christian culture of North Africa.

In his review of his own writings Augustine advises us to read his works in the order in which they were written, if we wish to follow the progress of his thought.[1] With that injunction in mind we propose to examine chronologically a remarkable series of texts illustrating Augustine's view on the spiritual growth of man in terms of the soul's movement toward union with God:[2] Two points in Augustine's thought will provide the context for our study of these passages: (1) his three-level ontology, and (2) his psychology of the tripartite soul.

As Augustine looked at the whole of reality he saw
bodies existing on the lowest level of being, souls on the
second level, and God dwelling at the top. There are only
these three kinds of 'natures': the corporeal is subject to
change in both space and time; the psychic changes tem-
porally but not spatially; the divine nature is absolutely
changeless. Furthermore, he insists that there is no intermediary nature between man's soul and God.[3] The spirit
of man may choose to look upward to God and eternal
verities (the *ratio superior*) or to took downward to bodies
with their many changes (*ratio inferior*). This schematism is
value oriented, for Augustine obviously thinks that the
good life for man depends on his turning upwards to God
(*conversio ad Deum*). As he says in *Letter* 18: 'That highest
[nature] is essential blessedness; the lowest, that which can
be either blessed or wretched; and the intermediate nature
lives in wretchedness when it stoops to that which is lowest,
and in blessedness when it turns toward that which is
highest.'

Within the working of the human spirit, Augustine
distinguishes three specific functions: mind (*mens*) is the
soul as knowing; memory (*memoria*) is the soul retaining its
contents; and will (*voluntas*) is the soul as acting in any
way. These are not three distinct faculties, in the Scholastic
sense of the term; they are simply three aspects of man's
mental activity. Thus Augustine explains: 'Since memory,
understanding and will are not three lives but one life, nor
three minds but one mind, it follows certainly that they are
not three substances but one substance.'[4] The human soul
(in the broadest sense, *anima*) is called *animus* when
Augustine wishes to stress its conscious features. It is called
ratio (reason) when considered as looking toward any object: '*ratio sit quidam mentis aspectus.* '[5] Finally, it is called
spiritus, in Augustine's terminology, when one is thinking
of its incorporeal nature and functions.

Having established these preliminaries, let us now
examine a chronological series of passages dealing with the
approach of man's spirit to God.

In one of his youthful psychological treatises, *The Greatness of the Soul* (A.D. 388), Augustine described for the first time seven grades of soul energy.[6] The lowest level, animation (*animatio*) is that on which the soul gives life to its body, *'praesentia sua vivificat.'* A step higher is sensation (*sensus*), which is the soul perceiving through the sensory organs of the body. The third level is the use of artistic skills (*ars*), the force of the soul reasonably directing man's actions in all the arts of living, whether useful or fine. Fourth is the grade called evaluation or virtue (*virtus*) which involves the discernment of good things. This entails a purification of human effort and is the beginning of man's spiritual/moral growth. Next is the level of stabilization (*tranquillitas*) in which the soul rests quietly in itself, *'in seipsa laetissime tenet.'* Sixth is the grade of fixation (*ingressio*) in which the soul directs its attention toward the highest object of vision. Finally there is contemplation (*contemplatio*), the serene vision of truth.

By way of comment, we may note two things in this text. In the first place it is a cognitive analysis of man's ascent to Truth. And among these seven levels we have but four steps in man's spiritual progress, for that begins only at the fourth grade.

In another work of the same period, *On Genesis Against the Manichees* (A.D. 388-390), we find seven stages of spiritual development described allegorically.[7] Augustine suggests that the first day of creation signifies man's gaining the light of faith: *'fidem Dominus visibiliter apparere dignatus est.'* The second day means that man distinguishes things of the flesh from those of the spirit: *'quo discernit inter carnalia et spiritalia.'* The third day prefigures man freeing his soul from the stain of passions: *'mentem suam . . . a labe et fluctibus tentationem carnalium . . . secernit.'* He takes the fourth day to mean man's vision of spiritual truths in the light of the Immutable Truth: *'videt quae sit incommutabilis veritas, quae tamquam sol fulget in anima.'* The fifth day means

man's acting to serve his brothers: *'in actionibus . . . prop-
ter utilitatem fraternae societatis.'* The sixth day suggests
the submission of one's soul to the control of justice and
reason: *'anima . . . rationi et justitiae serviens.'* Last, the
seventh day stands for man's resting in the hope of lasting
peace: *'speret homo . . . quietem perpetuam.'*

Noteworthy in these allegories are the facts that all
seven steps are of spiritual significance, the introduction of
divine illumination at stage four, and the stress on social
activism in stage five. This is not so much a psychological
analysis as it is a pious meditation on the flowering of faith
within the soul. There is little doubt that the seventh step is
some sort of union with God.

A year or so later, in the work *On True Religion* (A.D.
389-390), Augustine presented another cognitive series of
steps.[8] (1) Immutable law is seen to be higher than reason
itself: *'At ratione praestantior lex immutabilis.'* (2) God is
this law: *'Deus summa ista lex est, secundum quam ratio
judicat.'* (3) Unity in bodies is but a vestige of the unity seen
by the mind: *'Unitatis in corporibus est vestigium, sed ipsa
unitas nonisi mente conspicitur.'* (4) Eternal values, such as
wisdom, beauty and goodness, are discovered above one's
soul, in God: *'noli foras ire, in teipsum redi, in interiore
homine habitat veritas . . . transcende et teipsum . . . Illuc
ergo tende, unde ipsum lumen rationis accenditur.'* (5) As
spiritual remedies, Augustine suggests that reflection will
cure sensuality, and charity will take care of pride. (6) True
religion (*religio*) is not a matter of fanciful imagery (*'in
phantasmatis nostris'*); the worship of earthly or watery
things (*'terrarum cultus et aquarum'*), or the perfected soul
in itself (*'vel ipsa perfecta et sapiens anima rationalis'*). (7)
Religion binds us to the one, omnipotent God; as Truth he
abides above our minds with no intervening creature (*'inter
mentem nostram . . . et veritatem . . . nulla interposita
creatura est'*).

Here we may observe in the domain of reason another
version of man's ascent to God. Even though he starts with
immutable truth and recognizes quickly that this is divine,
Augustine takes seven steps to make explicit the meaning
of man's approach to God. This is a continuation of the

theme of his earliest philosophical dialogues, in which thought moves from corporeal things to incorporeal.[9] Some interpreters regard this passage in the work *On True Religion* as a key analysis of man's spiritual progress.[10]

In *The Lord's Sermon on the Mount* (A.D. 393-394) we find a quite different seven step series toward blessedness.[11] (1) Fear is the beginning of blessedness: *'initium autem sapientiae timor Domini.'* (2) Meekness signifies a certain stability in one's eternal heritage. (3) The sorrow of those who mourn turns one from earthly joys to God. (4) Hunger makes us lovers of truth and immutable goodness. (5) Mercy brings the achievement of blessedness. (6) Cleanheartedness, purgation, prepares one for the vision of God. (7) Peace-making brings us to perfection: *'in pace perfectio est.'*

What we have here is a combination of the Beatitudes with the gifts of the Holy Spirit. Much of the analysis of spiritual progress in this text involves affective dispositions, such as fear and sorrow. No longer a set of stages in the life of reason, it is an advance toward spiritual peace in the affective order. However, perfection in this final peace involves the subjection of man's emotional tendencies to the direction of reason, of the mind, and of the spirit.[12]

A similar advance through the seven gifts of the Holy Spirit is offered in *Christian Instruction* (A.D. 397):[13] (1) Fear turns one to the knowledge of God's will. (2) Piety leads to respect for Holy Scripture. (3) Knowledge turns our love toward God. (4) Fortitude brings one to take delight in eternal values. (5) Mercy cleanses sordid thoughts and turns one to love of neighbor. (6) Cleanliness of heart leads us to the vision of Truth, even though we see it obscurely. (7) Wisdom brings full enjoyment of final peace.[14]

It is noteworthy that the steps described in *The Lord's Sermon on the Mount* and in *Christian Instruction* depart from the psychological analyses of the earlier works. The first period of his episcopacy finds Augustine devoting much time to the study of Scripture. Although this turned his attention in part from the Platonic psychology evident in the early dialogues, Augustine did not abandon his efforts to discover a rational explanation of the stages in man's spiritual journey to God. The texts from his middle period, which we will now consider, exhibit the continuing influence of Plotinus and Porphyry as well as a growing competence in biblical exegesis.

MIDDLE PERIOD: A.D. 400-416

From the *Confessions* to *The Trinity* Augustine is of course engrossed with the problem of man's spiritual growth but no longer with seven stages of ascent. Rather, the pattern has been simplified to one that became commonplace in medieval spiritual exercises. Ascent becomes a three-stage schematism: withdrawal from the world of bodies, concentration on the soul in its most incorporeal features, and elevation of attention to God above the soul.

A much-quoted sentence in the *Confessions* (A.D. 397-401) says precisely this: 'thus admonished to turn back to my very self, I entered into my innermost parts under your guidance . . . and I saw . . . above my mind the immutable Light.'[15] The pattern is clear: from outside the mind, to inside the mind, to what is above my mind. It would be possible to illustrate this triple-graded progress from many other texts in the *Confessions* but there is another passage in which seven steps may be seen.

And so, step by step (*gradatim*) from (1) bodies, to (2) the soul which senses through the body, and thence to its (3) interior power to which the sense organs report about external things . . . further to (4) the reasoning power . . . which lifted itself to (5) its understanding . . . whence it discovered (6) the Immutable itself . . . and in the flash of a trembling glance (7) reached up to That Which Is.[16]

Later in the famous vision at Ostia, when Augustine and his mother rose to some sort of spiritual contact with God, the climax is reached 'with a click of the heart' (*toto ictu cordis*).[17] This suggests an affective, rather than a cognitive, experience.

Whether there is also some indication of mystical experience in these and similar passages in the *Confessions* is much debated. Dom Cuthbert Butler called these experiences 'identical in kind with those described by the later mystics.'[18] Gerald Bonner agrees.[19] E. Hendrikx, on the other hand, calls Augustine 'a great enthusiast but no mystic.'[20] However this may be, it is quite clear that the theme of conversion to God, the volitional turning of one's will toward the highest good, is the central theme of the *Confessions.*[21] We are well beyond a purely rationalistic search for truth.

A dozen years later Augustine was asked by the Lady Paulina to explain how one may 'see' God. His answer is a lengthy letter important for our understanding of what may happen in the final stage of man's approach to God.[22] He first distinguishes ocular vision—the soul seeing through the eyes of its body—from the mental vision of such facts as 'that you are living, that you have a desire for God, that you wish to fulfill that desire, that you know that you are alive and willing and seeking, that you do not know that you are alive and willing and seeking, that you do not know how God may be seen,' and so on.[23] Then, and not for the last time, Augustine faces two apparently conflicting texts from the New Testament: Mt 5:8—'Blessed are the pure of heart: for they shall see God'—and, in contrast, Jn 1:18—'No one has at any time seen God.'[24] His solution to this puzzle suggests that while no one sees the nature of God, clearly and directly, in this life, some people may see God, in this life, through some sort of 'appearance' which conceals God's nature.[25] What Augustine now stresses is man's need to will that such a vision occur. He cites his older contemporary, St Ambrose, in support of this claim that one must really wish to see God, before he can be seen, even obscurely.[26]

Etienne Gilson regarded this *Letter* 147, *to Lady Paulina,* as an important text for Augustine's differentiation of the natural intellectual seeing of truth from the supernatural vision of God. The whole second Part of Gilson's classic *Introduction to the Study of St Augustine* is an expansion of this theme of the approach to God, through willing.[27]

If the *Letter to Paulina* be dated A.D. 412/413, then within a year or so Augustine had returned to the problem of the vision of God in the last Book of his *Literal Com-*

mentary on Genesis (A.D. 414). There, in an effort to explain St Paul's rapture as a spiritual experience, Augustine
takes the injunction, 'You shall love your neighbor as yourself,' as an example and then describes in relation to it
three kinds of vision.[28] He says that we see the letters in
which this precept is written by looking through the eyes of
the body (*per oculos corporis*). On the second level of
vision, we may see through the spirit (*per spiritum
hominis*) the meaning of the word neighbor. This is an act
of 'cogitating' a person (who is not present, as would be the
case on the first level of vision) through images that are
retained in interior sensation. It should be noted that this
usage of 'spirit' is not identical with later Christian terminology but owes something to Pauline language and to
Plotinian psychology. The third and highest level of human
vision is accomplished through mental intuition (*per con-
tuitum mentis*), whereby one sees immaterially the meaning
of love, without having any image of it. This, according to
Augustine, is imageless thought.

The implication of this discussion is that St Paul saw
God on the level of the third type of vision. There is a
growing emphasis in this period of Augustine's thinking on
the affective side of these higher experiences. Willing and
loving add a new dimension to man's ascent to God.

In *The Trinity,* at about this same time (A.D. 412-416),
Augustine examined analytically the union of the soul with
God in the act of loving. At the start of the last Book (15) on
The Trinity, he wrote:

If we recall where it was in these Books that a trinity first began to show
itself to our understanding, the eighth Book is what occurs to us; since it
was there that, to the best of our power, we tried to raise the aim of the
mind to understand that most excellent and immutable nature, which is
not our own mind (*ad intellegendum illam praestantissimam naturam
quod nostra mens non est*). But when we came to treat of love which in
Sacred Scripture is called God (*ad caritatem quae in sancta scriptura
Deus dicta est*) then a trinity began to dawn upon us a little, that is: the
lover (*amans*), that which is loved (*quod amatur*), and love (*amor*).[29]

Going back to the eighth Book, written possibly some years
earlier, we find this text:

You certainly do not love anything except what is good, since good is the earth . . . an estate . . . a house . . . a beautiful poem. . . . This thing is good and so is that, but take away this and that and look at good itself (*et vide ipsum bonum*), if you can. So will you see God; not Good by a good that is other than Himself but the Good of all good. . . . So, God is to be loved, not as this and that good, but the good itself. For the good that must be sought for the soul is not one above which it is to fly by making a judgment but to which it is to cleave by loving (*bonum animae, non cui superuolitet iudicando sed cui haeret amando*) and what is this except God? Not a good mind, or a good angel, or a good heaven, but the good good (*sed bonum bonum*).[30]

These texts from *The Trinity* have been quoted at some length in order to show the context in which Augustine, in his middle period, puts spiritual progress in terms of the love of goodness itself. He still speaks of trying to understand God (*ad intellegendum illam praestantissimam immutabilemque naturam*) but this is now a movement within the ambit of divine charity.

LATE PERIOD: A.D. 418-429

We come finally to the time when Augustine began to stress the way in which divine grace affects man's spiritual life. In this period he became concerned with the teachings of Pelagius, whom he had hardly known before A.D. 415. Augustine felt that Pelagius was minimizing the role of God's grace in the growth of the human spirit. Since Pelagius claimed the support of Ambrose's writings, Augustine now turned to a more thorough study of the sermons and commentaries of the famous Bishop of Milan. The result of this anti-Pelagian activity is obvious in the treatise on *The Grace of Christ and Original Sin* (A.D. 418).[31] First Augustine states that men cannot avoid sin without the aid of grace (*agitur de auxilio gratiae, quo ad non peccandum adjuvamur*). Then he quotes and agrees with Ambrose's *Commentary on Luke* (2, 84) that 'no man is able to undertake anything without the Lord' (*nemo custodire sine Domino*). He adds that Ambrose also taught that any growth in man's love of God results solely from the gift of grace (*etiam ipsam dilectionem, qua quisque amplius diligit, ad beneficium gratiae pertinere*). Augustine is

now clearly teaching that only some people are called by
God to spiritual beatitude. Quoting Ambrose again (*On
Luke* 9:53) to the effect that God calls those whom he
deems worthy (*quos dignatur vocat*) and makes any person
religious whom he so wills (*et quem vult religiosum facit*),
Augustine approves and adds: 'For this reason, unless God
enable one to do a deed, who can do it?' (*Quapropter, nisi a
Deo fiat, ut hoc faciat, qui hoc facit?*)

Man's complete spiritual dependence on God is the
theme of these mature years. Augustine placed less stress
on the psychic *ascent* of the soul to God and more emphasis
on God's *condescension* to man. These anti-Pelagian
writings fascinated many theologians during the Reformation and induced some to dwell upon the weakness of
the human will, left to itself, and to concentrate on the
problem of predestination.

These emphases run throughout the *Enchiridion, on
Faith, Hope and Charity* (A.D. 421). True liberty (*libertas*),
he wrote, comes only from divine grace (*ista libertas unde
erit . . . nisi redimat?*).[32] Quoting St Paul (Ep 2:8), 'By grace
you have been saved through faith,' Augustine adds that
faith and liberty are both gifts from God, the whole thing is
given by God (*totum Deo detur*). Eternal life, the reward of
good works, is called the grace of God by the Apostle
Paul.[33]

The City of God, in its last Book (A.D. 425-426), continues this teaching that spiritual progress depends entirely
on divine condescension. Indeed we find here Augustine's
own words for spiritual growth, *institutio spiritalis*:[34]

So then, in regard to spiritual growth (*institutio spiritalis*), whereby a
man is formed in piety and righteousness, the Apostle says, 'Neither is he
that planteth anything, nor he that watereth, but God that giveth increase' (I Co 3:7); so also must it be said that he who has intercourse and
inseminates does nothing, but rather God gives the essential form (*nec
qui concumbit, nec qui seminat, est aliquid; sed qui format Deus*). He
alone, coupling and connecting in some wonderful fashion the spiritual
and corporeal natures, the one to command, the other to obey, he makes
a living being.

In such spiritual development seven steps may again be
discerned: (1) animation (*anima*); (2) consciousness (*mens,*

ratio, intelligentia); (3) intuition of truth (*perceptio veritatis*); (4) love of the good (*amor boni*); (5) wisdom (*sapientia*); (6) moral virtues (*prudentia, fortitudo, temperantia, justitia*); and (7) desire fixed on the highest good (*desiderium summi boni*).[35]

This remarkable text from *The City of God* draws together his sevenfold analysis of spiritual progress found in the early works and his mature emphasis on man's complete spiritual dependence on God.

Two writings from his last years maintain this view. In *Grace and Free Choice* (A.D. 426-427) we are told that, 'God works in the hearts of men to incline their wills wherever he wills, whether to good deeds according to his mercy, or to evil after their own deserts.'[36] And the theme of divine condescension is again stated: 'God will give you understanding . . . Wisdom itself comes down from above, as the Apostle James tells us.'[37] Then, in the *Predestination of the Saints* (A.D. 428-429), the elderly Augustine reminds us that all our accomplishments stem from God:[38]

Therefore in what pertains to religion and piety . . . if we are not capable of thinking anything as of ourselves, but our sufficiency is of God, we are certainly not capable of believing anything as of ourselves, since we cannot do this without thinking; but our sufficiency, by which we begin to believe, is of God (*sufficientia nostra qua credere incipiamus ex Deo est*).

He goes on to say that, like St Cyprian before him, he had thought as a young man that faith is in us from ourselves (*a nobis esse in nobis*) but he now realizes that faith is preceded in us by God's grace.[39]

There is no doubt that Augustine was aware of a considerable shift in his views on moral and spiritual development. Yet we find six themes recurring throughout.

I. The threefold pattern: withdrawal from the world, concentration on the soul, rising above the soul to God.

II. Stress on religious conversion as man's will turning to God.

III. A suggestion of mystical experience, even if its character be somewhat ambiguous.

IV. The tendency to combine psychological ascent with divine descent.

V. Spiritual love (*caritas*) adds a new dimension to the highest understanding.

VI. The climax of spiritual growth comes in a final peace of the spirit, described in poetic rapture in the last Book of *The City of God*:

> What will the spirit of man be like, when it has no vice at all, and gives way to no one, nor yields to any, nor fights even a praiseworthy battle against anything—when it is perfected in the most peaceful virtue (*pacatissima virtute perfectus*)? How sure then will its knowledge be of the grandeur and beauty of all things—a knowledge without error or labor, in which the wisdom of God will be drunk from its very source (*ubi Dei sapientia de ipso suo fonte potabitur*), accompanied by the highest happiness and stripped of all trouble (*cum summa felicitate, sine ulla difficultate*)?[40]

Surely this is the elderly bishop trying to convey to his readers what he, and they, may look forward to in heaven.

Vernon J. Bourke

St Louis University

DIONYSIUS THE PSEUDO-AREOPAGITE:
THE GNOSTIC MYTH

Dionysius (Denis: fl. c. 500) is the name given an anonymous author long reputed to be Dionysius, an Athenian converted by St Paul. His works synthesized Christianity and Neo-Platonism, the religious philosophy which profoundly influenced Augustine. The works of Dionysius, written in Greek, became known in the West through the ninth-century translation of John Scotus Eriugena, an orientophile scholar at the court of the Frankish king, Charles the Bald.

Gnostic: from gnosis, knowledge. *The knowledge by which man grasps and is unified with the wisdom and the love of God.*

The seminar has the general title 'The Spirituality of Western Christendom,' and since the students have to contend with several lecturers and cover an enormous span of history, it might not be amiss for me to state at the very outset my understanding of 'spirituality.' I take spirituality to mean religious man's personal experience of bridging the gulf between sacred and profane through participation in the really Real. Hence, spirituality refers to the dialectic of transcending the profane state while yet remaining in it. The media of such transcending are myth, ritual, and the community of believers of whom religious man knows himself to be part. Spirituality is not a solipsistic exercise, but a social phenomenon, and without a common world view, a common symbol-system, a common cosmos of meaning expressed in myth and ritual, there can be no personal experience of participation through understanding and ritual actualization. We are studying expressions of this experience which vary widely in space and time and hence employ highly variegated symbols, some of which have been rationalized to a high degree. We must never forget, however, that even in the state of advanced rationalization they remain symbols which need interpretation. Trying to

13

elicit the spirituality of a given individual or of a group is, in fact, an attempt to learn to read the symbols they employ and through them the myth that forms them into a coherent, meaningful symbol-system.

Let me add at this point a brief remark about a particular difficulty with which I find myself confronted. Unlike my worthy colleagues, I am saddled with two lectures. That in itself may be the result of sheer madness, but it is only the beginning of my troubles. I am to report on two phenomena, the spiritual stances of which seem diametrically opposed. Pseudo-Dionysius mixes with early Premonstratensian eschatology as well as fire does with water, and I think you will understand me when I admit to feeling like the Roman Janus, looking simultaneously in two opposite directions and feeling threatened by a kind of interpretive schizophrenia.

I could excuse myself by the fact that, after all, the Pseudo-Areopagite and Prémontré are separated not only by some six centuries, but also by some thousand miles, to wit, that they belong to two incomparable cultures. Such facile excuse will not do, however, for both antipodes understand themselves as Christian, and if there is anything to what I just said about the social character of Christianity, it must be possible to penetrate behind the irreconcilable symbols to the myth or myths which hold them together.

These myths (for we are really dealing with two distinct myths) I call, respectively, the gnostic and the apocalyptic. Christianity has often, and rightly, been described as a syncretistic religion. But syncretism here does not mean mixing as much as it means dialectical synthesis which one could express in the apparently contradictory 'Already-—Not Yet' of earliest Christianity. God has already come to man, and man has already returned to the eternal peace in God through faith; he has already become a καινὴ κτίσις, a new creation. The great circle is closed. Through the divine epiphany in the descending enlightening revealer, man sees the heavens open and he enters spiritually, leaving behind nothing but the husk of the body. This is the gnostic myth, the myth classically restated in the work of the Areopagite.

The apocalyptic myth, which was rediscovered in the Latin church around 1100 A.D., holds, on the other hand, that God *will* come to man; this profane world of factual experience must be utterly destroyed to make room for the new creation, but man, conscious of the historicity of his condition, may already live in hope, in straining anticipation of the future of God coming toward him, and thus he may dialectically employ his energies to hasten this future by substituting love for ordinary worldly affairs.

This Christian dialectic is as old as the New Testament itself, even though it found its first technical expression only in that great christological dogma of the fifth century: 'Fully God and fully man.' Fully present and fully future. To sustain the coagulation of the two myths is difficult and few theologians were, like the towering Augustine, capable of giving it systematic expression. With most, it became a matter of accent. Word-symbols are clues. In the gnostic myth, the symbolism is spatial and the key word in the dionysian literature is 'above.' Hence participation means ascent and merger. In the apocalyptic myth, the symbolism is temporal and the key word in the historical symbolism of the twelfth century is 'then.' Hence participation means anticipation. One road leads to mysticism, the other to eschatology and revolution.

It is important, I believe, that we keep this Christian dialectic in mind. We are looking at two sides of the same coin. The *corpus dionysiacum,* with its enormous influence on the medieval mind, never held or even gained a monopoly. Christian mysticism never quite 'made it,' by comparison to, say, Hindu mysticism—though Rudolf Otto may have overdrawn the contrast. This is so because, to borrow a Tillichian phrase, Christian mysticism was from the beginning 'baptized' in the name of the man Jesus of Nazareth. On the other hand, the exuberance of chiliasm, although forcefully reawakened after an Augustine-induced sleep of some seven hundred years and ascending to powerful influence at the edge of the age of modernity, did not make it either. But chiliasm may have proven the stronger of the two, at least as far as Christianity is concerned.

THE CORPUS AREOPAGITICUM

I would like to turn, first, to a brief sketch of the pseudo-Areopagite and his work as well as his effect on the middle ages. Then, we will take a closer look at his system of thought, and finally, I should like to consider a few points of what one might call a critical evaluation in which I want to return to the notion, already indicated, of the Areopagite as the successful purveyor and christianizer of the Great Gnostic Myth.

As the *corpus areopagiticum* we describe a body of literature consisting of four relatively short works and some ten letters of an unknown author. The four works really constitute something akin to the Ekkehardian *opus tripartitum*: two volumes, on the celestial and ecclesiastical hierarchies respectively, were meant as a symbolic theology through which the mind of the reader may be led upwards from the *significans* to the *significatum,* from the symbol to the reality symbolized, or from sense to intellect. The third volume, a treatise on the *Divine Names* which is later in origin and deals with the interpretation of divine attributes as they occur in the Christian scriptures, is really a *Prinzipienlehre,* i.e., a systematic attempt to elicit ontological and epistemological principles. The fourth volume, a work of only a few pages, is entitled *Mystical Theology* and describes—not unlike Bonaventura's famous *Itinerarium mentis ad Deum*—the ascent of the human spirit (the νοῦς, the words 'mind' or 'reason' would be misleading here) to the ecstasis of unknowing, to the experiential participation in the Unknowable, or to union with the Divine.

The identity of the author of this body of writings is shrouded in well-nigh complete mystery. In an obvious reference to the apparently sole philosopher-convert of Paul's futile foray into Athens, reported in Acts 17:34, he calls himself Dionysius, and occasionally he tries, somewhat awkwardly, to sustain this fiction through oblique references to his experiences with apostles and apostle-disciples. We need not waste time on this pseudonymity. It collapses in the face of the author's casual mention of Ignatius of Antioch who died in A.D. 117 and whose letter to the Romans the Areopagite, wittingly or unwittingly, misquotes. Much more important, and more frustrating, is the attempt to penetrate at least peripherally the obscurity of his identity by culling scraps of information, allusion, and innuendo from his writings. Professor R. Hathaway, in his recent work, *Hierarchy and the Definition of Order in the Letters of Pseudo-Dionysius,* gives a long list of tentative identifications which reflect the arduous, most exacting and penetrating scholarship that has gone into this unsolved detective case over the last hundred years. I will not bother you with details and names except to say that you have a choice among some twenty-two names of people living at any time between A.D. 129 and 544. This is, of course, in addition to those unregenerate souls who, some five hundred years after Laurentius Valla, still believe in the alleged identity of the author's own choosing. The year 528 must be the *terminus ad quem* since in that year Severus of Antioch cites 'Dionysius' in his treatise, *Against the Apology of Julian.* The *terminus a quo* would seem to be the death of Proclus in 485.

The truth of the matter seems to be that we have no inkling of who the author is. We do not even know with certainty that he was a Christian, or, if he was, whether he was a recent convert, let alone if he was a monk, a layman, a priest or a bishop. What we do know is that he quotes Plotinus (c. 205-270) occasionally and Proclus (c. 410-485) copiously, that he was not only quite familiar with, but lived the spirit and vocabulary of late neoplatonic philosophy as it had been cultivated at the dying school of Athens just prior to its forced closing in 529. By the same token, the author quotes the Christian scriptures haphazardly and very selectively though he had no doubt read them well. Luther's verdict seems as correct as it was intended derogatorily: the pseudo-Dionysius was *'plus Platonisans quam Christianisans.'*[1]

Much of this escaped the theologians of the middle ages, largely because the early commentaries of Maximus Confessor on the Areopagite smoothed the dogmatically rough edges of his work and made the author not only acceptable to the Church but one of the best-liked and most-read writers of the Fathers. To be sure, Thomas Aquinas complained about the Aeropagite's studiedly obscure, confused, and confusing language, but this did not deter him from writing his own commentary on the *Divine Names,* as did a whole string of other luminaries such as Hugh of St Victor, Thomas Gallus, Robert Grosseteste, Albert the Great, and Bonaventure.

The dionysian corpus first made its way to the West during the so-called Carolingian Renaissance when, in 827, copies were sent from Byzantium to the Paris of Louis the Pius. Soon it was—appropriately enough—translated by Hilduin, Abbot of St-Denis. This was the first of four medieval translations and was followed by those of John Eriugena, Joannes Saracenus, and Robert Grosseteste. However, the real heirs to the dionysian spirit were the thinkers who extend in a line from that great loner of the ninth century, John Eriugena, via the Victorines, Bonaventura, and Ekkehart to that universal genius of late medieval thought, Nicholas of Cusa (1401-1462). That is to say, the dionysian influence, while by no means limited to anti-aristotelian thinkers, is no doubt strongest in the tradition preserving the platonic-neoplatonic mystique. This influence did not come to an end with the Cusanus. On the contrary, it continued powerfully into Renaissance platonism and onwards in both Catholic and Protestant mysticism although in the mainstream of post-tridentine Catholicism and in that of the Reformation the dionysian spirit plays no more than a marginal role, often suppressed by suspicious institutions, emasculated first by the victory of aristotelianism and then by that of empiricism, yet never dying and never dead. Indeed, I believe, the myth of which it is a potent expression is irrepressible and does rather well without our premature pity or scorn.

THE PLATONIC TRADITION

Turning now to the content of the Areopagite's work, I suggest we first recall three axioms of the platonic tradition on which it rests, and without which these writings make no sense. I will call these axioms those of *realism, causality* and *identity*.

The axiom of *realism* says that the real is 'spiritual,' it is εἶδος—idea. Nothing material can be real in itself because it is subject to change, whereas the real is permanent and changeless. Correspondingly, no certain knowledge of reality can be obtained through sensory perception (though most knowledge begins there), because such perception is limited to material objects. If we do nevertheless attribute reality to physical objects, we do so only because these objects manifest or reflect, in a more or less deteriorated and partial fashion, an underlying idea in which they 'participate.' Do not judge by what you see: I may have a crooked nose, receding hairline and blackened teeth. Never despair. You are not seeing the real me, you are seeing an imperfect realization of the idea of humanness; you see a form, a shape which in turn is 'informed' i.e., receives its form, by what we call the soul, more correctly, the idea soul. Bodily you see shape, noetically you see idea and form. Bodily you see six feet and shrinking, noetically you see height and measure and proportion. The real world lurks behind the phenomenal world. Only by transcending the second through the ideas structured into our minds can we reach the first, the real world of pure forms. From this axiom follows an important corollary: Ontology and epistemology are ultimately one and the same. Only that which *is* can be known to exist and only that which is *real*, is. Since knowledge, however dim it may be, *is*, it not only refers to the real but partakes of it.

The axiom of *causality* (ἀρχή) says that the world is ultimately one. Multiplicity is deterioration, differentiation, a falling away from the one absolute cause which *qua* cause causes everything that is yet without being caused or being identifiable with anything that appears to be. What we call cause is cause only because it participates in *the* Cause. The universe is, as it were, a giant unfolding of the primal cause. Conversely, no matter where we begin, the chain of causality invariably leads us, via intermediate causes, forms, and ideas, to the highest and ultimate cause itself, the One in which all mulitplicity and differentiation is virtually contained.

This axiom, too, has an important corollary. Since not

all forms of differentiation are the same and since there are various kinds and degrees of multiplicity, it follows that there is a gradation of forms and ideas. The more universal an idea, the more real it is and the more it resembles Oneness; the more particular an idea is, the lower it is on the ladder of reality and causality. There is then a 'hierarchy' of intelligible forms and ideas corresponding to a 'hierarchy' of causes.

The axiom of *identity* says that the Real is the Good. The order of being is the same as the order of morality since the Good *is* and cannot *not be*. Anything that *is*, to the extent of its being, is good, though, of course, as there are degrees of being, so there are degrees of goodness. Absolute evil is unthinkable except as absolute non-existence. Anything that is, is good in proportion to the degree to which it participates in its idea and, ultimately, in the idea of the One and the Good.

Armed with these axioms, we are ready to take a look at the Areopagite's system, and in doing this I will limit myself largely to the treatises on the *Divine Names* and the *Mystical Theology*. Central to this system is the concept of the sacred. I deliberately avoid the term 'God,' not only because our author generally prefers other terms, particularly the term 'the One,' but because I think there is a system-internal reason for it which will become apparent as we go along.

Our first question must be: Can the sacred be known? The answer to this question must obviously be in the affirmative, for if the sacred could not be known in any way, we could not ask the question. We therefore reformulate: How is the sacred known? It is known on three levels, as it were: (1) from tradition; (2) through reflection; and (3) ἀγνώστως, i.e., through unknowing. From tradition the sacred is known as God—(today we would say, as Person); through reflection it is known affirmatively as Being and negatively as Non-Being, affirmatively as Goodness and negatively as Non-Goodness; through unknowing, that is, through experience alone, it is known ineffably through an immediate intuition which can be linguistically expressed only in such metaphors of paradox or pure negation as the

Nameless Name, the Darkness beyond Light, or simply Darkness.[2]

We must start from Scripture, and we must realize that in it all levels of knowledge are already contained. The writers of Scripture were inspired and illuminated with special knowledge. Hence Scripture is the only infallible guide to knowledge[3] and contains in itself the 'sacred science'[4] precisely because it is the revelation of the sacred which is Spirit. Wherever the Spirit speaks in terms drawn from the corporeal world, it does so by accommodation to the simple man, the unitiated. The understanding of the spiritual truths (νοητά) of Scripture, however, requires advanced capacities of reflection upon its underlying principles and is possible only to the initiators and initiates of the lower rank.[5] The ultimate step of unknowing, finally, is beyond the distinction of ignorance and knowledge.

At the moment we are interested in Step Two, that sacred science or philosophy of understanding the spiritual truths in Scripture which leaves behind all corporeal symbols. The first thing we must learn is that the sacred is spirit illuminating the cosmos and, in it, man and his spirit. The second thing we must learn is that the sacred is *absolute* spirit, so that all spiritual knowledge not only originates from it but is in fact participation in the absolute spirit's eternal knowledge of itself. There are two problems here, both of which are important to the understanding of the Areopagite's thought and both of which have to do with the ultimate identity of the *ordo essendi* and the *ordo cognoscendi.*

Absolute Spirit is by definition unintelligible and unknowable. Since the sacred is absolute spirit, nothing can be known or said about it, nor can it reveal itself. Yet Scripture gives the sacred names, that is, it describes the 'nature' of the divine. By the same token, we may say that the term 'absolute transcendence' is unintelligible, and therefore meaningless, because it would 'swallow up' the distinction between transcendence and immanence. Yet Scripture clearly does distinguish between *God and creation* while asserting creation to be *God's creation.* The Areopagite vainly tried to find a way out of this dilemma by

adopting the neoplatonic theory of emanation. The sacred
as absoute transcendence is the One which is beyond
thought because beyond all differentiation; it is the absolute unity which is the unifying source of all unity; it is
hyper-essential essence, 'a world beyond utterance, beyond
name and every kind of being. It is the universal cause of
existence while itself existing not.'[6] Nevertheless, it is com-
municable; it lovingly reveals itself by illuminations which
correspond to each separate creature's powers. The
unknowable is knowable *ex parte* because our human
minds are, however faintly, ϑεοειδεῖς, godlike images or
structures.

At this point the second problem arises: If knowledge is
purely spiritual, the phrase 'bodily knowledge' is a contradiction in terms. Yet human beings are bodily beings
and Scripture does not hesitate to apply bodily names to
God. How exactly are we to conceive of the relationship
between the spiritual and the corporeal? Here, the
Areopagite's answer is crisp and clear and again borrowed
from the neoplatonist theory of emanation. If we speak
negatively, there is no body, let alone bodies as such. Body
qua non-spirit is inconceivable because its thought implies
its existence and its participation in being, and because it is
impossible to think non-being. In fact, the cosmos is essentially spirit since its cause is spirit. Even a rock is spirit, for
even though it is impermeable, it reflects the light which
illumines all just as it partakes in the Being which gives
being to all.[7] Strange as it sounds to our ears, the sentence
'the rock is' can only mean 'the rock "knows" ' though of
course with a knowledge far below that of rational, or for
that matter of sentient, beings.

Emanation

The key concept in all of these reflections is obviously
the concept of *emanation*. (Later we must deal with its pendant, the concept of *remanation*.) As a way of getting at the
Areopagite's use of this concept, let me simply list a number of affirmations which are held together by this concept:

The sacred *qua* goodness is the ultimate cause of all that exists;

The sacred *qua* oneness is immanent to all that is, and all things that are participate in it to various degrees;

The sacred *qua* spirit renders the cosmos spiritual: only spirit has being;

The sacred *qua* illumination is known by knowing itself;

The sacred *qua* absolute is the negation of all that is as well as the negation of the negation or, more correctly: the not-negation of all that is.

Put into the language of the Christian tradition: God *qua* God, or God in himself, is unknowable and properly referred to in silence. If words must be used, God must be affirmed in terms of pure contradiction, as not-anything or being nothing. As God *ad extra*, however, that is as creator and cause of everything which is, he is in everything which is and hence knowable as unity (by which our author means the trinity); and all positive human knowledge of God is knowledge derived from his creation, hence knowledge of the creator as Cause, Goodness, and Being.

When we speak of emanation, we speak only of the Cause causing, not of the Uncaused Cause:

It is not our purpose to reveal the hyper-essential Being in its hyper-essential nature (for this is unutterable, nor can we know it or in any wise express it, and it is beyond even the unity [=trinity], but only to celebrate the emanation of the absolute divine essence into the cosmos of things.[8]

Emanation means 'outflowing': All that is flows out from the absolutely simple primal One beyond space (which, being divisible, is not simple) and time (which, being sequential, is not simple). Emanation may be described, but only metaphorically, as eternal process. Accurately speaking one may only say that it *is*. We cannot really ask, 'how does it come to be?' unless we want thereby to indicate metaphorically its Very Being. Thus cautioned, we may say that the sacred *qua* goodness overflows into the cosmos and thus sets the emanational process in motion. Of all the names that Scripture gives to the creator, goodness is the supreme and most adequate because indivisible goodness distends itself by its very existence. Appropriating a favorite simile from his neoplatonic teachers, the Areopagite compares the Good to the sun; as the sun emits its undivided rays upon all things without diminution and thereby calls them into being and sustains them, so the sacred goodness 'shines' or extends itself into the cosmos of beings. But here the feeble similarity ends, for whereas the illumination of the sun *produces* life, the divine goodness *is* illumination and being.[9] To put it bluntly: As the circumference of a circle is its center extended, so the cosmos is goodness extended. It follows that all that is is good[10] and beautiful[11] because of its participation in the Good.[12]

The principle of goodness is not, however, sufficient to explain the cosmos as outflow of the One. (This, by the way, is the term Pseudo-Dionysius prefers to all others, such as God, Being, Good, etc., referring to the sacred. It is borrowed from the platonic tradition, particularly from Plotinus and Proclus). Obviously, the cosmos is multiple being and form, and it is equally obvious that not all things are equal with regard to perfection, being, life, and wisdom. At this point two other principles come into play, viz., the principles of *differentiation* and *order,* or *'hierarchy'* as the Aeropagite calls it, coining a new word which was to acquire an important and permanent place in the Christian tradition.

We give the name 'divine differentiations' to the beneficient emanations of the absolute divinity [and] hierarchy is a sacred order of rank (τάξις ἱερά).[13]

The cosmos represents a holy order by virtue of the proximity or distance of multiple beings to the primal cause. Borrowing another plotinian analogy, our author refers to the radii of a circle: Differentiation begins just beyond the center in which all radii are one. The farther removed from the center a point on any radius is, the less oneness it shares with and the more different it is from other points on other radii. Translated, this means: There is a deteriorating order of being, goodness, wisdom, etc.

Nearest the unknowable center, but already differentiated, are the ideas or exemplars:

All the exemplars of existent things must preexist in [the One] under the form of hyper-essential unity. For it produces essences only by an outgoing from essence. And we give the name 'exemplars' to those laws which, preexisting in the divine as a unity, produce the essences of things . . . laws whereby the hyper-essential preordained and brought into being the entire cosmos.[14]

From the ideas or exemplars follow all other beings in the descending order of rank and spirit. Uppermost are the pure spirits (the neoplatonic 'gods,' but the scriptural 'angels')[15]; next come the rational souls, followed by the irrational souls of the animal world, the merely moving souls of the vegetative world, and finally the lifeless forms of anorganic matter.[16] These steps correspond, on the scale of knowledge, to immediate or simple knowledge (we would say 'intuition'), mediate knowledge of discursive reasoning, perception, vital movement, and mere existence.[17] All steps in this descending order thus imply the diminution of spirit, i.e., of reality, goodness (perfection), and knowledge. The diminishing anti-type is the ever-increasing 'lapse' from the archetype.[18]

Before leaving this emanationist scheme, we must emphasize, however, a final principle implicit in it, that of *continuity*. Each higher order passes on, or reflects, the primal illumination of the Spirit, every successive rank being a fainter analogy of its preceding rank and every superior order being the type of its next inferior order, while all ranks are tied together in the continuity of effluence through the unceasing illumination of the divine goodness yet held in their allotted and immutable station through the divine justice which Scripture calls righteousness:

Everything is good only in proportion as it approaches more or less to the Good, since the perfect goodness penetrating all things . . . extends even to the lowest things, being entirely present to some, in a lower measure to others, and to still others in lowest measure according as each is capable of participating in it.[19]

All things participate in [the divine] nor does it depart from anything that exists.[20]

The divine righteousness ordains all things 'defining proportion, beauty, order, arrangement and all disposition of place and rank for each in accordance with that place which is most truly right'.[21]

Remanation

The pendant to *emanation* is *remanation*. In the absolute sacred cause emanation and remanation are, of course, identical, as are goodness and being. Since the multiplicity of the cosmos is but one immense theophany and hence an analogy of the sacred, emanation must find its completion and perfection in remanation. In order to understand this more fully, we must grasp the Areopagite's concept of *eros* which will, in turn, lead us back to his notion of the divine Goodness.

In simple terms, remanation means the return of all things into the One from which they emanated; the undoing of differentiation and multiplicity, the perfection of the imperfect, the unknowing of knowledge. Again, we would be well-advised to use terms such as 'process' or 'motion' only metaphorically. In the Areopagite's world nothing moves but the false images in the 'false consciousness' of the cave-bound prisoner of Plato's *Republic*. Motion is necessarily predicated of multiplicity, but all multiplicity is contained or—in the words of our author,—'pre-exists' in the absolute One. With this caveat in mind, let us as cave-men make bold to say that all things flowing out from the One flow back into It.

But what is it that accounts for this movement or rather, the δύναμις, ἐνέργεια, power that produces the movement? The answer is *eros.* Mind you, not ἀγάπη, but ἔρως. Eros is, once again, another name for the nameless.[22] Perhaps it is not going too far to say that the term *eros* holds the key to the understanding of the Areopagite's system because *eros* is conceptualized experience. In a telling passage (part of an effusive, intense, almost hymnodic celebration of *eros,* a kind of philosophical Canticle of Canticles) the author defines *eros* thus:

[Eros] means a faculty of unifying and conjoining, and of producing a special commingling together in the beautiful and good: a faculty which preexists toward the Beautiful and Good, and is diffused from this origin to the end, and holds together things of the same order by a mutual bond, and moves the highest to care for those below, and fixes the inferior in a state which seeks the higher.[23]

Here we have all the elements that go into the make-up of the mystery of *eros*. *Eros* is inherent to goodness, cause of causes; *eros* is not illumination, but the very *power* to illuminate which permeates the entire cosmos. It brings into dialectical harmony order and freedom, rank and its own transcendence, the apollonian and the dionysiac, and it directs all towards the One which is both End and Beginning, the darkness of death which is the fullness of Life.

Let me dwell on this for a minute. The sacred, the Areopagite says, is that which all things desire.[24] It is not only absolute cause, i.e. origin and goal of all things, originating, maintaining, and perfecting them, but it is also the erotic force that draws them.[25] Indeed, the creator yearns after all things and attracts all things through the essence of his goodness. What else is the cosmos but the child of love? What else is creation but the Good yearning for the Good?[26] More yet: What we call 'emanation' is but the unknowable unknown in ecstasy. And so the Creator

is drawn from His transcendent throne above all things to dwell within the heart of all things through a hyper-essential and ecstatic power whereby He yet stays within Himself. . . .

For the sacred is not only both object and subject of *eros,* but its very power moving itself toward itself . . . being its own self-revelation and the bounteous emanation of its own transcendent unity . . . overflowing from the Good into the cosmos and once again returning to the Good.[27]

Thus *eros* creates and maintains all spiritual beings, imbuing them with itself, that is, with the divine desire through which they possess their being.[28] *Eros* insures the hierarchical order in that the higher ranks providentially care for the lower, passing on to them the illuminating rays of the divine Sun by reflecting the sacred like a well-aimed mirror,[29] while beings of the same rank are co-ordained by it through the mutual bond of communion.[30] The lower ranks strain toward the higher, as the human soul strains towards the angelic powers mounting towards the abundant origin of all things.[31] Thus *eros* is the great dialectical principle. It creates order while negating it through freedom; it insures status while transcending it; it imperfects perfection while perfecting imperfection. It is the mainspring of emanation and remanation, the mystery of beauty and harmony. As the cosmos is the sacred in erotic ecstasy, so the sacred is the cosmos in erotic ecstasy, for as the Good yearns for all things, so all things yearn for the Good. Those beings which by virtue of their rank have mind and reason seek it by knowledge; those which have only perception, by perception; those without perception, by movement; and those which are lifeless, by their very aptitude to exist.[32]

By now it should come as no surprise to us to hear that the goal of eros is ϑεώσις, deification, reached through the divine illumination drawing upwards holy spirits through ϑεωρία, κοινωνία, and ὁμοίωσις, which I would tentatively and all-too-pallidly translate as spiritual insight, communion, and assimilation. As the Areopagite himself says: 'through deification from the sacred many beings are made gods so far as the godlike capacity of each allows,'[33] since hyper-*eros* bestows deification by giving the faculty for it to those beings that are deified.[34] Indeed, 'the sacred gives itself for the deification of those beings that turn to it.'[35] Of course, not all beings have the same god-like capacity—we have already pointed out the difficulty of detecting the divine illuminating spirit in a rock. Yet it is there, faintly and dully to be sure, but there all the same, and so it, too, partakes in the unifying and unified erotic ascent toward the One which it unified in itself with itself. How is this possible? Again, I let the Areopagite speak for himself:

> The Sacred though in itself unlike any other being nevertheless bestows a divine similitude on those that turn to it and strive to imitate those qualities which are beyond all definition and understanding. It is the power of the divine similitude that turns all created things towards their cause . . . All similarity in the world possesses its quality through having a trace of the divine similarity and thus accomplishes the unification of the creatures.[36]

As I mentioned earlier, the Areopagite wrote two treatises on hierarchy, one on the *Celestial Hierarchy* and the other on the *Ecclesiastical Hierarchy.* In concluding this section on emanation and remanation, I suggest that the substance as well as the intentionality of these works is but an elaboration and application of the concept of the divine similitude, or 'analogy,' that patterns and 'eroticizes' the cosmos. The hierarchies are the cosmic liturgy. In fact, hierarchy is synonymous with the dialectic of emanation and remanation. At the beginning of the third chapter of the *Celestial Hierarchy,* the Areopagite defines the term thus:

In my opinion hierarchy is a sacred order (τάξις ἱερά), a knowledge, a power, (ἐπιστήμη καὶ ἐνέργεια) assimilating itself as far as that is possible to deiformity (ϑεοειδές). In proportion to the divine illuminations given it, each being is lifted up towards divine imitation (ἀναλόγως ἐπὶ τὸ ϑεομίμητον ἀναγομένη). And even though the beauty which belongs to the sacred—being simple, good, and the principle of all initiation—is inimitable, it yet makes each being participate, according to its dignity, in the light which is in it, and it perfects it in divine initiation harmoniously fashioning the initiates into the immutable resemblance of its own form.[37]

Emanation and remanation are thus two sides of the same coin. It is only because of our spiritual inferiority that we need see them dialectically related. Emanation and remanation constitute a giant and eternal cosmic cycle whose oneness is the oneness of the sacred itself. I am tempted to use a modern simile drawn from astronomy: The cosmos is the sacred exploding and distending into a super-nova only to contract and collapse again into and beyond itself into the cosmic hole of non-matter. Indeed it is difficult—in spite of all efforts since Maximus Confessor to baptize the Areopagite—to avoid the inner logic of the dionysian system which drives toward the identification of the sacred with the cosmos or, to put it into the terms of the Judeo-Christian tradition, to say that God and the World are one. If I nonetheless hesitate to draw this conclusion, it is not because of the somewhat tortured distinction between *deus in semetipso* and *deus ad extra,* or because of the ambiguous relationship between *eros* and analogy, but because of the Areopagite's mystical center. In order to explain what I mean by that, I must take you on a little detour, partially retracing our steps and looking at already familiar terrain from a different angle.

Affirmation and Negation

We said that the *ordo essendi* and the *ordo cognoscendi* are essentially one since both are the result of divine illumination. At this point, however, we are interested only in the *ordo cognoscendi,* and, more specifically, in the Areopagite's method, which, as we might expect, conforms exactly to the dialectic of emanation and remanation through the correspondence of *via affirmativa* and *via negativa.* Or, the descending order of differentiation corresponds to affirmative knowledge as the ascending order of unification (or reduction) corresponds to negative knowledge.[38] Thus the affirmative method begins with the most universal concepts and ends with the most particular ones. Added up, it achieves a concept of the sacred as cosmophany.[39] In the *via negativa,* on the other hand, one ascends from the particular to the universal by stripping away all qualities 'in order that we may attain a naked knowledge of unknowing. . . .'[40] Added up, it achieves a concept of the cosmos as theophany. To put it in yet different terms: the *via affirmativa* systematically asserts and relates the meaningfulness of symbols while the negative method destroys, step-by-step, all symbols—first the corporeal ones, next the emotional ones, then the conceptual ones, and finally the intuitive ones. Referring to Moses who, having passed through purification and illumination, achieved the mountaintop only to find that he could not see God, but only the place where God dwells, our author comments:

I take this to signify that the divinest and the highest of the things perceived by the eyes of the body or the mind are but the symbolic language of things subordinate to that which transcends them all.[41]

At the risk of gross oversimplification, let me characterize the two methods in this manner: Scripture gives God
all sorts of names, from the highest—Good, One,
Being—over a long series of intermediate names—Lord,
Powerful, Justice, Life, Father—to the lowest—Rock. And
rightly so, for all of these names aptly homologize a divine
analogy because they are borrowed from the divine
emanation. This is the affirmative method, the method of
the common man. On the other hand, the initiate knows
that precisely for this very reason (of hierarchical analogy)
these names are inadequate and improper. If—to take one
of the highest names—Oneness means the unity of composition, which is after all the only form of unity we know
from the sensible world, or, mathematically speaking, the
oneness which exists only by virtue of twoness and
threeness—then God is not-one, and by the same token he
is not-good, not-being, not-power, not-just, not-life, etc.

It is not our purpose to reveal the hyper-essential being in its hyper-
essential nature, for this is unutterable, nor can we know or express it
. . . but desiring to frame some conception and language about its ineffable nature, we consecrate as primarily belonging to it the name we
most revere [Goodness]. And in this, too, we are in agreement with the
sacred writers. Nevertheless, the actual truth must still be far beyond us.
Hence we have given our preference to the negative method because it
lifts the soul above all things cognate with its finite nature and, guiding
it onward through all the conceptions of God's being which are transcended by that Being exceeding all name, reason, and knowledge,
reaches beyond the farthest limits of the world and there joins us unto
God Himself, insofar as the power of union with Him is possessed even
by us men.[42]

The end of this passage indicates the next step we must
take: As the *via affirmativa* leads to the *via negativa,* so the
via negativa leads to the *via mystica,* as I would call it. Or,
as the meditation of sensory symbols leads to contemplation, in which perception and discursive reasoning
give way[43] to spiritual intuition, so spiritual intuition gives
way to unknowing when the soul becomes θεοειδής (godlike)
in immediate union.[44] This, only this, and not the negative
method as such, is the *via mystica.* As the dialectic of
emanation and remanation is transcended in the absolute

cause, so affirmative and negative methods are transcended
in the mystical way which culminates in the experience of
ἕνωσις (union) where language ceases in si-
lence. We should, however, speak of *via mystica* because it
continues the negative way and hence involves progression.
It is not itself *raptus,* but it *ends* in *raptus.*

Let me go back. If the affirmation 'God is good' must
be negated by saying that 'God is non-good,' this is not the
end. Obviously, this negation does not mean that God is
evil. Quite apart from the problem of theodicy, such a
statement would merely be another affirmation in need of
the negation 'God is non-evil.' God is neither good nor evil;
he neither is nor is not; he is neither god nor non-god. This
is the reason, of course, why I have all along avoided the
word 'God' and substituted the world 'sacred'—not
because this particular word could possibly escape its own
negation, but because it suggests what the Areopagite indicates through the use of the prefix 'hyper-,' and what led
Professor Gilson to speak of 'superlative theology' instead
of 'mystical' theology.[45] The sacred is beyond all distinction, and therefore beyond the distinction of affirmation
and negation. Language can only faintly indicate this
beyondness by negating the negation. The sacred is not
good (negative), it is not-not-good (negation of negation),
that is, it is hyper-good, hyper-one, hyper-being. Meister
Eckhart could much later say the same thing: God is non-
being and being-itself, and hence above all qualifications.
God cannot *be* yet have no being. It follows that God and
being must be identical. But this is necessary only because
of human thought and human language and itself stands in
need of negation. Negations are thus the strongest form of
affirmation: *Deus est aliquid altius ente.* Or, to borrow two
phrases from Cusanus, the *via mystica* is the *docta ignorantia* which intuits the *coincidentia oppositorum* in which the
absolute or infinitely maximal coincides with the absolute
or infinitely minimal in absolute simplicity. For the absolute is above every contradiction and opposition; it contains, as it were, the opposites not in their opposition, but
in their coincidence. All positive predicates of God in the
positive, i.e. historical, religions therefore comprehend

merely the relationship between God and creature, but not God's being in itself. Hence affirmative theology demands negative theology, and only the negative leads to the experience of *raptus*. Even though Cusanus expressly tells us that he did not get the idea of the *docta ignorantia* from the Areopagite, it seems clear to me who the father of this line of thought is:

The nameless is called by all names . . . the One is all multiplicity; [The hyper-essence of the sacred having no distinctions yet embracing all distinctions] is oneness above unity; it is namelessness and multiplicity of names; it is unknowableness and perfect intelligibility; it is universal affirmation and universal negation in a state above all affirmation and negation.[46]

Evil is nothing and hyper-being is nothing, but whereas the first is nothing because of lack, the latter is nothing because of abundance, hence the nothingness of death coincides with the nothingness of superabundance in the identity of infinity.[47] This is what is meant by the Apostle's word of the Foolish Wisdom (I Cor 1:20-25), the unknowing which is 'a hyper-essential understanding of the hyper-essential sacred and which lies in the sacred's hyper-essence surpassing discourse, intuition and being itself.'[48]

In the act of unknowing, all contradiction negates itself:

for while the transcendent cause possesses all the positive attributes of the cosmos, it does not possess them since it transcends them all so that there is no contradiction between affirming and denying that it has them, inasmuch as it precedes and surpasses all deprivation being beyond all positive and negative distinction.[49]

And thus the *via mystica* enters that 'hyper-essential darkness which is hidden by all the light that is in existent things,'[50] where

the hyper-essential stands revealed in its naked truth to those alone who have passed through the opposition of good and evil, and pass beyond the topmost altitudes of the holy ascent and leave behind them all divine enlightenment and voices and heavenly utterances and plunge into the darkness where truly dwells, as Scripture says, the One which is beyond all things;[51]

where entering the Light, all natural activities cease and the μυστικὴ ἕνωσις is achieved;[52]

where the true initiate is united by his highest faculty, through the passive stillness of all his reasoning powers, to it which is wholly unknowable, of which thus by a rejection of all knowledge he possesses a knowledge exceeding his own understanding.[53]

It is the divine Eros which makes man desire to come 'to this darkness which is beyond light' and 'to attain to the vision through the loss of sight and knowledge.'[54]

Let me conclude this section on the Areopagite's system with a quotation in which, describing the inspiration of his fictitious teacher Hierotheos, he in fact describes his own mystical experience in a nutshell: The true mystic initiate, says he,

'not only learns, but suffers the sacred.'[55]

THE GNOSTIC MYTH RESTATED

Nothing remains for me but a kind of critical postscript which—in the interest of time and in deference to your patience—I would like to present in form of a few theses, each followed by a brief explication.

My first thesis: Morphologically, the writings of the pseudo-Areopagite constitute a grand restatement of the great gnostic myth through which gnosticism experiences a belated, but nonetheless victorious and full, integration into that great syncretistic religion which we call Christianity.

By 'myth' I do not, of course, mean 'fable,' the caricature of those who think they can run away from themselves, or (to belabor the great Cusanus once more) the ignorance of those who think they know as opposed to the ignorance of those who know that they do not know. Rather, I mean by 'myth' the symbolic representation of hierophany in language; the presence of the sacred, the disclosure of the really Real, of that which ought to be but is not, or is no longer, or is not yet.

Without in any way trying to make a universally valid statement, I contend that there are in Christianity two great archetypal myths which I call the gnostic and the apocalyptic. In the gnostic myth, the sacred is experienced as present through re-presentation, as the ever-renewed and ever-renewing ἀρχῆ, the origin and archetype of all that is experienced in the phenomenal world of every-day life. In the apocalyptic myth, the sacred is present through anticipation, as the overpowering, disturbing-beckoning, and threatening-comforting new which is to be grasped, the end of all that is, and the promise of a new world and a new man.

The great gnostic myth has as its central symbol the cosmos in the Greek sense of the word, i.e., the ordered and therefore beautifully harmonious universe. The cosmos is hierophany. It is divine, for it is the overflow of the divine *pleroma.* Theogony, cosmogony, and anthropogony are essentially the same, for all is one, all originates in the one *pleroma,* and returns to it in timeless cycles as the cosmic bodies circle in the perfection of eternal renewal.

Yet cosmogony is deterioration, differentiation, fall. The circle deteriorates to a spiral, and the spiral to a straightline away from the *pleroma* and toward the infinity of nothingness. The archetypal illumination becomes dimmer and dimmer, but it is never extinguished. It is always on recall through the *imitatio* of its faintest traces in the remaining sparks of spirit and *eros.* And so, through the agency of the enlightening divine revealer, the return and renewal part of the cosmic cycle begins. End meets beginning and beginning end. Eon follows eon in unending simultaneity. The Great Circle is closed and we do not know if ever it had opened. From One through many to One. From integrity through disintegration to reintegration. Whether it be the Brahmin *yugas,* or the Persian great years, or the Greek *eons,* this world is integral, reality is plausible, even rational, and hence true and good, and its norms simple. The demons are banned. Change is ultimately impossible, indeed demonic. Is this incredible optimism or the yearning for security in an empirically absurd world? Whatever the cause, nothing new threatens the familiar; all conflict pertains to body and mind, but the spirit transcends it into integral order. Hope is not for the future. What can the future hold but more of the same, the necessarily recurring threat of disintegration, loneliness, scarcity, contingency, and powerlessness? No, one hopes ultimately for extinction of the self in the darkness of the One from which it 'fell' with inexorable necessity and to which it must return even as death must return to life.

INTERPRETED MYTH

My second thesis: The language of the Areopagite is philosophical, but philosophy itself is but interpreted myth.

Many have puzzled over, and been puzzled by, the language of the Areopagite. Thomas Aquinas found it exceedingly obscure, yet he was determined to make sense out of it. Is the speaker a philosopher trying rationally and systematically to comprehend reality? Or is he a theologian (certainly not a christologian) trying to restate, extrapolate, and interpret the Christian credal tradition in the thought forms of his day? Or is he an obscurantist, if not occultist, playing on the dark instincts of man? Is he a scientist or is he a poet? Whatever he is, he is above all else *homo religiosus* and that means *homo mythicus.*

Dispute over the Areopagite's divided loyalty—to neoplatonism and to the Christian tradition—is idle. Both are structurally as well as experientially religious. The great anonymous begins with a traditional philosophical assumption, viz., that one may conclude from the effect to its cause. With him this is not a scientific but a religious assertion; the real world of phenomena (we would say the empirical world) does not and cannot of itself disclose any permanent meaning structures. It is indeed a powerful symbol, but all the same *only* a symbol. Without interpretation it is absurd. With interpretation, however, it discloses order and meaning, and the interpretor is Logos (notwithstanding its own negation). Much later Luther will say *"scriptura sui ipsius interpres."*[56] The Areopagite says scripture is nothing of itself, but through the Logos becomes symbol: *Sacer mysterium est semetipsae interpres.* The mind devours the body, cognition devours action, contemplation cognition, and the darkness of unknowing all knowledge. And yet this final paradox is ultimately the experience of rationality, reason undoing reason in a final self-*destruct*, but *self*-destruct, the supreme assertion of optimistic faith in reason. Good is what corresponds to reason, evil what opposes it. Every being is good insofar as it obeys the limits imposed upon it by its own rational form. Evil is what breaks through the informed limitation and thus threatens being itself. But the form of man is his rational soul.

As a philosopher-theologian who opted for the theory of emanation, the Areopagite failed, at least in regard to two fundamental issues: the emanation theory can neither affirm absolute transcendence nor account for the reality of evil. Like his teacher Proclus, the Areopagite can find rational meaning only in the affirmation of the good and the denial of evil. At this point, he is in sharp conflict with the Christian tradition, for reasons to be mentioned presently. However, I want to repeat emphatically: the *theory* of emanation may have failed, but the *myth* of the emanation-remanation cycle could not, and indeed cannot, fail.

INTERMEZZO

Anticipating the Non-conclusion of my Second Lecture

Man is in the process of becoming. This is the poignant formulation of a contemporary Marxist author who, I believe, captures the spirit of our time. What or who man is going to be, he does not know. He does have notions about what he will be, or at any rate what he should be, but he drags these notions from premises all-too-small to permit a conclusion, viz., from the dialectic of experience and tradition, from tradition critique. Whether or not he can direct his own process of becoming, whether this process is inevitable or pliable, knowable or unknowable—all this is open to contradictory evidence and answers. Certain is only this: man is at present not what he ought to be, could be, and, one hopes, he will be.

I have deliberately chosen a Marxist spokesman

because I wished to make the point that the sentence 'Man is in the process of becoming' is a religious sentence; more accurately, it is a mythical sentence made up of religious symbols. I propose that the logical object of this sentence—really real man, fully realized man, true man—is homologous with the traditional term 'sacred,' and that the intentionality of this sentence is essentially identical with that of the Platonic sentence according to which the goal of human life is the ὁμοίωσις τῷ θεῷ, or in the Areopagite's version: ἕνωσις, union, assimilation to and identification with God, apotheosis. These are traditionally symbolic ways of stating the myth that man may be truly and fully man only in the One (Plotinus), as καινὴ κτίσις ἐν Χριστῷ (Paul), in the darkness of Light (Ekkhart), in the coincidence of all opposites (Nicholas of Cusa), in the absolute spirit (Hegel), in his archetypal self (Jung), in the identity of his true humanity (Marx), in the depth of his species-consciousness (Feuerbach), in the vision of *el hombre nuevo* (Castro), or in the *raptus* of LaVerna. Is your hair bristling by now? How can all these be the same? If all are the same, nothing is the same. If all is religion, nothing is religion. I am not denying that there are deep and important, indeed fundamental, differences, but I do say that these differences are differences in the symbols, not in the structure, of the Myth. The sacred and the profane are dialectically related; in the structure of human experience one cannot be without the other, but the *eros* transcending the dialectic is equally built into the structure. Tertullian was almost, but only *almost,* right when he claimed in his famous aside that *anima naturaliter Christiana.*[57] He would have been right had he said: *anima naturaliter mythica.*

SALVATION AND THE TEMPORAL PROCESSES

My third and final thesis: For the Areopagite salvation is escape from time. As a consequence of this, he cannot see history as hierophany.

I quote: 'The primary salvation of the world is that which preserves all things in their proper places without change, conflict, or deterioration.'[58] What is time? Time is deteriorated eternity, change, *totum simul.* The sacred is not the creator of time and history (as the great bishop of Hippo had already discovered) but is itself the eternity of the ages, the measuring principle of eons, the reality underlying time and the eternity underlying existence in time.[59] What we call history is neither the really Real nor its stage. Rather, the temporal processes themselves are symbols. Events are nothing in themselves. As the sacred creates itself in its creatures, it knows itself in their knowledge of itself and it acts in their actions. History therefore has no progression: the Kingdom is the unknowing of history.

The Areopagite knows Christ the Son, but he seems not to know the Jesus of Nazareth. Like the Corinthians, he seems to say: 'Glory be to the Lord Christ—Jesus be damned.' (1 Cor 12:3) He knows the spirit but not the body. Unlike his great predecessor, the first Christian 'mystic,' the author of the so-called Gospel of John, he cannot really say 'the Word became Flesh,' incarnate. He loves to quote the Paul of Romans 11:36 ('For from him and through him and to him are all things'), but he steadfastly ignores the other Paul, the Paul of 1 Thessalonians and 1 Cor 15, Paul the eschatologist. History is predicated of body; it is the story of the cross in A.D. 33 (or thereabouts). It is change, purposeful change perhaps, but at any rate real change and progression. The first Resurrection is *not* the second Resurrection, but only its historical anticipation.

We started out by speaking of the Christian dialectic, the dialectic of the already and the not-yet, the above and the forward, the solitude of the *logos* and the fellowship of bodies. The Areopagite dissolved this dialectic into its first antipode (his *logical* dialectic notwithstanding). As Bonaventura rightly observed, he is 'the prince of the mystics,'[60] not the prince of reform and revolution. In a way his spirit ruled the middle ages, but only in a way. In the next lecture, we will look at the rediscovery of the other pole of the Christian dialectic, the apocalyptic-eschatological pole.

One final word: I began by defining spirituality as

religious man's personal experience of bridging the gulf
between sacred and profane through participation in the
really Real, but I also insisted that spirituality is not the
solipsistic experience of an individual, but a social
phenomenon mediated through a common symbol system.
I think the Areopagite's thought bears me out. The union
of which he speaks is not theory or fiction. Regardless of
the failings of verbalization and conceptualization, it is experienced reality. Nor is it the Areopagite's own product,
but rather that of the social world of which he is a part.
And thus he himself, or rather his thought, becomes a symbol of a reality the ultimate meaning of which escapes us.

One question remains: If spirituality is the experience
of participation in the really Real, must such an experience
necessarily be that of union or may it also be one of
anticipation?

Guntram G. Bischoff

Western Michigan University

EARLY PREMONSTRATENSIAN ESCHATOLOGY: THE APOCALYPTIC MYTH

The Premonstratensians were an order of canons regular founded in 1120 at Prémontré, near Laon, France. The founder, Norbert of Xanten (c. 1080-1134), had previously been a canon of St Victor and had frequented the courts of the archbishop of Cologne and of the Holy Roman Emperor, Henry V. After a conversion experience in 1115, he made futile attempts at reforming his brother canons before beginning a career as an itinerant preacher. Even after founding his order at Prémontré, he continued to travel extensively on preaching tours. His zeal for reform and his strong-mindedness won him many enemies, but also impressed the devout, among them the pope, who appointed him archbishop of Magdeburg, and the emperor, who made him imperial chancellor for Italy the year before his death. His Life *is contained in the MGH SS XII (1856) 663-706. Excerpts of this same life appear in the AA SS Jun. 1 (1695) 819-58.*

Eschatology: from eschata, *the last things. The study of the last things, i.e., the ultimate end of each human soul and of mankind and the created universe generally.*

Apocalyptic: from apokalyptein, *to uncover, disclose. The teaching that the created world will be utterly destroyed when the fullness of God's plan is disclosed.*

Our second topic is 'Early Premonstratensian Eschatology.' The term 'eschatology' needs some preliminary clarification. It is a composite term, and its first part, *eschaton,* translates into the English words 'last,' 'final,' or 'ultimate.' If something is last or ultimate in the logical order of thought or being, we should retranslate 'last' by the word 'absolute,' and by doing so we would return to the world of Pseudo-Dionysius. But the word 'last' can also refer to the temporal order, in which case it is synonymous with 'end,' the end of time in the future. And this last is the sense in which I intend to use 'end' in speaking about early premonstratensian eschatology.

41

As you recall, we concluded the previous lecture with a question: If spirituality is religious man's experience of participation in the really Real, must such experience necessarily be that of union or may it also be that of anticipation? I would like to hyphenate the word anticipation: *anti-capere* means to grasp against the future, to wrench from the clutches of the unknowable abyss of future. In this sense, 'anti-cipation' is a faithful translation of the Greek *prolepsis*.

Behind that final question lay what I called the christian dialectic of the already-not-yet, the above and the forward, the beyond and the future—that is to say, the dialectic which results when the gnostic myth is juxtaposed to the apocalyptic myth. Before we can go on, I must be a bit more explicit about what I mean by the 'apocalyptic myth.' I have defined myth as 'the symbolic representation of hierophany in language, that is to say, the story of the manifestation of the sacred, the disclosure of the really Real, of that which ought to be, but is not, or is no longer, or is not yet.'[1] The apocalyptic myth tells the story of God's imminent coming to his waiting people, the story of the imminent final theophany whose very occurrence implies the utter destruction of the present social order and, hence, a completely new beginning. There are in the apocalyptic myth therefore two constitutive elements which we may call the dualistic and the social. By dualism I mean radical discontinuity: not renewal of what is old, decrepit, and exhausted but a totally new beginning, a new creation *ab ovo;* not reformation but transformation; not reform but revolution; not continuity and progression but hiatus and rupture. Unlike the gnostic myth in which we have carefully and laboriously to search out a social dimension since *logos* is neither individual nor social, but generic, the apocalyptic myth is social myth *par excellence.* Its interest is not cosmos but community; not hierarchy but history; not nature but empire.[2]

THE APOCALYPTIC MYTH

Let me state briefly some of the implications of this elemental structural analysis and at the same time penetrate a little more deeply the opacity of the apocalyptic myth:

—There is no bridge leading from the present social order to the order to come. The present order is, as it were, an order characterized by the absence of the sacred; its 'order' is really chaos. The present must be destroyed so that the future may come to be.

—The imminent new creation means primarily the creation of the new man, man who is truly what he is meant to be and what he ought to be. The *homo homini lupus* will be changed into *homo homini homo verus*.

—But if there is no bridge, how can there be hope? If there is to be an utterly new man, what is to be his image; what the content of the words *homo verus*? And how can absolute future be known? How can that-which-is-not-yet know what it will be; how can the unborn know himself in the fullness of perfection? At this point, we must again escape into metaphor: All this is possible because the coming hierophany casts its own shadow ahead of itself. The sacred reality *is* totally obscure as yet, but because it permits, as it were, a preview of itself, it may be glimpsed by those who have the gift of prophetic vision. The new order already now becomes partially realizable by the anticipation of its final consummation. Indeed, those who already now live in the shadows of the coming theophany not only set an example for all others but, by doing so, actually hasten the coming of the new order.

In his untiring effort to comprehend the nature and structure of myth, Mircea Eliade has tried to make it clear that all myths ultimately deal with ontogeny. I think he is right, if we realize that ontogeny is a concept based in the experience of *logos* and not in that of time, or, to say it differently, if we distinguish the concept of ontogeny from the experiences of *arche* and *eschaton*. What would have happened if, instead of the gnostic myth, the apocalyptic myth had informed the structure of christian dogmatics; if the topos of eschatology were not treated at the end, but at the beginning; and the topos of creation were treated not at the beginning, but at the end?

Chiliasm

Of the various expressions of the apocalyptic myth, I consider the most important, or at any rate the one I am most interested in at this point, that of chiliasm. I use this term in the loose, not the strict historical sense. The symbolism of the thousand years,[3] and the symbolic figure of a personal messiah, I do not consider constitutive of chiliasm. I would therefore define chiliasm as the proleptically experienced perfect society of the end-time. Chiliasm does not describe the new creation as such; it describes it *in statu anticipationis.* It does not, to use modern terminology, describe it in terms of the romantic distinction between the monster of *Gesellschaft* and the quaint idyll of *Gemeinschaft;* rather it describes it as the perfect community of the end-time.

One should not confuse the apocalyptic myth with the various hybrids which result from its amalgamation with the gnostic myth. I have two particularly in mind: the anaclitic and the progressive versions. The anaclitic version envisions, at the end of history, the restoration of paradise. Repristination is its key symbol, and the structure of the gnostic myth is easily discernible in this. It is the father of all models of renewal, restoration and reformation, and it has exerted a powerful influence in the history of Christianity.

The progressive version combines the gnostic structure of ontic continuity with the apocalyptic structure of temporal linearity. It ties the hierarchical order and continuity of cosmic being to the linear and irreversible sequence of human being in time. According to this hybrid, progress means more than mere becoming or change. Progress means continual improvement, gradual perfection toward a definite goal. One of its parents is the experience of human growth—birth-childhood-adolescence-adulthood—combined with the Greek idea of *paideia,* i.e. what we today might call self-realization. This was present in christian theology as early as Irenaeus. Its other parent, however, is the experience of the irreversibility and non-repeatability of events which lead up, in a straight line, to The Event yet to come. This element, too, was already present in Irenaeus, to whom the end was more than the beginning and recapitulation more than a return to the origin. He was, moreover, a chiliast expecting a new order quite out of the purview of the old creation. As Th. Mommsen has rightly pointed out, however, the full-fledged idea of progress as we know it first appeared in the thought of Augustine. This was not by chance for he, like no one else, knew how to synthesize the neoplatonist and the christian traditions. One might say that the *locus classicus* of the idea of progress is his famous outline of the second half of *De civitate dei,*[4] where he states that he wants first to describe the *exortus,* then the *procursus* or *excursus,* and finally the *finis* of the City of God. *Arche* and *eschaton,* but wedged in between is the course of real history, understood as progress towards its end.

This is of considerable importance for our present purpose, for while the apocalyptic myth in its elemental and pure structure is by no means unknown to the Middle Ages, it was in the main available only through its augustinian reinterpretation as progress. The correct label for this reinterpretation is not apocalypticism or chiliasm, but 'theology of history.'

I need not remind you that the apocalyptic myth, particularly its chiliastic expression, is not a late-comer to Christianity. On the contrary, Christianity was born with it and of it. I would not hesitate to claim that no one can fully understand and appreciate the history of Christianity who cannot see Jesus of Nazareth also as the prophet of an incipient chiliastic movement. As primitive Christianity encountered the Greek tradition, however, the gnostic myth gradually overlaid and eventually buried the apocalyptic myth. Although it seemed dead, it never died. It survived, paradoxically, in large part because of Augustine himself, and we are interested here in its reemergence in Latin Christianity around 1100.

The first thing that usually comes to mind when one speaks of the reemergence of chiliasm in the Middle Ages is the figure of the great Calabrian visionary, Joachim of Fiore († 1202). Anyone who has read him or read about him and his influence[5] knows the potency of the rediscovery of chiliasm. But I am interested in the development of the ideas which led up to Joachim. Most textbooks and monographs[6] jump in one giant leap from Augustine to Joachim while I am intersted in the 'missing link.' I look for the first stirrings of the chiliastic idea, the reemergence of the notion of a perfect *ordo,* a community of the perfect arising within the imminent future of historical time and anticipating, preparing for, and indeed hastening, the coming of the End.

RUPERT OF DEUTZ

Access to our inquiry comes through the *Commentary on Some Chapters of the Rule of St Benedict* by Rupert of Deutz.[7] This work is an early representative of the type of polemical literature which accompanied the rapid expansion of Cistercians and regular canons after the second decade of the twelfth century, and of which the exchange between Bernard of Clairvaux and Peter of Cluny is a classical example. The triangular controversy between Cluniacs, Cistercians, and regular canons is of particular interest to our present study in so far as it was focused at the opposition between old and new; it pitted the validity of the old and true original order against the worthlessness of deviant innovation. With the tenor of its traditionalism, this kind of valuation is, of course, the *cantus firmus* of all medieval reform, and scholarship has been generally agreed in considering the maxim 'renewal through repristination' as the hallmark of the great canonical and monastic reform of the eleventh and twelfth centuries. This view of the self-understanding of the reformers no doubt finds formidable support in the available evidence, yet we must question its exclusive validity.

Rupert, head of the benedictine abbey of Deutz, located across the Rhine river from Cologne, acted as defender of the old order when he published his *Commentary* early in 1126. As its title suggests, the work was primarily directed against the Cistercians whose 'novel' ways had just been introduced into the archdiocese of Cologne. No names are mentioned, but the identity of the opposition is no mystery. A cistercian abbot, Henry, and his small band of followers had arrived from Morimond in 1122. Almost at once they had begun a vigorous propaganda campaign, and more recently they had been surreptitiously applying pressure on some of the more naive black monks to induce them to leave their old ways and join their white rivals.

Our present concern is with the fourth and last book of Rupert's *Commentary*. There the author inveighs sharply against the views of a certain regular canon. No matter how great a nuisance, the Cistercians were still monks and Benedictines; their zeal, however misguided, demanded respect. It was a different matter with these new canons, who appeared to be neither canons nor monks yet claimed to be better than both. In the course of refuting these new and dangerous claims Rupert quotes *verbatim* a portion of his adversary's argument, the elucidation of which is my chief concern in the technical part of this lecture.

I remember [writes Rupert] hearing you say something which I am not sure how to understand nor of which spirit it proceeded. For you said: 'After the Babylonian empire grew to be huge, it ceased growing and another succeeded it, namely the kingdom of the Persians and Medes; and this in turn was superseded by yet another, that is to say, the kingdom of the Macedonians.'

Then you added these words as if in similitude of the foregoing. You said, 'Thus it must come about in the future—indeed, it must begin to happen now—that the greatness and height of those who have flourished until now in the monastic way of life, mostly the Cluniacensians . . . will be humbled and thoroughly reduced while the rule passes to the humble rising up.'[8]

The significance of this passage cannot be overestimated. It is obvious that Rupert's adversary does not consider the rise of his own community in terms of repristination. On the contrary, he consciously and approvingly sees in it the emergence of a new order and he looks expectantly toward the future for its full realization. The context makes it quite clear, moreover, that he expected this new order to surpass even the Cluniacs in perfection.

In order adequately to interpret this important though fragmentary piece of evidence, we must first attempt to ascertain the historical background. Then we should seek to establish the identity of its proponent and, if possible, its place in the context of what else may be known of his thought.

THE CANONS REGULAR AND THEIR REFORMS

Thanks to the thoroughness of recent research, we are today quite well-informed about the origin and course of the canonical reform. It began in the early decades of the eleventh century, but the reform came fully into its own only with the second half of the century. It fed on the explicit critique of the *Rule of Aachen,* especially with regard to carolingian legislation mitigating the common life and personal property. In the face of strong conservative opposition the reformers turn increasingly to the Fathers, particularly to Jerome, Augustine, and Gregory the Great, to substantiate their claim that they merely wanted to restore the primitive tradition to the Church. This gregorian phase of the reform finds its natural consummation around 1070, with the adoption of the moderate so-called *regula tertia* of Augustine which, added to such existing authorities as the *Rule of Benedict,* makes up the legislative body of rules and customs known as the *instituta patrum.*

Toward the end of the eleventh century there arose from within the reform a movement of an entirely different character. It grew out of spontaneously formed colonies of clerics, often associated with laymen and women, who gathered in some desolate place around the figure of a clerk-hermit. Marked by considerable heterogeneity in detail, the movement in the beginning was united only by its insistence on radical asceticism. A sudden focus was found, however, when these groups adopted the so-called *ordo monasterii.* The origin of this exceedingly severe rule is obscure, but the reformers adopting it attributed it unhesitatingly to the authority of Augustine. This truly extraordinary step seems first to have been taken, probably in 1115, at the community of Springiersbach, located on the middle Moselle in the archdiocese of Trier. Some five years later, Norbert introduced the *ordo* to the newly founded community at Prémontré.

A heated controversy resulted, but this time *within* the reform, as to who was in possession of the perfect recipe for repristination of the true apostolic tradition. Would it be the *ordo antiquus* of the moderates or the allegedly purer, more faithful, and more perfect *ordo novus* of the radicals? Once more the polemic was couched in the opposing terms of old versus new, even while both groups united in their contempt of the traditional *Rule of Aachen* and its cluniac progeny. But the use of the terms 'old' and 'new' now had a different ring: the *ordo novus,* precisely because it claims to restore the original more purely and more faithfully, *is* in fact more perfect than the old order.

Eberwin of Steinfeld

Rupert's point-by-point refutation of his opponent's claims makes it clear that his adversary was a devotee of the *ordo novus.* It also helps us to establish his identity, for at the time Rupert wrote there existed only a handful of communities which followed the *ordo monasterii,* and Rupert's detailed allusions make it virtually certain that his opponent was Eberwin, provost of a community of regular canons at Steinfeld, in the Eifel mountains not far to the south and west of Cologne.

Sources concerning the origin and early history of Steinfeld are, unfortunately, exceedingly sparse. The place had been a deteriorated benedictine convent prior to 1121, but in that year Frederick I, archbishop of Cologne, invited regular canons from Springiersbach to take possession of it and he granted a charter to the new community. It appears that in 1126 Steinfeld was still associated with Springiersbach. Soon after this year, however, Eberwin severed whatever institutional relationship his community had had with Springiersbach and affiliated with the order of Prémontré. We do not know what prompted this change, but Eberwin retained his position at the head of the community until his death, in 1152.

Considering the paucity of our sources, we are fortunate to possess a letter Eberwin wrote some eighteen years later to Bernard of Clairvaux.[9] This letter is of the greatest importance for the elucidation of Eberwin's thought and may be dated sometime between 1140 and 1143. Its chief purpose was to inform the abbot of Clairvaux about the discovery and inquisition of several heretical groups of laypeople in the city and archdiocese of Cologne, and to enlist the eloquence of his pen in the effort to put down this bewildering phenomenon. The main body of the letter has recently been subjected to detailed analysis because it constitutes a prime source of information on the obscure beginnings of medieval heresy. Its introductory section, on the other hand, seems so far to have escaped notice, and it is this part with which we must concern ourselves.

Eberwin begins by praising Bernard for his *Sermons on the Canticle,* the first sixty-two of which he seems to have known. Comparing the great abbot to the steward of the wedding feast of Cana who dispensed the miraculously produced new wine, Eberwin urges him to continue his work. But he qualifies his request at once by closely prescribing the way in which he would like to see interpreted the next verse, Canticle 2:15. He says: 'From the fifth jar you must now dispense drink to us, most holy father!'—that is to say, as we hear a little later on:

... the time has now come for you to ... enter into the fight against the new heretics who everywhere ... boil up from the bottomless pit as if their prince were being loosed and 'the Day of the Lord at hand'.

Eberwin's correlation of the fifth jar with the eruption of heresy is not just a fanciful oddity but part of an exegetic scheme in which each of the six jars of Cana is interpreted to refer to troubles characteristic of the church at various times of its history. By this exposition, Eberwin comes to terms with the bewildering new kind of heresy which puzzled him the more in that the faith of its adherents seemed stronger than any to be found in the Church. And their high ideals of virginity and radical asceticism seem virtually identical with those upheld by Eberwin's own order. Surely, he concludes, they must be those perverse liars prophesied by the Apostle in his letter to Timothy.

It may be well to pause briefly to summarize the three chief elements of this introductory portion of the letter:

Eberwin is convinced he is living in the last days of the present world;

His conviction is related to the rise of a new kind of heresy;

His appraisal is confirmed through the application of a certain method of biblical exegesis.

Our next aim must be a fuller and more adequate delineation of Eberwin's eschatology, if we are to understand it within the contemporary framework of cognate thought.

We begin by inquiring into the provenance of Eberwin's curious exegesis of the Cana-pericope. It is possible, of course, that Eberwin's interpretation of the miracle at Cana was original with him, but the power exerted by traditional forms in the exegesis of his time makes this very unlikely.

Considering Eberwin's high praise of Bernard's early sermons on the Canticle, we might expect him to have derived his interpretation from the work of the great abbot. Bernard had indeed dealt with the miracle of Cana, toward the end of *sermo* 54 in which he comments on *Cant.* 2:8.[10] Bernard, however, had interpreted the passage solely in its moral sense, and nothing was farther from his mind than to find historical allusions in it. Eberwin did not derive his interpretation from Bernard.

The exegetical tradition of what we might call the historical symbolism of the Cana-pericope is very scant. As far as I can see, it occurs only three times prior to 1100: in

Augustine's widely read *Commentaries on the Gospel of John;*[11] in a brief and unaccentuated passage of the *Liber formularum spiritalis intelligentiae* of Eucherius of Lyons,[12] and in the ninth (?) century work of the elusive Haimo.[13] Both Eucherius and Haimo copy Augustine.

Derivation from Augustine, on the other hand, would seem to commend itself if for no other reason than the ready availability of his commentaries, the authority of their patristic author, and the presumable loyalty of the augustinian canon Eberwin to his founding father. Yet a number of difficulties present themselves at this point.

Augustine focused on the significance on the water in the six jars prior to its conversion into wine; this symbolizes the prophecy of Christ through the six ages of the world; the six jars refer to the full course of universal history and not just to the sixth age, which is the age of the Church—as it is with Eberwin. Hence, the figure of the steward plays no major role in Augustine's exposition; the conversion into wine signals the change from historical prophecy to eternal fulfillment, from partial understanding to the full understanding which no longer belongs to the historical order but enables the Christian to see the *Logos* in the entirety of his historical manifestations. This interpretation accords perfectly with Augustine's concept of history, as we shall see, but it is foreign to Eberwin's exegesis. Eberwin did not derive his interpretation from Augustine.

We suggest that Eberwin's historical exposition of the Cana-pericope was inspired by the *Commentary on John* from the pen of his old adversary, Rupert of Deutz.[14] This work had been written at the abbey of Siegburg, near Cologne, and was finished by 1116. It had made a considerable, if not always favorable, impression on Rupert's contemporaries as it was the first full commentary on John's gospel since patristic times. Relying heavily on Augustine's work, the monk at Siegburg had borrowed, with only minor modifications, the great bishop's equation of the water jars with the six ages of the world. Otherwise Rupert had taken considerable liberties with the exegetical tradition—a feature characteristic of the entire work of the monk who knew himself to be endowed with a special grace of *intelligentia spiritalis.*

Time is short and I will spare you the marshalling of evidence in support of my contention. May it suffice at this time to state that the evidence is *not* unequivocal and that the validity of my contention depends on the further results of this study. Before we pursue this question, however, it is necessary to examine more closely Eberwin's outline of church history.

THE AUGUSTINIAN CONCEPT OF HISTORY

Because of its inherent dualism, the augustinian concept of history attaches no significance to history after Christ. To the bishop of Hippo, history is merely the temporal phase, or level, of the essentially atemporal battle between the two cities. Just as historical time is, strictly speaking, the time of fallen man, lacking all definition apart from the operation of the *Logos,* so history is meaningful only as redemptive history. From this point of view, it is only consistent that the Christ-event should appear as the climactic and effective end of the course of history. Perhaps one should more adequately formulate the Augustinian definition of history as being interrupted creation—an idea which can be traced directly to Irenaeus. Once the second Adam has retrieved the position in God's plan at which the first Adam failed, history is effectively ended. Christ consummates the delayed portion of the process of creation, but he does so no longer in the order of historical time, but in that of eternity.

This concept of history cannot master the fact of continued and continuing history after Christ other than through its complete spiritualization. This is precisely the course taken by the mature Augustine of the *City of God,* and in this form it dominated the western concept of history without challenge until about 1100, and sounded at the time the deathknell of all forms of chiliasm in the West.

Augustine achieved the complete spiritualization of history after Christ through an ingenious interpretation of the chiliastically intended passage on the double death and the double resurrection in Revelation 20. The Church, already redeemed to spiritual participation in the eternal city, exists exempt from history. Her temporal body, awaiting exaltation, has in and of itself none but a sacramental significance. It exists 'punctually,' as it were, within a socio-cultural order totally devoid of redemptive significance. Speculation on the date of the end of the world is not only undesirable, but unnecessary, since any present time is essentially and existentially end-time. Nothing materially new may be expected in the order of time save the manifestation of its end through the second coming of Christ.

In his untiring efforts to come to terms with the problem of history, Augustine experimented with a variety of symbols for the periodization of history. While all of these applied only to history before the Christ-event, we now see why he preferred the six-fold scheme, derived from the *hexaemeron,* to all others: it alone was fully adaptable to his dualism of time and eternity. It is this scheme which Augustine read out of, or rather into, the Cana-pericope also.

The difference between Eberwin's view and Augustine's is immediately apparent when we compare them. Augustine's perception of the punctual, hence un-differentiated, unity of the Church's existence has yielded to a view that detects movement. The time of the Church is now divided into the six ages, symbolized by the six jars of Cana, *because* the Church exists in historical time and because such historical existence is significant. The timeless unity and homogeneity of the Church's existence have clearly become a problem. Change is now perceived within this existence, and—what is more important—this change is viewed as a graduated process in which the flow of church-history accelerates toward its end. From op-position by the Pharisees and Scribes, to open persecution by the pagan empire, to the surreptitious subversion by the great heretics of the patristic age, to the hypocritical and insidious Christians of the time of the *res publica christiana,* to the incipient outbreak of new and open heresy at the end of history, to the final appearance of Antichrist, the history of the Church discloses the mystery of a dramatic process heading for its finale.

The implications of Eberwin's view may be summarized in terms of three intimately related aspects. A gradual intensification of the diabolical forces of persecution and subversion strongly accentuates the awareness he had of living during the end-time. This awareness—as well as its concomitant, a heightened anticipation of the immediate future—would tend to narrow the standards by which to distinguish the true and perfect Christian from the sham-truth and pseudo-perfection of the diabolical imitator on the one side and the tepidity of the so-called Christian, lay or clerical, high or low, on the other side. Finally, the periodization and gradation of the process of church history would eventually lead to a relocation of the Christ-event on the scale of universal history, away from its augustinian place. It would then no longer mark the end of history, but its center, and, because of the inherent teleology of the entire scheme, the focus would inevitably shift from the past to the future. At the same time, this 'leveling' of the Christ-event would tend to render it incomplete. Christ's work would have to be completed, in one way or another, before the end of history renders completion impossible.

This last implication might well be challenged as an impermissible, because anachronistic, anticipation of joachimite ideas. I would not deny this, except to point out that intellectual history is filled with ideas, the implicit and inherently logical consequences of which are not immediately and expressly drawn because of the weight of tradition. Yet the fact that Eberwin himself was, however gropingly, close to drawing just such consequences is incontestibly evident from his earlier remark to Rupert that the end of history, while near, was by no means to be considered imminent. On the contrary, Eberwin had argued, the Church would grow to perfection through the new and elite order during some future time *within* the historical order. Rupert understood Eberwin's argument in this way, and we have no reason to doubt his account of it, especially in view of the careful emphasis he placed on Eberwin's remark that the rise of the end-order was not entirely a matter of the future, but that it was already in the process of actualization.

Anselm of Havelberg

If we admit the novel character of Eberwin's application of the traditional six-fold scheme, may we also assume that the obscure Eberwin was the originator of this potentially fateful change? Augustine cannot have been the father of this thought, for its chiliastic potential is entirely contrary to his effort to overcome chiliasm by spiritualizing its expectations and its hope. If our problem is at all one of direct dependence, its solution as yet escapes us. We are, however, in the fortunate position of being able to trace what may be an *indirect* dependence. In studying Anselm of Havelberg's *Liber de unitate fidei et multiformitate vivendi*[15] one is at once struck by the remarkable congeniality of ideas and an amazing similarity in detail between the bishop's concept of history and that of Eberwin. Anselm's work has been intensively studied in the past, and we may confine ourselves here to its last section which concerned the history of the Church.

Like Eberwin, Anselm not only envisioned a definite span of history after Christ, but he also periodized this span. Again like Eberwin, the bishop of Havelberg saw the red thread uniting all the various periods in the internal and external opposition inspired by Satan. Furthermore, we notice the same gradation in the intensity of this opposition, from the *cruor martyrum* to the *validissima persecutio* to be expected at the future coming of Antichrist. Unlike Eberwin, Anselm bases his exegesis on a text ostensibly much more suitable to his purpose, i.e. the vision of the seven seals and the four horsemen of the Apocalypse. In this way, Anselm also arrives at a division of church history into six periods, or *status* as he calls them, and it is no doubt this different biblical model which accounts, at least in part, for some points of divergence between Anselm and Eberwin.

A close comparison on the two series reveals that their details concerning the second, third, fourth, and sixth periods agree perfectly. Only the first and fifth ages show some slight divergence. In both cases Eberwin has the more consistent version. This also applies to one other minor difference. Anselm's synchronization of his biblical model with actual historical events becomes somewhat hazy toward the end, whereas Eberwin's outline leaves no doubt of the place of the present within his scheme. One cannot be sure whether Anselm assigned the present state of the Church still to the fourth or already to the fifth stage.

This amazing agreement between Eberwin's and Anselm's views, even to the point of identity, can hardly be accidental. Unfortunately, Anselm's work cannot be dated with even approximate certainty. The *dialogi,* the first of whose three books it purports to be, were probably written in 1149-50. It has been recognized for some time, however, that the *liber de unitate* cannot originally have been an integral part of the larger work. This makes it probable that the work was written first as a separate tract sometime between 1136 and 1149. Further complicating the evaluation of the *Liber de unitate* is a complete lack of biographical data on Anselm's early life. We know only that Anselm was a Premonstratensian when, in 1129, he was elevated to the see of Havelberg at the suggestion of Norbert, who, although he had been archbishop of Magdeburg since 1126, would not resign his abbacy of Prémontré until 1129. It is reasonable to assume that Anselm knew Norbert and his views before becoming bishop of Havelberg. If this assumption is correct, it may shed some further light on our problem.

Norbert of Xanten

Norbert, the founder of Prémontré, is not known ever to have engaged in writing, but we do know from two occasional and unrelated remarks that, from the summer of

1115, shortly after his conversion, to at least 1126, when he became archbishop of Magdeburg, eschatological ex- pectations strongly colored his views. In 1125, Rupert of Deutz recorded his side of a nasty quarrel he had had with Norbert some nine years previously, when the Premon- stratenian had been an itinerant preacher on a self- appointed mission inside and outside the diocesan boun- daries of Cologne.[16] At that time Norbert had been highly conscious of living during the final days of the world, the end of which he believed near. We do not know his reasons for this, but among them seems to have been his ob- servation of what he took to be the rise and spread of heretical teaching. Again, we do not know what exactly Norbert considered to be the marks of heresy, but he ap- pears to have understood it as his mission to unmask such heretical teaching during the time remaining to this world. Rupert, at any rate, had heard it rumored that Norbert claimed to have been empowered to cure no less than twelve dioceses of heresy through the remedy of his preaching.

Probably some time before 1126, Bernard of Clairvaux replied in a letter to the inquiry of Geoffrey, bishop of Chartres, as to whether or not there was truth in a report that Norbert planned to leave for Jerusalem. Bernard assured Geoffrey that he knew nothing about it, but that he doubted it because,

The other day, when I last saw him . . . he spoke of the coming of An- tichrist and, on my asking him when he thought this would be, he declared himself quite certain that it would be during this present generation. But when I heard the reasons he had for his certainty, I did not feel compelled to agree with him. He concluded by saying that he would live to see a general persecution of the Church.[17]

The terse allusions of the ever-busy Bernard defraud the curious modern reader of Norbert's reasons, but they are still sufficiently detailed to permit us to conclude that Norbert was at that time still very much aware of living during the final years of the world, that he expected the im- minent coming of Antichrist, and that he associated the im- pending events with a persecution of the Church, no doubt on the basis of apocalyptic passages of the New Testament.

Bernard's letter thus complements what we glean from Rupert's reminiscences. Norbert evidently did not change his eschatological views when he was persuaded to exchange his itinerant preaching ministry for the stability of Prémontré.

We may perhaps go yet a step further. Rupert's report suggests that Norbert had somehow associated the present end-time of the church with the rise and spread of heresy. We may not err in assuming that this view represented one of the reasons which Bernard disdained to communicate to the bishop of Chartres because he did not consider them persuasive. If this was so, we may have good reason to date Bernard's letter in the year 1124 or shortly thereafter; it was in that year that Norbert, at the request of the bishop of Cambrai, took a number of his canons to Antwerp in order to win back for the Church large numbers of 'heretics' who for more than ten years had been disaffected from it through the machinations of the notorious Tanchelm.

While the paucity of sources keeps us ignorant of any definite concept of history Norbert might have held, we notice that his eschatological views closely resemble those of Eberwin of Steinfeld and Anselm of Havelberg. Again, nothing is known about the personal relationship of the three men, but it can hardly be ascribed to coincidence that all three were members of the same order, and we may be justified in referring to their views collectively as the eschatology of the early Prémontré. This does not explain the momentous step, taken by both Eberwin and Anselm, of discarding the augustinian tradition by the periodization of church history. We suggest that this step was inspired by the work of Rupert of Deutz. Rupert was no stranger to the young premonstratensian community. Norbert, as well as Eberwin and Anselm, knew him personally. Norbert had spent the summer of his conversion, 1115, at the abbey of Siegburg. We have Anselm's own words to the effect that he had read Rupert's works. We know with certainty that Norbert knew at least one of them, and Eberwin may have been familiar with Rupert's commentary on John.

While we cannot discuss Rupert's theology of history in detail here, it is essential that we sketch at least one essential aspect of it. Rupert's first completed attempt to set forth his views is contained in his huge work *De sancta trinitate et operibus eius,* [18] which he finished in 1117 and which constitutes a continuous commentary on selected passages from Genesis to Revelation. Note that Rupert arrives at his view by way of exegesis. The Spirit who wrote the scriptures will also unlock the mystery of history through the *intelligentia spiritalis* of the exegete. This is, of course, quite faithful to the augustinian tradition, and we are not surprised to find Rupert following the master's dualism and even surpassing him in the spiritualization of history. Rupert's intention is reflected in the very title of his work. The inseparable unity of the Trinity both in nature and operation notwithstanding, the traditional distinction of the *opus proprium* of each of the divine persons permits Rupert to distinguish three major divisions within the total course of history. Just as the Father's work is particularly manifest in the *hexaemeron,* and as the Son's redemptive work characterizes the period from Adam's fall to the incarnation, so the Spirit's work of dispensing divine grace is the particular of the time of the Church.

This, in itself rather simple, outline becomes very complicated, however, because of the rigidity of the trinitarian scheme, and Rupert's plan eventually staggers under the weight of its own method. The essential unity of the Trinity demands that even though each of the three major divisions of history is characterized by the distinct work of one divine person, each must yet show a structure identical with that of the other two. Hence Rupert subdivides each of the major epochs into seven identical periods, according to the symbolism of the *hexaemeron* and of the seven gifts of the Spirit gleaned from Isaiah 11. This presents no problem in the first two epochs, which alone comprise history in the augustinian sense. But the inflexibility of the trinitarian scheme demands the same subdivision for the third epoch. The result is a curious ambiguity in the characterization of this period. Since the cycle of redemption has been completed with the appearance of the Second Adam, and the sixth age of the week of redemption is really ended with the resurrection of Jesus, the *hexaemeron* motif is no longer useful for dividing the third epoch or seventh age. This leaves for its subdivision only the Isaiah-motif of the seven-fold Spirit, but the price Rupert must pay for consistency is the impossible task of having to divide the indivisible presence of eternity and to historicize the non-historical, changeless rest of the cosmic sabbath represented by the seventh age.

The paradoxical result of Rupert's methodological dilemma is that in the end there results something quite new and in all probability quite unintended. Rupert no doubt meant the subdivision of the epoch of the Spirit to symbolize both the atemporal unity of the Church and also the partial application in the Church of the fullness of grace present in the God-man Jesus. No historical refer-ence was intended, nor could it be. The parallelity of the sabbatical seventh age to the remaining portion of the tem-poral sixth age, however, makes the appearance of a correspondence between the two unavoidable. Hence the subdivision of the former is reflected onto the latter and in fact periodizes the history of the Church. To this is added the element of progress inherent in the way traditional exegesis graduated the Isaiah passage. The result is an overview of the history of the Church progressing toward its end which is strikingly similar in structure to the models of Eberwin and Anselm. The spirit of wisdom, according to Rupert, is characteristic of the God-man Jesus, as is the spirit of understanding of the Apostles. The spirit of coun-sel refers to the rejection of the Jews, and that of fortitude to the pre-constantinian martyrs. The spirit of science is clearly identified with the time of the fathers of the Church, particularly Jerome and Augustine, while the spirit of piety coincides with the age of Benedict's monasticism. The remaining spirit of fear is then appropriately associated with the coming of Antichrist, at the end of the sixth age. Without as much as hinting at it, Rupert has placed his own time with precision into the last period but one, exactly as Eberwin would do a generation later, and yet Rupert has accomplished this feat without reneging on his loyalty to the augustinian model and tradition.

Having placed Eberwin's later thought as part of what we have called the eschatology of Prémontré, we must now return to his earlier argument, preserved by Rupert of Deutz, in order to determine their relationship more closely and thus to arrive at an understanding of the ideas of the provost of Steinfeld.

The heart of Eberwin's argument, as will be remembered, was the dual correspondence he saw between the course of pre-christian history and of the history of the Church on the one hand, and between the universal empires of Daniel's prophetic vision and the monastic orders of the Church on the other hand. As the Babylonian empire had had to decline and yield to the Persio-Median, and this to the Macedonian, so the Cluniacs were to give way to the new rule of the rising 'humble,' that is to say, to the radical wing of the canonical reform which observed the *ordo monasterii* and which was just then rising at Springiersbach and Prémontré.

Rupert, though outraged at what he considered the result of an illicit exegetical method, took Eberwin's argument very seriously, quoting it in full in order to refute what he rightly sensed to be its chiliastic implications. Eberwin's exegesis amounted, in fact, to nothing less than the overthrow of the augustinian tradition, and no matter how one might reason, the expectation that a future order would at last perfect the implementation of the true apostolic tradition could not be made to tally with the accustomed view of the already perfected corporate existence of the Church in a *mundus senescens*. To be sure, there was room for individual growth toward perfection within the established order, and perhaps for the gradual permeation of the social fabric by the christian ideal, but the traditional view had no place for the expectation of anything materially new before the end.

At this point a number of questions clamor for an answer. How are we to understand the apparent change that has taken place in Eberwin's later position, where no em-

phasis is placed on the eschatological order? What may
have led him to make use of the four-empire motif of
Daniel 2 and 7? And in which contemporary context did he
find this motif used? Finally, why did he fail to allude to the
Roman Empire, as consistency would have required, if we
are to assume that he meant the future order to be the
eschatological order of end-time? To attempt to answer
such questions on the slim basis of an almost aphoristically
brief quotation would seem to be tantamount to finding the
proverbial needle. If we may yet hope to suggest an answer,
such hope is solely due to the fact that, in the early 1120s,
the use of the Daniel motif was still highly unusual and
strictly limited to certain traditional literary forms.

We cannot at this time enter into a detailed history of
the exegesis of Daniel 2 and 7. But we must note, in summary, the types of contemporary literature in which the
four-empire motif had its place.

The book of Daniel as a whole plays no role whatever in
professional exegesis prior to about 1115. In this respect
nothing had been added since Jerome's *Commentary on
Daniel*.[19] The somewhat narrower four-empire motif,
however, appears in the literary contexts of universal
historiography, political theology, and ecclesiastical
eschatology. Of these, historiography must for our purpose
be excluded, for while it preserved the four-empire scheme
of Daniel, it did so merely in traces, being almost totally
dominated by the augustinian model of the six world ages.
The four-empire scheme did not become the structural
principle of historiographical effort until Otto of Freising's
famed *Chronicle,* written a whole generation after the time
we are discussing.

For different reasons it is necessary to eliminate from
our consideration the influence exerted by political
theology in which the four-empire motif lived on, primarily
in connection with Jerome's Rome-oriented eschatology
and the implicitly chiliastic eschatology of the sibylline
literature. It is unnecessary to point out once again the
well-established fact that the canonical reform generally
represented the avant garde in the fight against the claims
of imperial theology.

Eberwin's argument, as preserved by Rupert, confirms this attitude. He uses the Daniel motif not for its own sake, but because of its teleological relationship to the development in the Church. His interest is totally confined to the limits of the ecclesiastical horizon. The series Babylon-Persia/Media-Macedonia is designed not to convey the impression that the *ordo novus* is to be the last step in the development of the Church, but to state simply that the old order must now pass away and make room for the new, just as the general order of the Church had to follow the prechristian political order. We do not know whether or not Eberwin deliberately avoided mentioning Rome because he associated it with the as-yet-nascent political eschatology. Clear is only this much: he expected the future to be determined by a new ecclesiastical *ordo* and not by the fate of the empire, whatever it might be. It is thus not necessary to assume a complete turn-about in Eberwin's views within the next twenty years. To be sure a change did take place—the awareness of the impending end of the world became much stronger, and the concomitant flush of anticipation of the new order came to be replaced by a fear of disaster—but the basic ingredients remained the same, and one must not overdraw the contrast because of the dire occasion for Eberwin's letter to Bernard.

There remains for our consideration the use of the Daniel motif in the context of ecclesiastic eschatology. But here too, the Daniel passages played no more than a marginal role. The explanation lies once more in the dominance of the augustinian theology of history which successfully asserted itself against Jerome's 'roman' eschatology. Augustine had deliberately rejected the four-empire scheme in constructing his theology and particularly his eschatology, presumably because of the traditional association of this scheme with chiliasm and its alternative in the eschatology of eusebian political theology. For Augustine, Rome could have no significant place within the outline of redemptive history. What remains of the sixth age is determined not by the Roman Empire but by the preaching of the Church. (Essentially this same idea underlay Eberwin's argument.) The result of his rejection of the four-empire scheme is Augustine's judicious avoidance in his book on the *City of God* of quoting Daniel 2 and 7. The only exception to this rule is to be found in the numerous citations of Daniel 2:34f. It is characteristic of Augustine's attitude that precisely this verse became in his hand a weapon against the traditional Rome-theology; for the stone torn from the mountain to shatter the image of the world empires signifies none other than Christ, and through Christ it represents the Church rendering the earthly empire irrelevant.

The result of our rapid survey is largely negative. Eberwin is not likely to have been inspired to use the four-empire theme of Daniel 2 and 7 by Augustine nor did he receive it through the other literary channels conveying its tradition. We suggest once more that he borrowed it from the work of Rupert of Deutz.

Rupert was the first theologian since the end of the patristic age to turn his attention repeatedly and at length to the four-empire theme of Daniel 2 and 7. Within the space of ten years, he treated the Daniel passages on three different occasions. The last of these is of particular interest to us, for it concerns Rupert's grand theology of history published under the title *De victoria verbi dei.*[20] Not only does the Daniel theme supply the basic structure of this work, but Rupert wrote it sometime between 1120 and 1124, that is to say, during the same period which saw his encounter with Eberwin.

Rupert set out to describe the battle between the *Logos* and Satan. On the historical plane this battle is visible as that raging between the *ecclesia* and the empires of the world. Since, however, Satan is identical with the seven-headed monster of the Apocalypse, Rupert does not hesitate to prolong the four-empire scheme of Daniel both backwards and forwards into a series of seven empires: Egypt, the idolatrous Israel of Jeroboam I, Babylon, Persia, Greece, Rome, and the eschatological *corpus diaboli* giving birth to Antichrist. This last distinction between the Roman Empire and a separate diabolical kingdom of the end-time is particularly noteworthy because it runs counter to the traditional view, represented by Jerome, according to which the Antichrist will arise at the end of the Roman Empire and from within it. On the other hand, Rupert's scheme is quite consistent with the augustinian spirit, and this the more so as Rupert agreed with his great teacher on the essential point, that the coming of Christ meant the defeat of the Roman Empire. The wounds then received by the monster have been healed, to be sure, and to this extent it lingers on, but essentially it has been already overcome through the spiritual victory of Christ.

It is evident that Rupert had no room for imperial political theology. The historical dimension of the kingdoms of Daniel has been absorbed by their spiritual significance, and his sole interest was in the kingdon of Christ. Rupert was therefore unwilling to speculate on the satanic qualities of the renewed Roman Empire. Here as elsewhere his spiritual exegesis discounts historical and political reality. The real enemy of Christ is not Rome, but heresy within the church. This is the same horizon within which Eberwin moved, although Eberwin was less consistent than Rupert in the spiritualization of historical events. It is therefore likely that Eberwin used the sequence Babylon-Persia-Macedonia as a paradigm just *because* no importance attached to the finality of the Roman Empire, its traditional place having been taken by Rupert's eschatological *corpus diaboli.* Moreover, it was precisely this denial of Rome's finality which made room for the coming perfect order in the development of the Church.

It is curious to watch again how Rupert, wishing to do no more than to perfect the augustinian view of redemptive history, actually furnishes the tools for its demise. He could not understand how, in view of his own spiritual exegesis of the Daniel passages, Eberwin could so completely misconstrue their symbolic significance. It is almost as if he were reproving Eberwin, saying: you should have known better from reading my works. His refutation of Eberwin's argument shows this clearly. The four kingdoms of Daniel, says Rupert, refer to beasts without God, and they cannot be compared to the monastic or any other order within the Church. Furthermore, the historical succession of those kingdoms is incommensurable with the indivisible and timeless unity of the Church. Just like the waning and waxing moon,

the holy church—and especially the spiritual order which the Holy Spirit has ordained—may for a while be wanting in some place, but only to recover again; and although the church and its *ordo* is almost always bent and changed according to the various habits and customs of men and people, it will never be dissipated or destroyed.[21]

This is to say, Eberwin's new order of the humble cannot but be part of what has always been and always will be. To deny this would be tantamount to claiming that the Church has erred, that Benedict was not full of the one and unchangeable Holy Spirit, and that one might improve on the work of the Spirit of God.

Eberwin did not think so. Less than twenty years later, under much more trying conditions, and thus somewhat less confident, he still pinned his hopes on the *ordo novus* of the perfect.[22]

CONCLUSIONS

I should like to formulate four major results of our study, and at the same time raise a few questions and draw a number of inferences.

1. The current view, according to which the great reform of the eleventh and twelfth centuries is characterized by ideals of renewal and repristination, should be amended and it should be amended beyond the commonplace that renewal is never merely repristination, but invariably asserts itself in new cultural forms. The emergence of a new and un-augustinian eschatology in the Middle Ages must be sought in connection with the most radical wing of the canonical reform whose adherents followed the rules of the *ordo monasterii*. Eberwin of Steinfeld may well have been the first to express the idea that the coming of Antichrist will not be the next decisive, and final, event in redemptive history, but that prior to this one will have to expect the rise of a new and perfect order of the humble within the historical Church. This idea implies the

notion of development and it expresses, for the first time, the availability of immanent future time. It thus signals the incipient overthrow of the until-then sovereign rule of the augustinian concept of history and its eschatological pendant.

2. Eberwin of Steinfeld was probably inspired to his novel ideas by Rupert of Deutz whose thought—though unintentionally—prepared their way and whose writings would also seem to have had considerable influence on the formulation of premonstratensian eschatology. Since Rupert's thought was, moreover, known and appreciated by Honorius Augustodunensis and Gerhoh of Reichersberg, his work deserves much closer attention than it has so far received.

Many questions still remain. One would like to know what exactly it was that was conducive to the rise of such ideas in the radical branch of the canonical reform yet was not present in the various contemporary monastic reforms. What weight should be ascribed to socio-economic factors? Did there exist a kind of ideological affinity with the contemporary heretical movements along the lower Rhine valley, and did these nurse chiliastic ideas? Why did the new radical orders originate in the territory of the Empire or, at any rate, near its borders and in the shadow of its influence? These are only some of the questions that invite further research.

3. Eberwin of Steinfeld's new ideas may be described as incipient ecclesiastical chiliasm, if we understand chiliasm morphologically as the expectation, in the future, but still within historical time, of a period in which the presently deficient order of man will come to perfection. Such a definition not only rules out a definite duration to this order of perfection—such as the thousand years of antiquity—but it also disregards the theme of material abundance which survived in the chiliastic notions of contemporary sybilline literature. Perhaps Eberwin's more subtle version was the only form in which chiliastic ideas could assert themselves within the matrix of medieval ecclesiastical spirituality.

The new chiliastic notions were not initially incompatible with the traditional idea of the *mundus senescens* but they could not be reconciled with the augustinian view of the Christ-event as the climatic end of redemptive history. The world, and with it the worldly Church, grows old and decrepit, but the true Church meanwhile grows more purely toward final perfection. The traditional augustinian rationale for the remaining duration of the sixth and last age of history, namely, the need to fill the predestined number of the City of God through the missionary activity of the Church, is in effect overcome by the idea that the Church must reach a state of perfection *before* the end of history can come through the agency of Antichrist. Indicative of this change in eschatology is the terminology which contrasts the *ordo novus* to the *ordo antiquus* within the general period of the sixth and final age of the world.

4. Although for obvious reasons christian chiliasm has never occurred without the messianic component, it is morphologically necessary to distinguish between chiliasm and messianism. Beginning with Eberwin of Steinfeld, there appears in the history of christian thought a kind of messianism within messianism. Without detracting from the expectation of the coming supernatural kingdom of God through the agency of the returning Messiah-Christ, the idea arises of a coming, more perfect, state of the Church on earth through the messianic agency of a new order within the Church.

Initially couched in the model of the *vita arctior et contemplativa* of the monastic ideal, the expectation of a new order becomes a constant element of the theology of history and the non-scholastic eschatology of the next one hundred and fifty years. This expectation is, of course, attached to any order which happens to be new at a given time. Eberwin of Steinfeld associated it with the rise of the *ordo monasterii,* as did Anselm of Havelberg and Gerhoh of Reichersberg. The available evidence would tend to suggest that at least certain of the contemporary heretical lay movements nourished the same idea in the form of the expected or beginning realization of the true *vita apostolica.* Otto of Freising seems to have envisioned as the eschatological order a pure form of monasticism, probably of the cistercian type. Only a scant generation later, Joachim of Fiore left the cistercian order because it, too, had grown old, and the preparation for the imminent final spiritual order then came to rest on the narrow shoulders of the Floracensians. Some of his disciples associated the beginning of the perfect order with the Franciscans, and this view was still upheld toward the end of the thirteenth century in the theology of history which the ageing Bonaventura developed in his *Lectures on the Hexaemeron.*

The messianic structure of the perfect order remains, morphologically, the same throughout this period although the historical agent varies and the intensity of expectation and its chiliastic definition, change. Finally, it would appear that the chiliastic structure of the messianic order of the end-time has become a more or less permanent fixture of Western christian theology and it has survived even the process of secularization under the guise of new forms, such as versions of utopia, the classless society, the messianism of American political theology, or the claims of modern scientism.

To return at last to our initial question: What is the *proprium* of the spirituality of early premonstratensian eschatology? We are, no doubt, dealing with the personal experience of bridging the gulf between sacred and profane through participation of the really Real. But in which sense is this experience of participation distinguished from that which we studied in the first lecture? Let me answer my own question: Precisely at the point where for the mystic the experience of participation ends in the experience of union, for the apocalyptic or chiliast it ends in the experience of proleptic realization.

Permit me to end with a passage from a new book which has just appeared in English translation:

... apocalyptic does not represent an accidental historical phenomenon, but a possibility of understanding existence which is potential for any time, and therefore inalienable—a historical possibility even when it hopes for a historical impossibility, the end of history.[23]

Guntram Bischoff

Western Michigan University

BERNARD OF CLAIRVAUX:
THE MYSTIC AND SOCIETY

Bernard of Clairvaux (1090-1153) abandoned the life of a minor aristocrat in 1113 to enter the floundering new monastery at Cîteaux. With him he took thirty of his relatives and friends, including married brothers. This in itself indicates the charismatic sway which Bernard exercised over his contemporaries throughout his life. Chiefly through his efforts, the Cistercian order exploded in a single generation from three to over three hundred monasteries, and for persons high and low throughout Europe and the latin Middle East, the austere white monks became the most perfect embodiment of medieval christian ideals. Severely ascetic in his personal life and uncompromising in his demands on others, Bernard revealed a great sensitivity for beauty, especially the beauty of language in both speech and writing. He knew scripture and the works of the Latin Fathers thoroughly and was so imbued with their doctrine that he has been called The Last of the Fathers.

On Palm Sunday of the year 1098, which in that year was also the feast of Saint Benedict, twenty-two monks under the leadership of Robert of Molesme founded a monastery in a place known as Cistercium, a marshy woodland located in the diocese of Châlons and the duchy of Burgundy. The New Monastery—which is what the founders modestly and accurately called their new home—did not flourish: the pope ordered Robert back to Molesme, the community often came close to starvation, disease reduced their numbers, and the few hardy souls attracted to their hard life soon gave up in despair at its severity.

The seemingly imminent collapse of the young foundation was saved by the arrival of a man almost as young as the foundation. In 1111, Bernard, a son of the lord of Fontaines-lès-Dijon, had made up his mind to become a monk, and, in an action characteristic of his leadership powers, he brought with him in 1112 some thirty companions, more than doubling the community at Cîteaux.

Only four years after Bernard entered Cîteaux, he was chosen to lead a new foundation. So, in June of 1115, he and twelve fellow monks set out on a seventy mile trek to their new home in the Valley of Absinthe near Bar-sur-Aube. They changed the name of the place to the Valley of Light, Clairvaux. Largely because of Bernard's influence, the Cistercians were to possess 343 houses all over Europe by his death in 1153. But Bernard was not only the leader of a new wave of monastic reform, he became the leader of Christendom in the first half of the twelfth century. It would be difficult to find a parallel in any other period. Bernard remained abbot of Clairvaux all his life, but he was able to spend far less time there than he wished. Bernard was thrust into a role of leadership, a role he always regretted.

Perhaps more than any other event in Bernard's life, his role at the Council of Etampes reveals the extent of his influence on contemporary society. At this Council, Bernard was instrumental in settling the papal schism of 1130, and his decision won France for Innocent II.[1] And this was but a preliminary to Bernard's campaign in Germany, Italy, and Sicily, a campaign pursued successfully through letters, travels, councils, and disputations. In an age in which religion is important, as it was in the twelfth century, the man who decides who is to be the head of the institutional expression of that religion is a man of great power.

It is not necessary to describe the leadership which Bernard exercised; that has often been done. His role in launching the Second Crusade is well known; Bernard's preaching, letters, and miracles[2] aroused the European conscience to the point that he could write to Pope Eugenius:

You have commanded and I have obeyed, and the authority of your command has made my obedience fruitful. Since I have announced and have spoken [the soldiers of the Cross] have been increased beyond number. Cities and castles are emptied, and now seven women can hardly find one man to hold; so much so that everywhere there are widows whose husbands are still alive.[3]

Many scholars have shown Bernard's great contribution to theology and his influence on its development. His letters show Bernard as the preceptor of popes and the conscience of kings. In short, Bernard was the leader in so many aspects of early twelfth-century culture that it is impossible to examine his age without studying him.

Bernard's leadership leads us to ask the question: how is it that a monk—and a mystic—could play such a role? How is it that a man dedicated to withdrawal from the world had so much influence on the world? My contention is that Bernard could lead Europe to a crusade, decide who its leaders were to be and how they should act, and influence what its inhabitants were to believe, because his life embodied so many ideals of his age, some of which had not even crystalized until his coming. The ideals of early twelfth-century Europe were largely unified around spiritual values. Thus, it was possible for one man, who as a monk and mystic most perfectly embodied those ideals, to give expression to the spiritual values of his age. Because of his genius, Bernard was able to explicate the ideals and values implicit in society's choice of him as its leader. We must turn to Bernard if we are to understand the mystical spirituality of the twelfth century.

'Mysticism' is a word with a bad press today and it most often carries connotations of irrationality, superstition, spiritualism, obscurantism, or a side-show version of Orientalism. Mysticism is a difficult concept, and its explanation may necessitate an illustration.

Let us suppose that we have a friend who has been blind from birth. We are walking together one evening and we remark on how beautiful the sunset is. Our friend asks us: 'What is a sunset?' We may reply with an explanation of how the rotation of the earth places the horizon between us and the sun. This is a scientific explanation which is true as far as it goes, but our friend might justifiably question why we had described the sunset as 'beautiful.' We might say that the color, particularly the red, was magnificent, but our friend would surely ask us what 'red' was. A description of 'red' as an energy wave of a certain frequency would be accurate, but again not adequate. The difficulty is that our

experience of the sunset or of 'red' is not simply an intellectual awareness; it also involves an emotional and
volitional response. Not only do we know something in an
experience, we also feel and choose in that experience. An
experience is something unique because our reactions are
determined not simply by the object we experience, but also
by our predilections and past experiences. No one can ever
completely experience what we experience, and surely our
blind friend is unable to share our experience of the sunset
or of 'red.' In trying to share with him at least part of our
experience, we might have recourse to poetic language. We
might try to get him to 'see' red by describing it as 'warm.'
Red is not physically any warmer than green, but our
psychological reaction to red roughly parallels the way we
feel when we are warm, and so we describe red as a warm
color. We say what is literally false in order to convey what
is psychologically true.

When we ask a mystic for an explanation of mysticism,
it is not surprising that he, too, must respond in poetic
form. A mystic is a man who has had—or at least thinks he
has had—an experience of God. This experience, he
claims, is quite unlike other experiences in its source, but
like others in that it involves knowledge, choice, and
emotional response. The metaphor which Bernard of Clairvaux used to describe his experience of God was that of
sexual union between the Bridegroom (God) and the Bride
(the soul):

But let me tell you what I have attained to, or, rather, what I believe
myself to have attained to. And you must not regard as a boast this com-
munication which I make only for your own good . . . . But there is a
place where the Lord appears truly tranquil and at rest. It is the place
neither of the Judge nor of the Teacher, but of the Bridegroom, and
which becomes for me (whether for others also, I do not know) a real
bedchamber whenever it is granted to me to enter there . . . . If, my
brothers, it should ever be granted to you to be so transported for a time
into this secret sanctuary of God and there be so rapt and absorbed as to
be distracted or disturbed by no necessity of the body, no importunity or
care, no stinging of conscience, or, what is more difficult, no inrush of
corporeal images from the senses of the imagination, you can truly say:
'The King has brought me into his bedchamber.'[4]

If Bernard, and other mystics, must express themselves poetically, this expression does not detract from the certainty of the knowledge which they believed they obtained in the mystical or contemplative experience of God. The epistemological value of mysticism or (to use Bernard's word) contemplation is indicated by his own definition: 'Contemplation may be defined as the true and certain intuition of any object, or the certain apprehension of truth.'[5] The certainty of mystical knowledge becomes all the more important when one considers that for Bernard the primary object of contemplation is God, that is, Truth Itself:

> But let me speak first about the Image. The Word is Truth, the Word is Wisdom, the Word is Justice. Under each of these aspects He is an Image. An Image of what? An Image of Justice, an Image of Wisdom, an Image of Truth. For the Word as an Image is Justice of Justice, and Wisdom of Wisdom, and Truth of Truth; in the same manner as He is Light of Light and God of God. But the soul is none of these things, because she is not the Image. Nevertheless she is capable of them, and is desirous of them too, and perhaps it is with respect to this capacity and this desire that she is said to be made according to the Image. She is a noble creature whose greatness is shown in the fact that she possesses in herself so great a capacity for participating in the perfections of the Word; and, in her yearning for the same, she gives proof of her righteousness.[6]

God is seen by the contemplative under many aspects, all of which give insight of a profound nature into reality:

> There is in the home of the Bridegroom a certain place where, as Governor of the universe, he frames his decrees and disposes his counsels, appointing to all creatures their laws, their weight, measure, and number. It is a lofty place and a secret one, but very far from quiet. For although as far as depends on him, he 'disposes all things sweetly,' yet he disposes them and does not permit that one who has reached that point by contemplation should rest there peacefully; but by causing her to scrutinize everything with admiration, he wearies and disquiets her in ways no less pleasant than marvelous.[7.]

It was obvious to Bernard and his contemporaries that the knowledge of the nature of things obtained by such an experience is far superior to any other way of knowing. But not only the nature of things but the right ordering of them (justice) was at least sometimes open to the contemplative:

There is a place from which an immutable watch is kept over the reprobate rational creatures by the just vengeance, as severe as it is secret, of the most righteous Judge, 'terrible in his counsels over the sons of men.' Here the trembling soul beholds the Almighty, by a just but hidden judgment, refusing both to pardon the evil and to accept the good works of the wicked and, moreover, hardening their hearts, lest perhaps they should become contrite, enter into themselves, be converted, and he should heal them . . . . Do not be surprised that I have ascribed the beginning of wisdom to this second place rather than to the first. For there we do indeed hear wisdom teaching all things, as it were, in a lecture-hall; but here we actually receive wisdom. There our minds are instructed; here our wills are affected. By being so instructed we become learned; by being so affected we are made wise.[8]

By contemplating Truth the mystic becomes learned, and by contemplating Justice he becomes wise.

We have already seen[9] that God is also experienced by the mystic as a Bridegroom; it is under this aspect that the mercy of God is seen.

There [in the third place] we can plainly see that 'the mercy of the Lord is from eternity and to eternity upon those who fear him.' . . . I have therefore observed that [the elect] are as if they had never sinned, because whatever faults they may seem to have committed in time, none at all shall appear in eternity, for the Father's 'charity covers a multitude of sins.' . . . At the thought of this, I, even I, have suddenly experienced such an infusion of confidence and joy which altogether exceeded the earlier emotion of fear felt in the place of horrors, that is, in the place of the second vision. For it seemed to me that I was of the number of these blessed ones.[10]

Not always does the mystical experience encompass such grand visions. The knowledge Bernard claimed he received was sometimes very specific, so much so that it strikes the modern ear as strange and bordering on the humorous:

I am lying (and I say this for your consolation) if from the hands of this sinner to the joys above there have not flown the souls of monks, novices, and lay brothers, without any hindrance once they were freed from the prison of our mortality. If you ask how I know this, know that absolutely certain evidence of it has been given to me.[11]

Although Bernard's descriptions of the contemplative

experience which I have quoted so far seem to indicate that mysticism is essentially cognitive or intellectual, there is more to the story. For Bernard mystical knowledge was obtained in an ecstatic experience:

> Therefore, 'Let my soul die the death of the angels' also (if I may use the expression), so that escaping from the memory of all present things, she may strip herself, not alone of the desires, but even of the images of inferior and corporeal objects and may converse spiritually with those whom she resembles in spirituality! The name contemplation, it seems to me, belongs either solely or principally to such a mental ecstacy. It is the part of human virtue to live on earth unfettered by earthly desires; but to be able to contemplate truth without the help of material or sensible images is characteristic of angelic purity. Yet each of these two is a gift of God. Each is a true ecstacy. In each the soul rises above herself, but in the second far higher than the first. Blessed is the soul which can say in this sense: 'Lo, I have gone far off, flying away; and I abode in the wilderness.' It is not enough for her that she is transported out of herself, unless she can fly far away and be at rest. You have such a victory over the temptations of the flesh that you no longer gratify its concupisence nor yield assent to its enticements. This certainly is progress. You have surely gone forth from yourself. But you have not flown far, unless, by purity of mind, you are able to rise above the images of sensible objects, which are constantly rushing in upon you from every side. Until you have attained this, do not promise yourself any rest. You are in error if you think that the place of repose, the quiet of solitude, the perfection of light, and the dwelling of peace can be found any nearer.[12]

So far removed from the normal world of perceptions or even conceptions is this mystical experience that it might be better described as emotional than as intellectual. Or, rather, it is volitional, since it is achieved through a harmony of the wills of God and the soul. This harmony Bernard described as the mutual love of the Bridegroom Christ and the Bride the soul:

> Grace alone can teach it, it cannot be learned except by experience. It is for the experienced, therefore, to recognize it, and for others to burn with the desire, not so much of knowing, as of feeling it, since this canticle is not a noise made by the mouth but a jubilee of the heart, not a sound of the lips but a tumult of internal joys, not a symphony of voices but a harmony of wills. It is not heard outside, for it does not sound externally. The singer alone can hear it, and He to whom it is sung, namely the Bridegroom and the Bride. For it is a nuptial song, celebrating the chaste and joyous embraces of loving hearts, the concord of minds, and the union resulting from reciprocal affection.[13]

It was necessary for Bernard to use such poetic expressions in describing the union of the soul with God, because this experience was highly individual, incommunicable, ineffable. Bernard put it this way:

Furthermore, in such matters the understanding is altogether unable to transcend the bonds of experience . . . . None but the Bridegroom himself can tell us with what infusions of spiritual delight he ravishes the soul of his best-loved, with what aromas of sweetness he intoxicates her sense, with what inspiration he wondrously illuminates and refreshes her mind. Let there be for you a private fountain of graces in which the stranger shall have no share, nor shall the unworthy drink of it. For it is a 'Sealed Fountain,' a 'Garden Enclosed.'[14]

So far outside the bounds of ordinary experience is this mystical exaltation that Bernard could not ascertain even its coming or going:

I confess, therefore, that even to me—'I speak as it were in foolishness'—the Bridegroom has condescended to pay a visit, and indeed not once but many times. But although he has often come into my soul, I have never been able to ascertain the exact moment of his entrance. I have been conscious of his presence within me, I could afterwards recall that he had been present, sometimes I have even had a presentiment of his coming; yet I have never perceived him either in the act of entering or in the act of retiring . . . . But neither can he be said to come from within me, because he is good and I know there is no good in me. I have ascended to what is highest in me, and behold I have found the Lord to be higher still. Influenced by a pious curiosity, I have descended to explore the lowest depths of my being only to find he was deeper down. If I looked to my exterior, I perceived him beyond what is outermost. And if I turned my gaze inward, I saw him more interior than that which is in most . . . . For it is not to any movements on his part nor to any activity of my own senses that I am indebted for the knowledge that he has come into my soul. I have been made conscious of his presence from the feelings of my own heart, as mentioned already. . . .[15]

How is one to reconcile Bernard's cognitive and intellectualistic, if not to say scholastic,[16] description of contemplation with the volitional, non-rational, ecstatic experience about which he also tells us. Are they two different experiences?

Both approaches described the same experience, but from different points of view. Bernard was conscious of the tensions between his various descriptions of the mystical experience, and he resolved those tensions by appealing to the simile of the lips of the Bride. The two lips of the Bride, the understanding and the will, are kissed by her Divine Spouse:

> Rightly thus does the Bride, when seeking him 'whom her soul loves,' not trust herself to the senses of the flesh nor follow the vain reasonings of human curiosity; but she solicits a kiss, that is, she invokes the Holy Spirit from whom she shall obtain both the food of knowledge and the seasoning of grace. And it is well known that it is true knowledge which is imparted by means of a kiss, and it is accepted with love because it is the token of love. Consequently, the knowledge which puffs up, which is unaccompanied by charity, does not proceed from a kiss. But neither can this kiss of love be claimed by those who indeed 'have zeal for God, but not according to knowledge,' for the grace of the kiss communicates at once both the light of knowledge and the warmth of love. It is in truth 'the spirit of wisdom and understanding,' who, like the bee bearing wax and honey, has the wherewith to light the lamp of knowledge and to infuse the sweetness of devotion. Wherefore, let not him who has understanding of truth without love, nor him who has love without understanding, ever imagine he has received this kiss. With it error and coldness are alike incompatible. So, for the reception of the twofold grace of this all-holy kiss, let the Spouse on her part get ready her two lips, namely, her intelligence for understanding and her will for wisdom. Thus glorying in a perfect kiss, she deserves to hear these words of consolation: 'Grace is poured abroad on your lips, therefore has God blessed you forever.'[17]

Even this simile does not adequately express Bernard's concept of the mystical experience, for it still maintained a dualism: the contemplative's ecstacy and vision, corresponding to the faculties of will and intellect. It was Bernard's conviction that love and knowledge not only accompany one another, but are truly one in the contemplative experience:

> It is only to his friends and lovers that God communicates his secrets, for to them alone was it said: 'All things whatsoever I have heard of my Father I have made known to you.' Indeed, as the blessed Gregory teaches, *love not merely merits but is itself this knowledge.*[18]

We can see that, for Bernard, the effect which contemplation has on the will does not mean that the mystical experience has no epistemological value; rather the truths to which the mystic attains—or better, which are revealed to him—embrace his whole being and are not simply intellectual. The contemplation of God as Truth is involved in the mystical experience, but the perception of Truth on this level involves love of him who is Love. This is a super-rational perception in which God is seen in a way having many more dimensions and implications than the word 'truth' contains. Indeed, Bernard, in an attempt to convey the distance between the mystical experience and the ordinary world of knowledge, choice, and emotion, compared his experiences to death:

Therefore I also can be guilty of no absurdity when I describe the ecstacy of the Spouse as a kind of death, not the death which terminates life, but that which delivers her true life from danger, so that she may say with the Psalmist: 'Our soul has been delivered as a sparrow out of the snare of the fowlers.' For in the present life the soul is always surrounded by the snares of temptation, which have, however, no power to frighten her as often as she is transported out of herself by some holy and irresistible attraction, if yet the mental exaltation and ravishment be so great as to lift her above the common and usual modes of thinking and feeling. So we read in Proverbs: 'A net is spread in vain before the eyes of them that have wings.' For what has such a soul to fear from sensuality, since she has lost even the faculty of sensation? No longer conscious of material impressions, though retaining still the principle of life to the body, she is necessarily inaccessible to temptations from the senses.[19]

The exalted state which the mystic attains was, according to Bernard, the source of a many-faceted and extremely complex sort of knowledge. This knowledge was not only of use to the mystic, but a potential source of information for pope and peasant, emperor and humble cleric, many of whom appealed to Bernard for advice and usually got it. Bernard spoke on the great issues of his day and, because he was thought to be close to God, the men of his age listened and, most often, agreed with what they heard.

But all of this ignores a very important question. How is the mystical experience attained? What is path to the Christian perfection which Bernard believed a necessary prerequisite to union with God in contemplation? As Bernard put it:

> This [mystical] canticle can neither be heard nor sung by souls that are weak and imperfect and only recently converted from the world, but only by those who are advanced and sufficiently enlightened. For these, by their progress under the grace of God, have so grown that they have now come to maturity and the marriageable age, so to speak, measuring time by merits rather than by years. They are ripe for the mystical nuptials of the Heavenly Bridegroom. . . .[20]

For Bernard, the first step in the mystical life, the fundamental Christian virtue on which all else spiritual was based, was humility.[21] But humility did not mean to Bernard what it often means today; humility was not simply going about with hands folded and eyes meekly lowered. Bernard defined humility as self-knowledge, a true knowledge of oneself.[22] In order to be a real, a genuine man—one who truly follows in the footsteps of the perfect man, Jesus[23]—one must realize what a man really is and the way one should act to be a man. Humility or self-knowledge requires the grace of God,[24] but also thorough self-examination by the Christian. He must take time from his usual occupations to think about or to meditate upon his ideal and his actual self. By nature man is, as Bernard put it, the 'noblest of earthly creatures, image of God [and] living likeness of the Creator.'[25] On the other hand, to be realistic about oneself one must face up to the fact that one has betrayed oneself by acting in less than human ways. In humility, Bernard said, one is imitating the man who most perfectly fulfilled human nature, Jesus Christ. Humility is self-knowledge; pride is self-deception. And it is through a rational process of self-examination that one comes to know the truth about oneself.[26]

> He, therefore, who wants to know truth in himself must first get rid of the beam of pride, which prevents him from seeing the light, and then erect a way of ascent in his heart by which to seek himself in himself, and thus after the twelfth step of humility he will come to the first step of truth.[27]

To gain the time necessary for the meditation which

leads to self-knowledge, Bernard thought it was necessary to give up other activities. This is asceticism. 'Asceticism' is a word with an even worse press than 'mysticism' these days, so it is necessary to spend some time defining it. Asceticism is not the rejection of that which is evil in order that one may embrace the good. It is rather a restatement of a universally accepted ethical principle: faced with a choice between two goods, one should choose that which is more beneficial to oneself. Bernard did not reject wife, family, and material possessions because they were evil,[28] but because the time he gained by not possessing them could be devoted to the quest for self-knowledge. Self-denial for its own sake led to pride; properly used it could gain the time needed for the development of the humility of self-awareness.

According to Bernard, the man who is truly aware of his own human condition can have empathy for others. Recognizing his own weaknesses, he can appreciate the weaknesses of others and not judge them too harshly.

The merciful quickly grasp truth in their neighbors, extending their own feelings to them and conforming themselves to them through love, so that they feel their joys and troubles as their own. They are weak with the weak; they burn with the offended. They 'rejoice with those that rejoice and weep with those who weep.'[29]

Just as asceticism is a means to humility, doing good for one's neighbor aids in the development of love for him. Bernard asserted that the measure of a man's capacity for union with God is his virtue, which is shown by his love for his neighbor.[30]

Humility, then, is the right ordering of one's ability to know; humility is knowing the truth about oneself and one's relation to God. Love is the right ordering of one's ability to choose; one should choose the well-being of all and work toward that end. The perfection of the intellect and of the will prepare one for mystical exaltation; but they are only a preparation. It is from such men that God chooses those whom he wishes to take to himself in the mystical embrace. In the end, it is God who gives, not man who achieves:

Both faculties, reason and will, the one taught by the Word of Truth, the other inspired by the Spirit of Truth, the former sprinkled with the hyssop of humility, the latter kindled with the fire of love, now from a finally perfected soul, are flawless through humility and unruffled through love, since neither the will resists reason nor does the reason ignore the truth. The Father unites this soul to himself as a glorious bride so that neither the reason can think of itself nor the will of its neighbor, but that blessed soul delights only in saying: 'The King has brought me into his chamber.'[31]

I must return again to the world in which Bernard lived and which he led. The method which Bernard described as preparation for the mystical experience was nothing more or less than the Christian life as the men of the twelfth century knew it. Indeed, they knew it largely through the teaching and example of Bernard and of other monks and mystics. The education of the monk and mystic embodied most perfectly the ideals—if not the practice—of most twelfth-century men. The spirituality taught by Bernard was the life-style prized by his contemporaries: one's happiness consisted in the long run not in what one did, but whether one did it out of love and in humility. It is no wonder Bernard was the acknowledged leader of his age.

John R. Sommerfeldt

Western Michigan University

WILLIAM OF SAINT THIERRY:
RATIONAL AND AFFECTIVE SPIRITUALITY

William of Saint Thierry (1070?-1148) is best known through the friendship he enjoyed with Bernard of Clairvaux, whose Life *he was writing when he preceded his friend in death. Born at Liège, he seems to have been educated at Reims, where he also entered monastic life. Around 1120 he was elected abbot of the Benedictine monastery of Saint Thierry, not far from the city, and as abbot he composed several works on the spiritual life. Weighed down with the duties of office and drawn to the stricter Cistercian observance, he petitioned Bernard for permission to enter Clairvaux, but was refused. After several years, he quietly transferred to a new Cistercian abbey at Signy. There he led a quiet, contemplative life, interrupted only when he raised an alarm, through the eloquent Bernard, against what he considered the heretical teachings of Peter Abelard. As he grew older, he felt drawn to the solitary life and is known to have visited a Carthusian monastery shortly before his death.*

Characteristic of the spirituality of William of Saint Thierry are ways of ascent, spiritual staircases by which the human soul mounts up from its present, fallen, state to the vision of God. These are not unique to William; innumerable other spiritual writers suggest similar patterns of ascent, periodizations which are in large measure a part of the Augustinian heritage of western Christendom. As the Praemonstratensians (and the Benedictines) attempted to fit the ages of the world and mankind into successive ages, so the Cistercians of the twelfth century attempted to convey analytically—psychologically, if you like—the growth and development of the human soul. Whether William of Saint Thierry explicitly stated and followed a way of ascent, or merely sketched one out in passing, sooner or later he was irresistibly drawn to construct at least one such staircase in every work.

Within the framework of these ascent patterns he explored, in several of his fifteen extant works, the differences between a rational and an affective approach to God. Situated as he was in the confrontation between the outstanding 'rationalist' of his day, Peter Abelard, and the most outspoken 'affectivist,' Bernard of Clairvaux, William—the man who set the one on the other—illustrated perhaps prototypically the dilemma of western man in the twelfth century. In order to analyze his opinion of the respective places of love and reason, we shall examine, within the context of the ascent patterns, his teaching on reason and its relationship to love.

So specialized a treatment may require some defense in a volume treating the more general topic, western spirituality. One important—even distinctive—facet of that spirituality has been given very short shrift here, the rationalist tradition. No 'scholastic spirituality' is being considered. By concentrating on something which was for William a 'problem,' furthermore, we can distinguish his spirituality from that of his contemporaries, and especially from that of his intimate friend, Bernard of Clairvaux. Although their teaching is very different on many points, any general introduction is bound to point more to the similarities than to the differences between two educated, twelfth-century, 'French' Cistercians. Reason posed no problem for Bernard, who did not emphasize it in his works. It was, however, a problem for William, or rather it became a problem after he encountered and reacted to the dialectical theology of Peter Abelard. More than his contemporaries and confreres William deliberately tried to bridge the gap which was developing between traditional monastic theology and the newer theology of the schools, between the praying theology of Evagrius Ponticus and the objective study of the data of revelation which Abelard himself named 'theology'.

Finally, the problem of choosing a rational or an affective approach to God was not unique to the twelfth century. It did not originate nor did it terminate there. In the persons of William (and Bernard) and Abelard, the dialectic between them was focused in a confrontation which symbolically sundered in the west the integrity of man's response to God. Affect and rationality went separate ways, and western man divided love from reason, action from thought, being from doing.

By concentrating on only one aspect of William's thought, we inevitably run the danger of distortion. William had chosen the monastic path to God. Reason was not an overriding preoccupation with him, except in one treatise which he wrote immediately after having read Abelard's *Theology*. To discern William's sudden awareness of the 'problem' and his resolution of it, we will examine reason's place in works taken from three periods of William's life: his years as a Benedictine abbot; his outraged reaction to Abelard; and finally, the final year of his life.

We begin by defining reason as William understood it. This we can do with some accuracy, especially for his later works, because William himself clearly defined it in a study *On the Nature of the Body and the Soul.*

The soul of man, he taught, is incorporeal and cannot therefore be localized.[1] In this way it is analogous to God, for 'as God is in the world,' he writes, 'so somehow the soul is in the body everywhere and everywhere entire. . . .'[2] The soul perceives through its understanding,[3] and is the greater part of man, quickening, giving life to, man's animal being.[4]

Reason is one of three faculties of the human brain. In the front of the brain lies the imagination, along with sensation—what William called 'animal power'. In the rear lies memory. Between them, 'in the middle, reason is placed as a queen and a lady, by which we are distinguished from beasts.'[5] 'For like a queen seated in the midst of the stronghold of her city, reason discriminates, receives, and disposes.'[6] Reason directs the body; it causes the hand to write, the lips to speak.[7]

Animals, devoid of reason, are governed by their senses,[8] but the spirit of man governs and judges his senses.[9] Having none of the physical protection afforded beasts by nature, man has yet managed to achieve dominion over potentially dangerous animals.[10] Why? Because human reason has given him the power of subduing them and rendering them subject to himself.[11] 'Wherefore,' William advised his readers, 'behold and cherish, o man, the dignity of your nature . . . constituted to have dominion over all things. [12]

In his physiology, William made a distinction between *reason,* a part of the brain, and *rationality,* the ability to use reason. Just a vision (the ability to see) is one thing and the eye another,[13] so rationality differs from reason. Reason is one of three faculties of the brain; rationality is one of three powers of the soul. As reason is located between imagination and memory, so rationality mediates between concupiscence (the ability to desire) and irascibility (the ability to be angry).[14] Rationality moderates. It is the middle, determining faculty. So, for example, anger can be beastly and therefore bad, or it can be rational and good.[15] Because of reason's mediation we can speak of charity as being grounded in irascibility:[16] if the soul is to love good, it must be angry at iniquity. Such rational anger 'is a disposition of the mind not other than the love of God and neighbor, and the hatred of vices. The hatred of vices because it is the love of God and of man. . . .'[17]

Reason and rationality direct man naturally toward God. Reason reflects God; he is the *lumen illuminans*[18] and man is the *lumen luminabile.*[19] If man uses his natural faculties as God created and intended them to be used, he can mount up by them to the very presence of the Creator. Even man's upright stance manifested to William man's natural striving upwards and his regal dignity.[20] Man has been created and called by God and drawn by nature to seek the oneness of God himself. William interpreted Christ as saying:

'I and the Father' and love 'are' not three but 'one,' we are one God. You, a rational mind, cogitation, and your love, are one man, made to the image of your author, not created to equality with him. Not begotten, you have been formed, yet you are not the one who forms. Draw back from those things which are beneath you, less well-formed and less comely than yourself. Come up to the forming form, that you may become comelier, because the more you are pressed against him by the weight of love, the more you will take on from that very likeness.[21]

It is this natural impulse upwards—to use spatial terms, as

William does—which led him to construct in his meditative works ways of ascent to God. Despite his distinction in this one treatise between reason and rationality, he usually spoke only of reason, by which he seems to have meant both the ability and the faculty.

In *The Nature and Dignity of Love,* which I think must have been William's first work,[22] the abbot of Saint Thierry proposed a tidy way of ascent to God which he appeared to think he could mount and, in fact, implied he had mounted. Patristic and logical, it consists of four steps or three dynamic stages: one begins by setting one's foot to will and steps up to love (*amor*); from love one advances to charity, and then moves into the final step, wisdom.[23] The entire process is analogous to human growth. It is a continuing development, the maturing of a single being rather than four separable or separate states of being. Old age, William reasoned, is distinct from infancy, yet every old man was once a child. '. . . so too with the increase of virtues, the will grows into love, love into charity, and charity into wisdom.'[24]

Even after setting out the four stages and elaborating them at some length, William cautioned his readers against separating them too strictly:

Every wise man who makes this ascent ought, however, to know that the steps of this ascent are not so much like the rungs of a ladder, that each of these affects[25] is necessary only at one time and not at another. Each affect has indeed its own time in the order and its own place, by which it seems—with the cooperation of the other affects—to achieve its part more painstakingly. But they all cooperate and travel together. They all forge ahead and they all follow.[26]

As its title demonstrates, this early work of William dealt specifically with love, its source, its types and its goal, and the author took care to define it. Annoyed by the pervasive influence of Ovidian definitions and practical suggestions, William the abbot reminded his monks that christian love, unlike carnal love, is born in God alone and bestowed by God alone.

Its first birthplace is God. It is born there, nourished there, reared there. There it is a citizen, not a tourist but a native. For love is given by God alone, and it endures in him. . . .[27]

He who created all things has made love a part of the nature of his creature, man. Love (*amor*) is the natural weight which bears man godward—an Augustinian notion.[28] Man's affections may be drawn to many things, but love, essential, unswerving affection, should not be squandered on creatures but directed toward its creator and only to him. Only in returning love to its source can human affection be completed and made whole.

In treating of love, the second stage of ascent, William found it necessary also to treat of reason. In this early work he spoke of reason as a second eye by which, with love, God may be seen. Reason aids and instructs love; love illuminates reason. These two eyes, both natural faculties implanted in all men by the creator of all nature, function best together:

But in this faculty of sight there are two eyes forever trembling with the natural tension of looking to that light which is God: love and reason. When one makes the attempt without the other, it does not get very far. When they help each other, they can do a great deal, just as when one eye helps the other. . . . When, as I said, they help each other, and reason teaches love and love illumines reason, when reason moves along into the affect of love and love agrees to be confined within the limits of reason, they can do great things.[29]

Despite its utility, Abbot William did not see fit to make reason a separate step. In remained ancillary, a sober companion to a more exhilarating ability.[30] Reason plods along cautiously, picking its way from the known to the unknown while love soars up to meet God. 'Reason,' he observed, 'appears to advance through what is not to what is. Love disregards what is not and rejoices to retreat into what is.'[31] Reason devoid of love remains a dull tool, unable to do more than deduce God's existence. Love without reason can be carried away into enthusiastic excess. Together, they focus the soul's attention on God.

As man's love reaches out toward God, it encounters God's love condescending. Human love, the love of desiring, enveloped within the love of God, becomes the love of enjoying.[32] When human affection is met by divine love, love for God becomes as well love from God and in God. This William called no longer *amor*/love but charity, 'illuminated love, love from God, in God, and to God,' who is charity.[33] Love longs to see God because it loves God. 'Charity loves because it sees,' he wrote, 'for charity is the eye by which God is seen.'[34] Love searches for God; the 'affect of charity' cleaves indissolubly to God.[35] William remembered Saint Paul's warning that so long as mortal life endures even charity can see only in part, only in an enigma and in a mirror.[36] Yet when the soul has seen God, however dimly and fleetingly, he believed, it somehow knows God with a knowledge he does not even connect with reason for this knowledge becomes wisdom, the final step of his ascent.

The Mirror of Faith

After becoming a Cistercian in 1135, William turned deliberately to meditative from instructive writing. Happily immersed in commenting on that favorite of medieval Cistercians, The Song of Songs, William chanced to read through the newly published *Theology* of Peter Abelard.[37] Without hesitation he broke off his commentary to study the book and to alert his best, and most influential, friends to the dangers he sensed in it. In his letter and in the *Disputation* which he addressed to Bernard and Geoffrey of Chartres, William concentrated on doctrinal errors which he believed Abelard had promulgated, and he lamented only in passing that the schoolman studied Plato with more caution and respect than he extended to holy scripture.[38] After delating the theological propositions of the Master of Dialectics, William wrote three books—four if we include his Life of Bernard. *The Enigma of Faith* and its companion, *The Mirror of Faith,* reveal by their titles—taken from Saint Paul's warning of the limitation of mortal vision—reveal a constant contention of William which now received new emphasis. Both works show unmistakably that Abelard's teaching and, more, Abelard's dilemma had seized the attention of the monk who had set up the hue and cry which resulted in the scholar's condemnation and excommunication.

In the *Enigma* William pondered the mystery and the mysteriousness of the Trinity, in his misprized attempt to explain which Abelard had, he thought, grievously strayed from orthodoxy. In the *Mirror* William took up once more the central, practical concern of his life: man's approach to God.

Abelard taught that 'by doubting we come to inquiry. By inquiring we perceive the truth.'[39] Bernard, alerted by William, charged indignantly that 'there is nothing in heaven above or on earth beneath which [Abelard] admits to not knowing, except [the words] I don't know.'[40] 'He presumes against reason and against faith,' Bernard railed. 'For what is more against reason than by reason to endeavor to transcend reason?'[41]

Despite his use of reason as a declamatory weapon, Bernard seems to have had no particular difficulty with the relationship between faith and reason, either before Abelard loomed on his horizon or afterwards. During the fray he accepted William's interpretation of Abelard's errors and in large part repeated William's correctives, adding his own impressive rhetorical flourishes.[42] By Abelard's method and its results, however, William was made acutely aware of the difficulties of relating reason to other human cognitive faculties. The storm which he himself raised seems to have brought him face to face with a dichotomy implicit in his own anthropology, and he seems to have resolved to spell out, for his own benefit and for the edification of others who, like Abelard, employed reason methodologically, the proper functions of these tools. In both the *Mirror* and the *Enigma* he worked out and published the relationship he believed should exist between reason and the other spiritual faculties. In doing so, he proposed, in the *Enigma,* a new way of ascent which he then developed in the *Mirror.* He listed three steps of increasing difficulty toward God and the knowledge of God. First, one must learn through diligent study what to believe. Then, he should discover how to express that belief both mentally and verbally. Finally, he may experience the reality of faith and begin to sense truths concerning God.[43] The first step demands faith grounded in obedience to authority, the second reason founded on faith, the third love, which completes faith and ushers in the wisdom of vision. In William's words:

The first step, based on authority, is of faith, having the form of faith, having been formed by proven witnesses of proven authority. The second is of reason, not human reason but that which is proper to faith, having also the form of sane words in faith and agreeing thoroughly with divine authority. To this [second] it belongs not only to think and to speak reasonably about God, according to the reason of faith, but to know how faith comes to exist where it is not, how it is nourished and aided where it does exist, and how it is defended against its enemies. The third [step] is one of illuminating or beatifying grace, completing faith, or rather beatifying it through love, advancing the soul from faith to vision.[44]

We see already in this first post-abelardian work a heightened emphasis on obedience to authority. Reason, furthermore, has been separated out for the first time into a distinct step of the ascent. One can only surmise that it was Abelard's plight which had brought this about. William's new concentration on reason becomes even clearer as he explicates each of the steps in *The Mirror of Faith.*

Faith is man's very first step on the lifelong pathway toward God, he insisted repeatedly.[45] Man begins at faith.[46] Faith is man's response to God, yet faith itself is a gift given to the believer by God. To this gift the recipient replies by the consent of his free choice, a choice made free through grace by Christ.[47] Freedom of will was not a subject on which William often discoursed—perhaps he felt Bernard had said it all adequately[48]—but when he did he spoke of it as one of man's greatest gifts. 'Give up asking, "Why did you not grant me humility," ' he had God order in his early *Meditations.* '[I did not] because I have given you something greater: freedom of choice.'[49] Faith, freely chosen, is God's due. Before anything else, mankind owes its maker the simple and pure assent of faith, free from hesitations and hedgings.[50] Such faith requires a deliberate decision. One chooses to believe, yet one can choose only because God draws one on.[51]

Within this traditional teaching William admitted to himself a new problem: With the best will in the world, man can be duped by ignorance and misled by falsehood. How can anyone, cut off from the vision of truth and hemmed in by misconceptions, know and profess the truth on which his salvation utterly depends?[52] He must believe, first of all, without any doubt, in the Holy Trinity, Father, Son and Holy Spirit. He must also believe without hesitation that God became man to effect man's salvation[53]—both doctrines on which he felt Abelard had erred.[54] Yet these are both truths which man cannot know unless an outside agent teaches him. Natural reason and sensory experience do not lead man to the Trinity or to the Incarnation. Before what William called 'the splendor of God's gospel' can illumine the human heart, therefore, man must be guided by the authority of that same gospel.[55] To believe meant to William to accept scriptural teaching on the authority of the teacher, humbly and obediently, without eliminating at random any unattractive or uncongenial doctrine. If a man fails to depend on authority at the very beginning of his spiritual journey, William insisted, he will inevitably stumble off the pathway of ascent, or even perish in the hell of unbelief.[56]

To clarify his position William distinguished between different types of faith. To believe without any intruding doubt, to have what he called a simple faith, is very pleasant. To apply reason to the task of understanding what one already believes produces doubt. This faith is less comfortable as it is more difficult. The struggle to understand lacks the sweet savor of simple faith, but it results ultimately in a more steadfast faith and it helps others in the same struggle. 'Simple faith savors, but it gives no light . . .' he admitted.[57]

To be unable to understand rationally something about

God and to admit it, William accounted neither sin nor shortcoming. On the contrary, he often stressed the virtue of recognizing one's own natural limitations. He did not, however, oppose the searchings of reason, provided the motivation was not idle curiosity but sincere desire for God.[58] Not to endeavor to know rationally everything about God which does lie within one's capabilities, he considered damnable rather than virtuous. To refuse to try, or merely to pretend to try, to understand what one can of God not only blocks one from God, it also begins an all but irreversible descent:

Just as it is not reckoned as sin not to be able to know something about God, who surpasses man, so too the person who is answerable to God, who does not strive to understand what he can, or does not yet understand as he might but pretends to make the effort he ought, will not only be condemned before God of ignorance, but will also be ordered to the punishment due his actions, so that he who chose not to know or to take action when he could, will not be able when he wishes to do so.[59]

The human mind tends by its nature to seek truth and, William says, 'the way of discovery is ordinarily reasoning (*ratiocinatio*), by which truth is found.'[60] He warned repeatedly, however, that if reason, the instrument for understanding human affairs, attempts by itself to break in upon divine truth it will fail. 'Although it mounts up in that direction, it blunders, it runs away, it totters.'[61] If reason first bows itself beneath the lintel of faith, if reason stoops beneath him who claimed to be the door, then reason, humbled by faith under the yoke of authority, may enter into the knowledge of God's very truth.[62]

To distinguish with greater precision between reason unsupported, which William had been forced to realize could produce confusion, and reason supported by faith, which he believed would lead to vision, William itemized the faculty in two categories. One reason assails while the other defends faith. Offensive reason he characterized as animal, knowing only carnal things and hesitating therefore before the unknown. This reason produces uncertainties and doubts in the soul because it is asked, or rather,it asks, to investigate what it has not experienced and cannot experience. On the other hand, defensive reason he placed as a spiritual faculty, able to discern the things of the spirit because it subdues its hesitations to authority and it remains wary lest it entertain the doubts which come.[63] Of itself rationality is restless and uneasy, he admitted.[64] It has a hard time realizing that it can operate on a level different from its usual, sense-fed one. The mind needs to be snatched, abducted, from its natural path— its usual way of perceiving things—and lifted on to the path of grace, to the interpretation of revelation accepted in faith.[65] Once reason has come to abandon any exclusive in- sistence on merely rational, sensible evidence and has assented to faith, it will be transformed into the zeal of love, whereby it may contemplate and enjoy what it only then begins to understand. Reason operating within faith not only aids and enkindles love, it becomes love. Then, William says, 'the fervor of natural rationality, as has been said, may be turned by the operation of grace, into the fer- vor of love, and importunate reasoning may become blessed contemplation, the knowledge (*scientia*) of having found, the joy of having been fulfilled.'[66]

Reason is one of man's natural senses, but until it is joined by and turns into the greater sense, love, it is re- stricted and incomplete. Part of the process of spiritual maturation, part of the ascent to God, for William was this realization. The greater capacity of love to understand God can best be explained if we look at William's theory of the human learning process.

Man has several natural senses and each has ap- propriate and inappropriate applications. By his physical senses man perceives the physical world. By his non- physical senses—rational and spiritual—he perceives what we may for convenience call the non-physical world. In William's paedagogy, physical senses carry sensory in- formation to the brain, which then interprets it by being conformed to the thing sensed and so comes to understand it. So, too, spiritual senses convey information about spiritual 'objects' to the soul, which is conformed to them and comes to understand. Reason is one of these spiritual senses; love is another. William explains:

Just as the outward senses of the body relate to bodies and physical things, so the inward senses relate to things like themselves, that is to rational and divine—or spiritual—things. But an even greater and worthier sense, and a purer understanding, is love. For by this sense the Creator is sensed by the creature; by this understanding he is understood insofar as God can be sensed and understood by creatures. For the sense faculty or the soul of man, when it seeks sensations, is by the action of sensing changed into what it senses. Otherwise there is no sensation. For example: physicians say that the sense of sight, in going out from the brain by the eye's rays, comes into contact with the forms and the colors of visible objects. When it has relayed this back to the mind, the mind is conformed to them and vision results. Otherwise the person seeing cannot see. The very same thing is true of the other senses. For its sense the mind has understanding (*intellectum*), by which it senses everything it senses. When it senses rational things, reason goes out to them, and when it has relayed the message back, the mind is transformed into it and becomes understanding. In those things which go out to God, the mind's sense is love.[67]

'The eye of the mind,' 'the mind's sense of sight,' William (echoing Augustine) called reason,[68] and it is man's best and highest way of coming to understand rational things. But God is not a rational thing.

As sense perception is changed into the physical object perceived, and reason is transformed into the rational object understood, so, too, love understands by being conformed to and transformed by its object, God who is love. Love is changed into the figure of God's substance, as the Apostle had promised.[69] 'For the soul loves,' William explained, 'and her love is her sense by which she senses him whom she senses, for she would not sense him unless she were transformed into him, that is, unless he were in her and she in him.'[70] When this happens, he goes on, 'our substance is transmuted for the better,' while God remains forever immutable.[71] Having been conformed through love to God, man shares in the godliness of Christ, 'who also bowed himself down to the fellowship of our humanity for this purpose,' William wrote, 'that he might make us partakers of his divinity.'[72] Not that human nature will ever be changed into the nature of God, he emphasized, but the loving soul will be transmuted by the work of God's Spirit, who is the love of Father and Son, into something which, while short of the divine, surpasses the merely human.[73]

The recognition of God which comes through faith pertains to this life, mortal and physical. Reason, properly channelled, carries man from faith to a more profound understanding. Love brings man an understanding which surpasses rational cognition as God surpasses the rational creature. That affective understanding belongs to eternal life; as Christ has promised it is itself eternal life.[74]

What does this ordering of senses, reason, and faith in *The Mirror of Faith* tell us about the reaction to early scholasticism of William and his generation? In probing earnestly and not unsympathetically Abelard's 'rationalist' doubts and difficulties, William—whether he realized it or not—was weighing the methodology of the schools against that of the cloister. He found the objective, rational analysis of schoolmen a viable tool so long as the analyst was committed in faith to the doctrine he investigated. The monastic methodology of loving response to the object of faith, he contended, reveals that object more profoundly because human love more nearly than reason approximates God. Steeped in the patristic tradition of applying faith to living, he remained convinced that reason and love are not opposing but complimentary faculties, each to be used in turn by schoolmen and monks—and all christians. Implicitly he maintained that the way of the monk succeeds better than the way of the schoolman because it is the response of the whole man. In his final treatise, addressed solely to monks, William showed that he had incorporated what he had learned from Abelard into his monastic approach to God.

THE GOLDEN EPISTLE

William's most widely-read treatise—in fact his only really popular treatise[75]—was written in the last year of his life, shortly after he visited the newly-founded Charterhouse of Mont-Dieu. This *Letter to the Brethren of Mont-Dieu,* or *Golden Epistle,* represents the final synthesis of William's spirituality and the incorporation of his Abelard-induced thrashings on the subject of reason into his own tradition and experience. In *The Golden Epistle,* more consistently than in any work after *The Nature and Dignity of Love,* William proposed and scrupulously followed a threefold way of the ascent. Citing First Corinthians, he wrote:

... even as one star differs from another in brightness so one cell differs from another in conversation, that is to say, the conversation of those beginning, of those advancing, of those that are perfect. The state of beginners may be called animal, of those advancing rational, and of those perfect, spiritual. [76]

The animal man, the beginner, is the person who is moved neither by reason nor by affection. He is like a dumb beast or like a blind man groping for light. Absorbed in his own physical existence to the point of ignoring—being ignorant of—his spiritual faculties, he needs to be taken firmly in hand by someone more 'advanced,' and by admonition and example led beyond himself. [77] He must be instructed to regard not his carnal but his spiritual being, William counselled. Before anyone can even begin to mount upwards, he must first learn humility and obedience, and to this end he must submit himself to authorities—to his novice master, to his seniors, to the Rule, and to his Redeemer.

In meditation and in study, this irrational and unaffectionate beginner should fix his attention on the words and acts of the Incarnate Lord, from whom he will learn humility and by whom his love will be enkindled; he should also attend the lives of the saints and the simple moral interpretation of scripture and the church fathers. [78] Unable as yet to advance beyond the familiar, physical world or to touch the unknown realm of eternal reality, the beginner must obediently confine himself to what he can master and not attempt to fly off in a premature excess of devotion. For this reason, William suggested:

He must be taught also to lift up his heart in his prayer, to pray spiritually, to draw back as far as he can when he considers God from corporal images and from bodies. . . . It is better and safer, as has already been said, that to such a man praying or meditating be proposed the image of the Lord's humanity, his nativity, passion, and resurrection, so that the weak mind (*animus*) which does not know how to think except in corporal images and bodies, may have something to which it can attach itself, to which according to its measure it may cling by the intuition of piety.[79]

Visualizing Christ, God and man, in physical terms may be an elementary and earthbound exercise, but it prevents the beginner from constructing false pictures of God. It enables him, however imperfectly, to learn to recognize God as God truly is, and so to draw a little nearer to reality.

When animal man, regarding Christ, has learned obedience and has ordered his being in accordance with nature, placing soul over body that is, he advances to the second state, that of rational man.[80] By his innate reason, the elderly William asserted, rational man is able to delve into the less obvious but more essential manifestations of God. Rational investigation stirs deeper longings in the seeker, but it is itself the objective activity of someone looking on.

These are the rational [William wrote], who through the judgment of reason and the discernment of natural knowledge *(scientia)* are both acquainted with and hunger for the good, but they have not yet been touched by affection *(nondum habet affectum)*.[81]

Having subdued his lesser part, his body, in the animal state, man in the rational state begins to put his spiritual being in order. To explain the growth of the spirit William borrowed from Augustine a distinction which he had not used before—although he had introduced the terminology, undefined, into his commentary on the Canticle. He contrasted the soul (*anima*-feminine) with the rational soul (*animus*-masculine—which is Abelard's word for mind, cognitive power, the arena of vice and virtue).[82] William begins with the Augustinian definition of *anima*:

The soul (*anima*) is an incorporeal reality, capable of reason, designed to give life to the body. This is what makes animal beings men, familiar with the things of the flesh, cleaving to bodily sensations. When it begins to be not only capable but in command of perfect reason, it immediately renounces its name of feminine gender and becomes *animus,* the participant of reason, fit to rule the body.[83]

Animus is the prince and participant of reason (*princeps et particeps rationis*). The distinction between it and *anima* is further explained to the satisfaction of William (who had no feminists with whom to contend) by the direction each takes:

For as long as it is *anima,* it effeminates easily into what is carnal; but the *animus,* or spirit (*spiritus*) meditates only on what is virile and spiritual.[84]

Having equated *animus* with *spiritus,* William went on a moment later to make *mens* synonymous as well.[85]

Created to seek what is good, man's spirit, his rational soul, fell through attachment to the flesh. Created in God's image and capable of reason,[86] man let himself—his soul and his will—become the slave of sin. The power of choosing (*arbitrium*) became captive, not, William asserted, that man entirely lost the power of choice, which he defined as the judgement of reason in judging and discerning, but that man has lost the freedom to will and to act.[87] This returns us to the initial step of William's first way of ascent, to the will, a natural appetite of the rational soul (*animus*) 'turned partly toward God and concerned with inward affairs, partly toward the body and external corporeal affairs.'[88] If spiritual growth is to continue and understanding increase, the will must turn to God and be liberated. It must experience *conversionem et liberationem.*[89] Once the will has been freed, reason also will be free. 'And then reason is truly reason, that is, a disposition of the mind (*habitus mentis*) coming together with the truth in all things.'[90] Once the will and reason are free, then the spirit (*spiritus*) begins to be moved, activated by a liberated reason, and it becomes *bonus animus et rationalis.*[91]

Once William had emphasized the human necessity of escaping bondage to sin and subservience to physical being, he had no reservation in acknowledging reason as man's finest means of piercing the sensory world. Reason is the tool by which man—by Boethian (Porphyrian and Aristotelian) definition a rational animal—naturally seeks truth. Like any tool, reason is honed by use but atrophies through disuse.[92] Borrowing again from Augustine, William presented five definitions of reason, and two of the rational process:

Reason is defined by those who make definitions or described by those who describe things in this way: (1) 'It is the rational soul's sense of sight (*aspectus animi*), by which it looks into truth not through a body but through itself, or (2) the very contemplation of truth,' or (3) the truth itself which is contemplated, or (4) the rational life, or (5) rational service in which it is conformed to the truth contemplated. Reasoning (*ratiocinatio*) is (1) the investigation of reason, that is (2) the movement of its sense of sight through those things which are to be examined. Reasoning seeks; reason finds.[93]

By the process of reasoning, he went on to say, reason discriminates, it draws distinctions between rational objects.[94] He made no apology for pointing out its utility to the contemplative Carthusians whom he expected, as rational animals, to use it.

In the entire universe, William went on to say, there is only one being more excellent and more wonderful than the rational soul of the rational animal, one thing which is 'worthier to seek, sweeter to find, more useful to possess,' and that being is God.[95] God made man for himself. In his own image he created man's rational soul, and it is this image which attracts man to God and renders him capable of returning to his Creator. Doubling his emphasis on man's rationality, William wrote:

For by him and for him has the rational soul (*rationalis animus*) been created, to the end that its whole conversion might be towards him, that he might be its good. Good from his goodness, it was created to his image and likeness, so that as long as it lives here, it may approach him as closely as it can by that likeness, away from whom it steps only by unlikeness, that he may be holy as [God] is holy, and in the future blessed as he is blessed. For it is the image of God. And because it is his image, it becomes capable of understanding him and it can and ought to cleave to him whose image it it.[96]

When the conversion is complete, when man is wholly turned to God, and God has become the object of an understanding which is fuller than merely rational, then man reaches the third state of spiritual growth, he becomes 'spiritual.'[97] Then the seeker is no longer concerned with knowledge about God and God's attributes. Then he seeks God himself, God as God is. At this point, William reiterated, reason is simply no longer the best tool; if he is to approach more closely to God's reality, man must employ that one remaining better, but still imperfect, tool:

Just as the rational soul (*animus*) discriminates among physical things by the body's senses, so it can discern rational or spiritual things only through itself. The things of God it can seek and hope to understand only from God. And it is lawful and possible for a man possessed of reason to think and to inquire sometimes about things which pertain to God—such as the sweetness of his goodness, the power of his strength, and things like that. What he is himself, however, what he is absolutely cannot be conceived, except to some extent by a sense of enlightened love.[98]

The spiritual are those whose wills, already liberated, have been turned into love.[99] In love, who is God the Holy Spirit, they will only what God wills and love only what God loves, and therefore they are like unto God.[100] In some ineffable way they see the ineffable,[101] and—as ineluctably they must who see God—they love God, for God cannot be seen and not loved.[102] They seek a still deeper understanding of God and their understanding differs vastly from that which reason and the senses produced. The knowledge which love produces is not *scientia,* knowledge of something outside oneself; it is *sapientia,* the savor (*sapor*) of what is most deeply within oneself.

Although reason cannot attain this savoring by its own efforts, it can conform itself to that wisdom once attained. Reason itself is the transitional faculty: 'As for what reason itself conceives in such matters,' William wrote, 'it is already on the borderline between knowledge and wisdom.'[103] Reason conformed to wisdom produces conscience[104]and directs man's life so that by his actions and his prayers he may become one spirit with God. 'Because he savors these things [of God] he is wise; because he is made one spirit with God he is spiritual.' The image of God is then renewed within man,[105] and he attains to a likeness of God on a new scale. This likeness, William wrote, 'is the perfection of man in this life.'[106] Only a few lines earlier he had already dismissed the excuses of the person who does not struggle on to the third, affective, sapiential level of growth by saying curtly, 'not to wish to be perfect is to fall short (to fail).'[107]

Even while he divided human faculties into ascending steps, William broke his own arrangement—he never saw any scholarly necessity for driving a logical scheme into the ground. Even while exalting love over reason, he repeated and re-emphasized his conviction that the two human faculties cannot be separated. Instead of being two exclusive or even progressive epistemological tools, love and reason—the two eyes, the two faculties of the soul—form in fact a single crescendo toward God, who enkindles and enlightens them both.

And when reason as it advances mounts up on high to love, grace comes down to the one loving and desiring. Reason and love which produce these two states often become one, as do knowledge and wisdom, which are produced by them. They cannot now be treated or thought of separately, they are now one—of one activity and of one virtue, both in the sensory state of understanding and in the joy of fulfillment. Although one must therefore be distinguished from the other, because reality presents itself this way, yet each must be treated and considered with the other and within the other.[108]

In the oneness of God, all things are one.

Finally, lest we entertain any lingering doubts as to the environment needed for this ascent to the knowledge of God, William makes it very clear that knowledge and reason, like wisdom and love, are contemplative pursuits. They are studies which love silence, calmness of heart, poverty of spirit, and peace from exterior pressures—not disputes, wranglings, and chattering.[109] The understanding, the knowledge, and the wisdom which William believed God calls men to seek by reason and by love could never result from the idle and pointless investigations which he called *cogitationes sine intellectu.*[110]

E. Rozanne Elder

Western Michigan University

GUIGO II: THE THEOLOGY OF
THE CONTEMPLATIVE LIFE

Guigo II (Guy, Guigo the Angelic; †1188) was the ninth prior of the monastery of the Grand Chartreuse, near Grenoble, France, until his resignation eight years before his death. His only known works are the Scala claustralium *and* Meditations, *the first written c. 1150. The* Scala claustralium *(Steps of the Cloistered Life) was translated into Middle English and exercised an influence not only on monks but on the piety of layfolk.*

The Carthusians were founded in 1084 by Saint Bruno and combined cenobitic (community) life with eremetic (solitary) life. Each monk lived in an 'apartment' which consisted of a workroom, a study, a bedroom, a chapel, and a garden where he raised vegetables. Because of their emphasis on solitude, all Carthusian monks were from the beginning ordained to the priesthood. The monks recited their offices, prayed and worked in their cells, but assembled in the common monastic chapel for Mass, Matins and Lauds, and Vespers. Noted for their austerity, the Carthusians have never been a large order, but they also never suffered the mitigations and decline which befell more numerous orders.

The twelfth century struggled to put things together, all the way from the analysis of the *quaestio* to the synthesis of the *summae*. The struggle took place on all sides, in literature, law, philosophy, and especially in theology. Hugh of St Victor, William of St Thierry, Bernard of Clairvaux, and Richard of St Victor among others were exerting the same effort in spirituality. Of those others one gifted author deserves wider attention for his synthesis of the spiritual life of the monk. Accordingly, this paper concerns the theological context of the *Scala claustralium* (The Ladder of the Monks) composed by Guigo II, the ninth prior of La Grande Chartreuse who died in 1188.[1]

The *Scala claustralium* belongs to that literary genre known as the monastic letter, a genre popular in the twelfth century. The prologue and the epilogue, both very brief, reveal the straightforward tenderness we know in so many of the monastic letters of the twelfth century.[2] Guigo is writing to his friend, brother Gervase, whose previous letters have called forth this letter. Guigo is sharing with Gervase thoughts on the spiritual life which Gervase has already known from his own experience. With the accustomed humility of these letters Guigo asks that Gervase be both a judge and a revisor of his thoughts.[3]

The *Scala claustralium* is not a casual letter, but minutely planned and carefully executed composition of fifteen chapters which include the prologue and epilogue. The *Scala* is elegant in content and in style—not the elegance of grandeur but that of a simplicity that pervades every facet of the letter. There is obvious restraint in this letter. Guigo has both the good sense and the courage to be selective. He chooses to say what is crucial to his message rather than to try to say everything. He wastes neither ideas nor words. This simplicity is reminiscent of the same quality in a letter of a Carthusian namesake who had been the fifth prior of La Grande Chartreuse, Guigo I.[4]

In the prologue Guigo states that he is about to share certain thoughts on the spiritual formation of monks (*de spiritali exercitio claustralium*),[5] Guigo's central message, one that came to him suddenly while he was engaged in manual labor, concerns the four steps of that monks' ladder that stretches from the earth to the exploration of the secrets of heaven. The four steps of the ladder are: *lectio, meditatio, oratio,* and *contemplatio.*[6] The subsequent tradition knows Guigo's steps well. Giles Constable, in particular, has shown that Guigo's *Scala,* passing sometimes under the name of Augustine, Bernard of Clairvaux, or others, became a favorite of the late Middle Ages.[7]

Guigo's genius lies well beyond the enumeration of the four steps in the spiritual development of monks. If he had contributed merely a listing, he could have culled and pruned a little longer list from the meditations of his predecessor, Guigo I:

Now these are the works of divine devotedness: contemplation, prayer, meditation, reading, the singing of psalms, performance of the sacred mysteries. The purpose of all these [is] to know and love God.[8]

Guigo's contribution, I believe, lies first in his understanding and insistence on the causal relationship of the four steps, their necessary inter-relatedness, and then in Guigo's concept of the ladder and its steps as symbolic in the neo-platonic sense.[9] Without an appreciation of the nature of Guigo's affirmations, we run the danger of being content with what may appear a little pedagogical schema of the spiritual life, neat and easy to commit to memory. Such a simplistic reading distorts Guigo's contribution and has disastrous consequences for anyone who would take the four steps to be a continuous forward ascent up the ladder of perfection. Guigo is aware of the deceptions consequent upon too superficial an interpretation of the meaning of the four steps. He warns that we need to look at these steps diligently.[10]

Distortion is an ever present danger when wisdom is capsulated in aphoristic phrases. The best of the consequent tradition has avoided a simplistic reading of Guigo's steps. John of the Cross knows the four steps:

Seek in reading and you will find in meditation; knock in prayer and it will be opened to you in contemplation.[11]

In his *The Dark Night of The Soul* John shows that he appreciated the profound nature of the steps of the ladder (which for John had ten stairs). There the Spanish mystic reminds us that '. . . upon this road, to go down is to go up, and to go up, to go down.'[12] John's insight has been shared by the truly wise all the way from Heraclitus to T. S. Eliot.[13] In the fourteenth century the author of *The Cloud of the Unknowing* had an appreciation of this same wisdom when he discussed the place of reading, thinking, and praying on the way to contemplation.[14]

Though the best of the tradition saves from distortion

major insights of Guigo, a full appreciation of what he understood and communicated requires a thorough investigation of the roots of his thought and of the situation from which he made his statement on the dynamic nature of the Christian's spiritual life. The ground work for this appreciation has been laid by the recent critical edition and by the very thorough introduction to it by Colledge and Walsh. Moreover, the limitations of this paper make it impossible for me to deal adequately with all the questions which arise from a consideration of the meaning of Guigo's four steps. My aim is to indicate the direction of such investigations by insisting especially on the need to study Guigo's work in context. From reflection on that context will come, I think, important insights into the central emphasis of Guigo's thoughts on the four steps: the dynamic process of the way to union with God and the interrelationship of the stages on the road to 'tasting the joys of eternal sweetness' (*eternae dulcedinis gaudia degustans*).[15] Guigo's succinct summary of the spiritual life of the monk, I am tempted to call it a *summula,* achieves this emphasis through his keen and economical observations on the properties and functions of the four steps (that is, of the *proprietates* and the *officia* of the *quatuor graduum*).[16]

In the twentieth century we have discovered the sad effects of a spirituality isolated from theological reflection and of a theology deprived of mystery. When we study the resources of the past, we risk the same consequences if we investigate these sources out of context. Let us then try to delineate in broad lines the context that we need to keep in mind as we reflect upon the meaning of Guigo's message.

Colledge and Walsh have already uncovered and traced the sources that constitute the roots of Guigo's *Scala.* Theirs was a task which required much patient research and perceptiveness. These editors have shown every page of the text to be filled with biblical quotations and allusions. To borrow a phrase from Marie-Dominic Chenu, Guigo's synopsis is a theology born of scripture.[17] Like other monastic theologians Guigo is an inheritor and continuator of the spiritual doctrine of Augustine and Gregory the Great, and like many other twelfth-century writers Guigo was influenced by Origen. Of his contemporaries, Hugh of St Victor had a direct influence on him. Hugh and Guigo were both concerned with understanding and synthesizing the meaning of the Christian spiritual life and prayer.[18]

I wish to insist on calling Guigo a theologian. I do so not because he is less if he is not a theologian but because his works, both his *Meditations* and, more maturely, his *Scala claustralium,* clearly demonstrate that he had made a penetrating and rigorous analysis of the meaning of, and the process involved in, the mystery of the Christian call to union with God. Guigo had also been able to communicate his understanding of the process of the life of faith precisely and clearly. The test of time and the critical eye of posterity have demonstrated that Guigo's work is far from a transitory piece of devotional literature or an accidental leftover from the past. Specialists in spiritual theology have known and appreciated this little classic, the *Scala claustralium,*[19] but it deserves to be still more widely known for its understanding of monastic spirituality in particular and for its theological understanding of the Christian call to union with God.

Classification of Guigo's work is not, however, an act of piety intended to enhance Guigo's memory. It is for our sake that we investigate and classify Guigo's contribution. We are the ones who need to know what Guigo did, and for that reason we need to pursue further the classification in Guigo's *Scala claustralium.* For it is in this pursuit that we have the opportunity of uncovering the context that reveals the meaning of Guigo's emphasis on the inter-relatedness and the symbolic character of the four steps of his ladder.

It is easy enough to see Guigo's context as that of the monastic theologians, a group which in recent years we have come to know better through the research and writings of Jean Leclercq, especially through his book, *The Love of Learning and the Desire for God.*[20] There surely is much more to be done in coming to appreciate the nature and the scope of monastic theology in the Middle Ages, but Jean Leclercq has made it unnecessary to apologize for this classification. Guigo clearly belongs among the monastic theologians. He is a Carthusian monk writing to a fellow monk about the meaning of the monastic life. Moreover, like those of other monastic theologians, Guigo's sources are chiefly biblical and patristic, and like the best known of all monastic theologians, Bernard of Clairvaux, Guigo saw his theory of the spiritual life as arising out of his experience of that life. He is also a monastic theologian in his use of symbols and images to convey the levels of meaning of which he has become aware. Guigo's theology, like monastic theology in general, is moral in the broad sense of that term. Moralizing is almost completely absent from Guigo's work, yet like Bernard of Clairvaux[21] Guigo was trying to move hearts. Guigo was not preaching a sermon but writing a letter so in the *Scala* the moral character is less strong than it was among monastic preachers. Guigo's role as a monastic theologian is one very important context for understanding Guigo's ladder and its steps.

Another context needed for understanding Guigo's theology is the contemporary twelfth-century appreciation for reason and reasoning. Guigo is clearly no early scholastic. Yet, he had been affected by the new reverence for reason and by the methods of the early scholastics. Guigo was interested in clarifying through definitions, divisions, and comparisons as he endeavored to communicate an understanding of *lectio, meditatio, oratio,* and *contemplatio.* Guigo set up his descriptions and definitions in a fashion not all that foreign to the dialecticians.[22] He probes the meaning of the four steps through his investigation of their properties (*proprietates*) and functions (*officia*).[23] Though Guigo is not an intellectualist in his approach to the description of spiritual experience, he defines the functions of the steps with a decided emphasis on the rational character of the process. In his definition of *lectio* Guigo speaks of the very careful investigation of the scriptures through the attention of the mind (*sedula scripturarum cum animi intentione inspectio*). He sees *meditatio* as the studious action of the mind, investigating the knowledge of hidden truth under the impetus of one's reason (*studiosa mentis actio, occultae veritatis notitiam ductu propriae rationis investigans*). *Oratio* is defined in terms of the heart and *contemplatio* in terms of the

traditional monastic imagery of taste, but through the
elevation of the mind in suspension to God (*mentis in
Deum suspensae quaedam supra se elevatio, eternae
dulcedinis gaudia degustans*).[24] Further investigation could
determine Guigo's use of *mens* in an era that was witnessing a departure from Augustine's usage.[25]

Guigo's recognition of the place of reason in the
spiritual life of the monk centers on the first two steps, *lectio* and *meditatio*. In fact, Guigo says that the acts of
reading and meditating in themselves, that is, apart from
the religious formation about which he is speaking, belong
both to those who are good and to those who are bad.[26]
While Guigo remained very much a monastic theologian,
he was not an alien in an age that had a new appreciation
for reason. He states quite confidently that both scripture
and reason demonstrate that the perfection of the blessed
life is contained in the four steps of his ladder.[27] Guigo felt
no obligation to apologize for his regard for and reliance
upon reason. This rational aspect of his work is another
context for understanding Guigo's theology of the four
steps.

Perhaps the most crucial context, and the most neglec-
ted, for understanding Guigo's theology of the four steps is
what I refer to as the symbolic character of Guigo's exposition. I am inclined to see Guigo's thought as symbolic
theology in the sense in which Chenu used that term to
characterize a movement in twelfth-century theology that
had flourished in the biblical exegesis of the Fathers and
which was further refined by the theologians of the twelfth
century.[28] This symbolic theology is the theological exposition that is rooted in the spiritual interpretation of
scripture. Chenu shows that the allegorical interpretation
of scripture is not only a technique but it is also, through
the technique, a way of articulating the Christian mysteries.
By allegorizing, the exegete uncovers the realities of the
Christian mysteries that are the basis for the symbols, events, and words of scripture. Through the symbolic nature of
scripture, one moves to the elaboration of Christian doctrine, to the meaning of mysteries. Technique and doctrine
are closely related in this essentially neo-platonic outlook.

In the twelfth century, e.g., with Hugh St Victor, there was
a movement away from exaggerated spiritual interpretation
because of a new respect for the literal and historical sense
of scripture. While Guigo is sober and restrained in his
spiritual exegesis, he is not inclined to align himself with
the new emphasis on the literal or historical sense. Actually, Guigo sees the literal sense as superficial and external. He sees no profit coming from the literal or external
meaning.[29] It seems to me, on the other hand, that Guigo
shows an explicit appreciation for the connection between
the technique of spiritual interpretation and an evolving
spiritual doctrine. The explicit reference occurs in his
Meditations. After using imaginative language about the
difference between ordinary food and the bread of angels,
Guigo says: 'Illuc reducit hominem unde traxit
imaginem.'[30] This bread of the angels has led man to the
very source of the image, to God himself.

When Guigo explores the functions of his four steps, he
does so by a spiritual exegesis of the text: 'Blessed are the
pure of heart, for they shall see God.'[31] Guigo says that this
statement, although short, is sweet and has many senses for
the nourishment of the soul.[32] He was trying to come to an
understanding of the functions of the four steps through his
exegesis and he was doing so against the background of a
basically biblical symbol, the ladder.[33] This symbol goes
back to the ladder of Jacob and was used in biblical and
Greek spiritual traditions. For a long time before Guigo it
had been accepted as a symbol of the soul's progress in its
ascent to God. The biblical symbol and the traditional
usage gave Guigo an opportunity to describe through
restrained allegory the soul's movement to union with God,
a union that culminates, as does the spiritual sense, in one's
becoming as if fully spiritual.[34] Guigo's description of this
process uses an extended allegory of Matthew 5:8. He uses
various texts from scripture, and his texts illustrate at the
same time the external process of movement toward God
and the inner mystery.

To his spiritual exegesis Guigo adds an adept and
restrained use of imaginative language to describe the
functions of the four steps. This use of imaginative

language and spiritual interpretation are related activities, means of delving into the mystery of the spiritual life. Of the four functions Guigo says: reading seeks, meditation finds, prayer demands, and contemplation tastes. He continues: reading provides solid food, meditation masticates and breaks up the food, prayer achieves a savor, and contemplation consists in the sweetness which rejoices and refreshes. Reading is on the surface, meditation gets to the inner reality, prayer consists in the demand by the desire, and contemplation in the delight of experienced sweetness.[35] Another context for understanding the four steps is then the use of symbolic theology both through exegesis and through imaginative language.

In his commentary on the functions of the four steps and in his treatment of such questions as the signs of the coming of the Lord in contemplation, and the reality and the meaning of the Lord's withdrawal after his visitation in contemplation, Guigo makes a unique contribution to the understanding of the process of spiritual growth and prayer by insisting on the causal sequence of the four steps. He maintains that the steps not only succeed one another but that they have a causal relationship. Reading is the foundation that sends one on to meditation, meditation prepares the way for desire, prayer impels one to the desirable treasure and to the sweetness of contemplation. It is, by the way, in this discussion that Guigo speaks of reading as belonging to the beginners, meditation to the proficient, prayer to the devoted, and contemplation to the blessed.[36]

Guigo very strongly asserts the inter-relatedness of the four steps. Reading without meditation is arid, meditation without reading is erroneous; prayer without meditation is tepid, and meditation without prayer is fruitless. Contemplation without prayer is rare or miraculous. He hastens to add, however, that we cannot put limits to God's power. He can give to whomever he wishes whatsoever he desires.[37] To Guigo it seems that one moves closer to God as one moves away from the first step of reading; yet he continues to affirm the ascent and descent theme of spiritual development, by pointing out, for example, that because the fragile and miserable human condition cannot sustain the gift of God's sweetness, God in his wisdom withdraws his presence.[38]

There is much more to which one would like to call attention in Guigo's *Scala claustralium:* his strong insistence about the gift nature of spiritual experience, his affirmation of the central placc of contemplation in the life of the monk, his practical advice on the meaning of the Lord's withdrawal and absence, the place of purification in *oratio,* and the brief imaginative descriptions of the gift of contemplation. To understand these points and others one would, I believe, have to do as we have done above, try to determine the contexts within which this delightful spiritual classic came into existence. That Guigo was a Carthusian hermit, a monastic theologian influenced by the tradition of symbolic biblical theology, a man of his own times with a regard for reason, a person with a gift for orderly thinking and a flair for simple metaphor are all contexts, the perception of which help us achieve an authentic understanding of the *Scala.* One cannot, however, say everything in one essay about Guigo's *Scala.* He was a person who knew how to stop. Toward the end of his letter he says: 'it is now time that I make an end to this letter.' At this point he also showed that he belonged to that long tradition of Christian letter writers who have ended their letters by requesting a remembrance in the prayers of their correspondents.[39]

Keith J. Egan

Marquette University

FRANCIS OF ASSISI: AN APPROACH
TO FRANCISCAN SPIRITUALITY

Francis of Assisi (1181/2-1226) turned abruptly from seeking fame and fortune to pursuing the absolute and unmitigated poverty which he believed Christ had demanded in telling his disciples to provide themselves with neither gold nor silver, clothes nor shoes (Mt. 10:7ff). Discarding all his personal possessions, and not a few of his father's, and giving himself utterly to the imitation of the poor Christ, he began preaching God's love. As initial ridicule gradually changed to admiration, followers flocked to join him. Never an organizer, he was persuaded to seek permission from the pope to establish an order and to compose a Rule. Before his death, he sought solitude on Mount Alvernia, where he received the stigmata, the wounds of the crucified Christ.

Thomas of Celano (c. 1190-1260) joined Francis around 1214. Two years after the saint's death, he wrote his first Life. Eighteen years later, at the behest of the order, he wrote a second, expanded biography. The hymn Dies irae *(Day of Wrath) has also been attributed to Thomas.*

The intent of the present study, as is indicated by the unpretentious but significant term 'an' in the title, is to offer *one* approach to that line of Christian spirituality which carries the label 'Franciscan.' This particular approach, which the present author considers not only valid but exciting as well, seeks to say something meaningful about Franciscan spirituality by examining the life-story and experiences of its founder, St Francis of Assisi.

The image of Francis which underlies this study is quite specific. He is viewed as a person to whom 'something happened' and as one who let 'this something' happen to him.[1] To discover just what it was that 'happened' to Francis of Assisi, we will find it very helpful to examine the very first biography of the saint, that written by Thomas of Celano[2] in 1228, and in particular those passages which deal with the process of conversion which he underwent.

In this first biography,[3] Thomas of Celano depicts the early life of Francis in rather somber colors. By so doing, Celano was able to emphasize the contrast between the 'unconverted' Francis and the later 'saint,' and thereby to give credit to God for working so mightily and effectively in him.[4] In spite of his 'sinful youth,'[5] however, Thomas of Celano emphasizes that the young Francis was a man of good heart. Francis, the biographer writes: 'was a very kindly person, easy and affable, even making himself foolish because of it . . . .'[6]

It was to this jovial, friendly son of a well-to-do business family that 'something happened.' What this was Celano explains in simple but dramatic words: 'The hand of the Lord therefore came upon him and a change was wrought by the right hand of the Most High. . . .'[7] What 'happened' to Francis? God stepped into his life very palpably. In the course of a long and serious illness, the grace of God touched Francis and began to transform him in so fundamental a way that he himself was surprised and troubled by the change. Racked by conflicting thoughts, he could not find peace anywhere.[8] Nor could he any longer find joy in the beauty of nature, as he had done before. 'The beauty of the fields,' Celano reports, 'the pleasantness of the vineyards and whatever else was beautiful to look upon, could stir in him no delight.'[9]

At the same time there began to grow within Francis an aversion to his former life-style. Celano describes the process of *metanoia* going on in Francis in this way: 'he began to think of things other than he was used to thinking upon.'[10] Nor was that all, for at this time Francis also turned his gaze inward and began 'to despise himself.'[11] This harsh phrase, so reminiscent of the process of 'dying to self' to which Jesus invites his followers (Lk 14:26; Mt 16:24), very likely refers to the experience of emptiness and meaninglessness which so often accompany a spiritual awakening.[12] This process of change was by no means an easy one for the young Francis. Celano testifies that the pull of the old life-style and plans to accomplish 'great deeds of worldly glory and vanity' were so strong in Francis at this time that he 'still tried to flee the hand of God. . . .'[13]

At the same time, the Lord in his patient way met Francis where he was at and invited him to go forward. Because Francis was still eager for knightly glory, the Lord sent him a dream in which he saw his home filled 'with the trappings of war, namely, saddles, shields, lances, and other things . . . .'[14] Francis interpreted this dream to mean that he would someday become a famous knight and he was thus greatly encouraged to go on searching and to have faith in himself and in his mission in life. In this way, Celano points out, did the Lord 'entice' Francis, for he was not yet ready to receive the Lord's invitation to 'rebuild the Church.'

While these changes were going on in Francis, he felt his life being 're-directed' along new paths. For example, there began to grow within his heart an ever-deeper desire for intimate union with God. Francis found in himself a great need to be alone, so he began to spend extended periods of time in prayer. Francis' 'safest haven was prayer,' Celano emphasizes, 'not prayer of a single moment, or idle or presumptuous prayer, but prayer of long duration, full of devotion, serene in humility. If he began late, he would scarcely finish before morning. Walking, sitting, eating, or drinking, he was always intent upon prayer.'[15] He sought out deserted places and caves, where he could give himself to God in prayer. He spent whole nights in abandoned churches, where, with the grace of God, he won many battles of the spirit.[16] That great change and growth were taking place in the young man's personality is dramatically attested to by Celano when he writes that 'one person seemed to have entered [the place of prayer], and another to have come out.'[17]

Another fundamental characteristic of Francis' deepening conversion, as it was interpreted by Celano, was his great desire to recognize and to follow the will of God in his life. This too was a painful and costly process. Francis, Celano states bluntly, 'strove to bend his own will to the will of God.' At this time the young man was still filled with inner tension and conflict. He was not yet innerly 'at one' with himself. All the while, however, he prayed 'devoutly that the eternal and true God would direct his way and teach him to do his will.'[18] This burning desire to surrender

himself completely to God even led Francis to divest himself of all his material possessions, and even of his clothing,
before the bishop of Assisi. The bishop, being very sensitive
to the moment, viewed this unusual act of disrobing as inspired by the Lord and containing a 'mystery,' the mystery
that Francis, by dispossessing himself so completely, was
becoming 'like Christ.' For just as the 'kenotic' Christ
surrendered his riches at the Incarnation (see Ph 2:6ff), so,
too, Francis renounced all his possessions for the sake of
Christ.[19]

Another important moment in Francis' on-going process of discerning God's will for him took place one day
when he attended Mass and heard a reading from the
Gospel describing how Jesus sent out his disciples on their
preaching mission. This text, which summarized the
apostles' life-style, moved Francis deeply and he approached the priest after Mass for a fuller explanation of
the passage. From him Francis learned 'that the disciples
of Christ should not possess gold or silver or money; nor
carry along the way scrip, or wallet, or bread, or a staff;
that they should not have shoes, or two tunics; but that they
should preach the kingdom of God and penance . . .' (see
Mt 10:5-14; Mk 6:7-12; Lk 9:1-6).[20] Hearing this explanation, Francis realized in the depths of his being that
this was what God was calling him to do. Unable to control
his joy any longer, he cried out: 'This is what I wish, this is
what I seek, this is what I long to do with all my heart.'[21]

This hearty exclamation of joy is very significant. It indicates that Francis was listening carefully and was attuned
to what the Lord was saying to him, that he was totally
present and receptive to this moment of inspiration. But
the words also indicate that something important happened to Francis at this moment. For a long time he had
been searching for a purpose and a direction in life. During
this time of searching he had experienced tension, conflict
and doubt within himself. Now all the disjointed pieces and
fragments of his life fell into place. Now, suddenly, he *knew*
very clearly what the Lord wanted of him. He *knew* what he
wanted to do with his life. Francis' dramatic words indicate
that he is now 'at one' with himself, that he has achieved a

high level of inner unity and integration, and that he has discovered new wellsprings of strength and courage within himself. Francis is now deeply 'in touch' with himself: he knows what he wants and longs for and he sets out to do it with all his heart. In these words Thomas of Celano records Francis' enthusiastic and wholehearted response to the inspiration he received: 'He immediately put off his shoes from his feet, put aside the staff from his hands, was content with one tunic, and exchanged his leather girdle for a small cord.'[22]

Francis, Celano points out, was 'no deaf hearer of the Gospel.'[23] He accepted and fulfilled the challenge of the Gospel he heard by surrendering all his possessions. This he did in order to become free for the service of God. Having thus cast away what he had, he began to preach peace, penance and the Kingdom of God. He observed the Gospel message by going about in shabby clothes, barefoot and without money, but also, even more importantly, by becoming *innerly free.* This he did by letting go of the worries, cares and anxieties which until then had cluttered his heart. Now he cast his cares on the Lord and trusted in him with a joyous abandonment. It was this inner freedom that allowed Francis and the brothers who later followed him to be ever attentive to the Word of God and to experience a deep joy in the Lord. 'There was great rejoicing among [the friars],' reports Celano, 'when they saw and had nothing that might give them vain or carnal pleasure . . . . And because once they had put aside solicitude for earthly things, only the divine consolation gave them joy . . . .'[24]

As for Francis himself, the more he surrendered himself to God, the more the Lord visited him with consolation and joy. According to Celano, Francis was 'strengthened by the Holy Spirit' and filled with 'the sweetness of grace.' Thomas of Celano further reports that '. . . the blessed father Francis was being *daily* filled with the consolation and the grace of the Holy Spirit. . . .'[25] He was often filled with such happiness and joy that he could not keep silent.[26] Even when thrown into the snow by two bandits, he did not lose his good humor and internal joy but continued to sing the Creator's praises in a loud voice.[27]

God, for his part, continued to touch Francis, ever deepening his original conversion of heart. One day, when Francis was deeply troubled by the sins of his past life, he approached the Lord in prayer, 'as he had done so often.' Francis placed himself in spirit 'before the Lord of the whole earth' and remained in prayer a very long time, repeating over and over again the words of the publican: 'O God, be merciful to me the sinner' (Lk 18:13). After a time the 'darkness' that had engulfed his heart began to be dispelled and an 'unspeakable joy and very great sweetness began to flood his innermost heart.' With the joy, too, came the cleansing experience and vivid awareness that all his sins were truly and eternally forgiven. There was 'poured' into him an assurance that he was restored to God's grace. Then he was 'caught up above himself' and absorbed in a 'certain light.' The capacity of his mind was 'enlarged,' so that he was able to see 'what was to come to pass' in regard to himself and to the fate of his brothers.[28]

Francis came out of this inner 'happening' deeply consoled and refreshed. In fact, he became a 'changed' person. Certainly this moment of experiencing the forgiveness of sins and of receiving the assurance of God's grace marks a significant stage in Francis' spiritual 're-birth,' that inner transformation which Jesus himself described to Nicodemus (Jn 3).

It is time to return to the main theme of this study. What 'happened' to Francis of Assisi? As Thomas of Celano makes clear in his description of the saint's conversion, he was 'touched' by God. Though many beautiful words have been uttered and written about Francis of Assisi, the fundamental truth about this simple but fascinating human being is that he was completely filled with God. One of the most exciting things about Francis was his vivid consciousness of actually having met and experienced the Lord in his life, and of having surrendered himself fully to the workings of God's grace. Not only Thomas of Celano and the other early biographers, but the saint himself in his own writings, testify to Francis' keen awareness of the Lord's presence in his own life and in the life of his followers. Francis' testament, composed shortly before his death, rings with the firm conviction that it was the *Lord* himself who revealed to him the kind of life he was to live. It was the *Lord,* Francis repeats over and over again in this autobiography, who inspired him to undergo the process of conversion. It was the *Lord* who led him among lepers, who gave him faith in the Church and in priests; it was the *Lord* who gave him brothers, who inspired him to write the rule, and who revealed to him the greeting of peace.[29]

This firm conviction that the Lord was leading him and acting very intimately in his life deeply influenced Francis in becoming the kind of person he was, but it also affected his approach to the life of the spirit. Indeed, the vivid, personal experience of God, the consciousness that God 'touched' him, can be viewed as the very core and center of Francis' spirituality and his approach to the Christian life. Whatever else of significance one wishes to say about Francis of Assisi or the movement he started can be viewed within this perspective. Certainly the Christian values which Francis espoused and shared with his brothers and sisters were based on and sprang from his experience of God. A few examples follow:

Brotherhood. Francis felt deeply that he was accepted by God, that God was his loving Father. He soon came to view himself as a 'son' of the Father. And not only he himself, but all persons who came into his life, and even the animals and inanimate creatures as well were 'sons' of the Father. Because all creatures were 'sons' and 'daughters' of the one Father in heaven, Francis looked upon them all as his brothers and sisters. And he wished to be of service to them.[30]

Poverty. Francis experienced God as the Almighty and Perfect One, as the Creator and Lord of the universe. Standing before this Lord, who was rich beyond measure, Francis experienced his own nakedness and nothingness. He realized that all he had, his life and his very self, were not his own but came to him from the bounty of the generous Gift-giver, his heavenly Father. Francis came to see himself therefore as the 'poor little one,' the beggar who stretches out his empty hands and has confidence that the Lord will fill them with good things.[31]

Obedience. Francis felt that the Lord was 'touching' and directing the course of his life. In response, he was keenly sensitive to the Lord's presence in every situation in which he found himself. And he was deeply obedient to the will of God as it became manifest to him through the words of Holy Scripture, through the guidance of the church, through the advice of persons and the promptings of his own heart.[32]

Gospel Life. God revealed to Francis that he should live 'according to the form of the holy Gospel.' Francis did so, not merely by adopting a life-style of itinerant preaching and poverty, but even more dramatically by observing, and encouraging others to observe, the great commandment to love God and neighbor.

The Following of Christ. Having experienced God in his life, Francis was eager to 'return' to the Father who created him. He therefore undertook to 'follow' Christ, for he realized that Jesus is man's only 'way' to the Father. Francis was particularly struck that Jesus emptied himself and surrendered himself to the Father, especially at the incarnation, but also in Gethsemane and on the Cross. Christ's love for the Father and for mankind was so great, Francis came to realize, that he gave up his very life for man. Francis therefore also sought to become a man of love and to surrender himself completely into the hands of his Father in heaven. These were the 'footsteps' of Christ which Francis 'followed.' And these inner attitudes he externalized by living in joyful simplicity and poverty and by being of service to others.

These values, and the experience of God which underlies them, indicate what Francis' life was all about. And they indicate what the spirituality which bears his name is all about. Francis was caught up in God; he sought to be ever attuned to the will of God for him. Because he was a man deeply in love with the Lord, he spent his life in praising and thanking God for his greatness and goodness. He invites all his brothers and sisters to join him in praising the heavenly Father: 'With all our hearts and all our souls, all our minds and all our strength, all our power and all our understanding, with every faculty and every effort, with every affection and all our emotions, with every wish and desire, we should love our Lord and God who has given us everything, body and soul, and all our life. . . .'[33]

Duane V. Lapsanski

St Bonaventure University

NORTHERN SPIRITUALITY AND THE
LATE MEDIEVAL DRAMA OF YORK

The evolutionary approach to drama and art so prevalent in the early part of our century has been thoroughly exploded during the years since World War II.[1] This development has been very fortunate, for it has forced upon us the recognition that any rigidly diachronic methodology must severely limit our discussion to events and details thoroughly wrenched out of their context. If the critical process does not therefore retreat into a formalist consideration of the literary elements of a play or the technical processes of a work of art, the possibility opens up of providing a criticism which is of necessity interdisciplinary because it is synchronic. The task does not exclude the historic perspective derived from close attention to the development of ideas, attitudes, or images, but it insists nevertheless upon understanding the work which is being subjected to analysis in terms of its interrelations with other factors and events simultaneous in space and time.

The plays and the art of the city of York during the late Middle Ages therefore require examination in a manner more satisfactory than to see them as primitive expressions of a didacticism rooted in the fourteenth-century Church. In the first place, neither the art nor the plays were really primitive. The amateur and quasi-amateur status of the plays, it is true, made them less sophisticated than the liturgical music dramas that were being performed in various cathedrals, churches, and monasteries until the sixteenth century, but they nevertheless shared traditions which assured that, on the whole, high quality would be

125

I. Nicholas Blackburn, Sr, and his wife Margaret in the glass of the East Window, All Saints, North Street, York.

preserved. The fact that they were middle class and popular should hardly prejudice us against them. The plays and the art express the central images and actions of the Christian story or religious myth, which we may define as matter held to be true in a deeper than literal sense. Both plays and art participated in the spirituality of the city during an age when civic piety was still the focal point of life in York.

The citizens of York in the fifteenth and early sixteenth centuries did not simply distinguish, as we do, between art and the myth, or between drama and the myth. To understand the structure of civic thinking we need to put aside our smug rationalism and our modern scepticism. When we today hear that a cross on the high altar in York Minster contained a piece of the column to which Christ was bound during the Flagellation,[2] we may remain unconvinced. Yet no doubt this cross was a thoroughly fine piece of workmanship, and when Archdeacon Stephen Scrope gave it to the Cathedral in 1418 he certainly meant to provide a gift which was both aesthetically pleasing and spiritually valuable. Both the piece of column and the cross would have reminded those who looked at this work of art that Christ's Passion was the central event upon which the Christian scheme of salvation depended, and we know that for the later Middle Ages the Passion and the Crucifixion took on new importance, for to a considerable extent they even supplanted the early Church's emphasis on the fact of the Incarnation and the event of the Resurrection.

If it were possible for a few moments to enter into the mind and heart of a spiritually inclined person looking with devotion upon the York cross with its fragment of the column, we would perhaps come to know a great deal more than we presently do about fifteenth and early sixteenth-century spirituality. Alas, the thoughts of our medieval ancestors are as inaccessible to us as the artwork on the gold cross on the altar, which had disappeared by 1509.[3] Certainly, however, art did provide the focus for popular meditation, and hence extant works are remnants of phenomena which really mattered in that age.

An understanding of the spirituality of the citizens of York during the late medieval period cannot be achieved

more completely than through the extant art, mainly painted glass, and the plays that were performed normally by
the crafts each year at Corpus Christi time. For convenience, the glass will receive attention at this point. Even
the Cathedral, which was distinct from the city and was the
domain of the clergy rather than the citizens, was adorned
with some glass given by the crafts.[4] In the instance of the
bell-founders' window, given in the fourteenth century by
Richard Tunnoc, the work of the guild itself is set forth by
workmen shown at their tasks. But in the city churches the
men of the crafts, along with the merchants, had to take the
major financial responsibility for adorning the windows.
For example, Reginald Bawtree, a merchant, left 100
shillings in his will in 1429 for a new window in All Saints,
North Street. The moving force in providing new windows
of the highest quality for this church was the pastor, Father
James Baguley, a rare man of learning who must have ap-
proved the design—in this instance, the Corporal Acts of
Mercy—and have insisted that the contract be let to the
very best glass painters available locally. This window, like
the famous Fifteen Signs of Doomsday window in the same
church, was surely painted in the workshop of John Thorn-
ton, previously of Coventry and made free of the city of
York in 1410 after the completion of his massive East Window in the Minster.[5] The difference in style between this
window and the Tunnoc window in the Minster is
remarkable, and a comparison of the two is indicative not
only of new techniques in glass painting but also of new
aesthetic values and of a new mode of spirituality even in
conservative York in the fifteenth century.

The Corporal Acts of Mercy window provides specific
examples of feeding the hungry, of clothing the naked, of
giving drink to the thirsty, of offering housing to the
homeless, of visiting prisoners and the sick. The figure
painting itself is much more highly individualized than in
the work of the previous century, and the attempt was
clearly to bring to life the scenes represented. In contrast,
the fourteenth-century bell-founders' window in the Minster is formalized and abstract. It is clear that by the fifteenth century citizens and clergy alike were coming to ap-

preciate a new kind of art which emphasized particulars, which brings to life scenes from devotional life.[6] The new style is indicative of changing modes of religious devotion. The craftsmen and the merchants now preferred to see in a more specific way how the events of the Christian story *might* have appeared. To be sure, conservative York was hardly the location where new modes of devotion and a new aesthetics could have originated, but this city with its extensive trade with the Low Countries nevertheless contributed something unique to the new trends.

The spirituality of the late Middle Ages in York, as in the Netherlands, was clearly very personal and quite emotional. The sight of a religious painting or a pious object was enough to release a flood of tears. The object of the continental painters from the Low Countries was to present the details of a religious scene in such detail that the imaginations of the viewers would be stimulated to the highest extent. The Northern Painters were not simply formalists, rather they used their discovery of perspective as the means whereby they might all the more carefully present iconographic details. In such a painting as the miniature illustrating the flagellation in the courtly *Hours of Catherine of Cleves,*[7] we see the carefully painted tiled floor as well as the sharply visualized details of the torturing of Christ during his Passion. The attention to detail had as its purpose the establishment of credibility. The aggressiveness and anger of the torturers is not only represented by their faces but also by the way in which the fist and scourge extend into the border of the miniature. In other instances, Northern painters tended to make literal even the symbolism of the Christian story. This kind of painting was scorned by Michelangelo, who sneered that 'Flemish painting pleases all the devout better than Italian. The latter evokes no tears, the former makes them weep copiously. This,' he asserts, 'is not the result of the merits of this art; the only cause is the extreme sensibility of the devout spectators.'[8] If one can believe the travel section of the *New York Times* (18 May 1975), pious tears are still evoked in Flanders by the sight of an object of piety such as the vial of Precious Blood brought to Bruges during the

Second Crusade.[9] That the spectators responded similarly
to the tableaux offered by the actors of the Corpus Christi
plays at York and elsewhere is proven by *A tretise of
miraclis pleyinge,* a lollard tract against the plays. This
treatise takes into account the argument that plays are like
paintings come to life, and curiously admits the aesthetic
effectiveness of the religious drama in England during the
fifteenth century. The plays inspired pious tears: 'Also, ofte
sythis by siche myraclis pleyinge men and wymmen, seynge
the passioun of Crist and of hise seyntis, ben movyd to compassion and devociun, wepynge bitere teris. . . .'[10]

EARLY AND LATE MEDIEVAL SPIRITUALITY

The sources of late medieval spirituality are well
known:[11] St Augustine, St Anselm, St Bernard of Clairvaux, St Francis of Assisi, the *Meditations on the Life of
Christ* attributed to St Bonaventura and in fact written in
part by him. A key figure is Anselm, whose writings figured
importantly in establishing the new interest in Christ's
humanity. Instead of emphasizing the divinity of Christ as
the supernatural power who overcomes sin and death
through the strength evidenced in the Resurrection, the
medieval church turned to the Saviour who experienced
human suffering and death and brings relief to man in
need of salvation. The shift is particularly noticeable when
vernacular plays are compared with the earlier liturgical
dramas which were presented as additions to the liturgy
from the tenth to the sixteenth centuries. The liturgical
plays have their roots in the earlier theology, and hence it
should come as no surprise that they were at first most
closely linked to the Easter ceremonies. The earliest of
these plays was apparently a dramatization of the story
of the three Marys at the empty tomb, where they are
greeted by the angel who speaks the famous words, 'Quem
queritis. . . .' This brief play has been proven, through an
examination of its music, to be a development out of the
Easter Introit.[12] It provided a controlled and ritualized re-
enactment of the event which was then considered to be of

the greatest significance in the life of Christ. A more elaborate version of the same story and utilizing the same tradition of drama is the famous *Visitatio Sepulchri* from the Fleury Manuscript; this drama does not lack emotion, but it is as stylized as the figures in eleventh- and twelfth-century art. The play, like the miniatures and sculptures, aims at stylized visualizing of the scene in a manner that gives very close attention to the essence of the event. As a rule, particulars are of little concern and are eliminated in the interest of perfectly realized form. Aesthetically, these plays are in many ways superior to the vernacular plays which made their appearance later, but they hardly convey the *humanity* of Christ which was demanded by the later spirituality.

When we compare such a play as the Fleury *Slaying of the innocents*[13] with the fifteenth-century vernacular play *Magnus Herodes* by the Wakefield Master in the Towneley cycle, we see that we have moved into a different world from that dramatized in the stately verse and music of the Fleury Master. In the Wakefield play, Herod's anger is more genuinely unrestrained, though his raging in early productions of the play presented in West Yorkshire was clearly not so lacking in control as in the Coventry play where the stage directions insist that he should rage both 'in the pagond and in the strete also.'[14] More commonly Herod's rage is shown in iconography by his glowering face, his crown tipped slightly awry, and his crossed legs.[15] When the Towneley Herod learns that the Magi have gone back to their lands by 'Anothere way' (l. 147), he shouts: 'Why, and ar thay past me by? for tyn I brast!/ We! fy!/ Fy on the dewill.' He attempts to beat his knights, and then announces that he is so angry that he is about to 'yelde my gast.' And he does not really settle down until, after he has heard the prophecies that enrage him further, one of his counsellors suggests that slaughter might be a good way to handle the problem; the infant Jesus is to be put to death 'on a spere' (l. 252). Herod's role becomes that of child-killer—a distinguishing mark which identifies him in the very late medieval glass at Fairford where he holds up a sword with an infant impaled upon it. The entire *Magnus*

Herodes develops at considerable length the futile attempt of an earthly king to destroy the human child who is also divine. Particular details are used to underline the nature of evil which will seem to triumph at the Crucifixion, when paradoxically the victim will become the victor. In the *Magnus Herodes* the soldiers, who later figure in the story of the Passion, are brutal and abusive (they call the mothers names—e.g., 'hoore,' l. 340); furthermore, they are ultimately cowardly, though not so cowardly as the base messenger named Watkin in the *Massacre of the Innocents* in the Digby manuscript.[16] Watkin asks Herod 'for Mahoundes sake' to make him a knight as a reward for his valor in infanticide, yet he quakes when he envisions the mothers: 'though the moder be angry, the child shalbe slayn,/ but yitt I drede no thyng more than a woman with a Rokke' (ll. 158-59). He is in fact eventually beaten by them, and is only rescued by the knights. Two examples of painted glass in the choir of York Minster witness to the popularity of the theme of the Killing of Innocents. In the glass in the South Choir Clerestory, Herod himself reaches out and stabs a child. In the *Magnus Herodes,* the soldiers who return to their king brag that they have murdered 'Many thowsandys' of children (ll. 418-19)—144,000, to be exact. For their exploits, Herod offers them ladies, castles, and towers, and then launches into his last speech in which he boasts for approximately fifty lines. 'I lagh that I whese!' he exclaims (l. 472), and finally he concludes with this absolutely incoherent advice to the audience: 'Syrs, this is my counsell: Bese not to cruell./ Bot adew!—to the deuyll!/ I can [speak] no more Franch.' Obviously the children whom he has killed are identified very closely with Christ himself, and these scenes from Christ's infancy look forward to those scenes which will take place between the betrayal and the death of the Saviour. Then again the threat to Christ's life will be made manifest when he is betrayed on a very human level by a follower who feels aggrieved and cheated. The multiplication of particulars in the *Magnus Herodes* underlines threats to Christ's humanity—a humanity that must suffer for the rest of humanity on account of the weakness inherited from our first ancestors. Even such a lively play as this must be seen as pointing to the human nature of Christ which figured so largely in the spirituality of the late Middle Ages.

THE HUMANITY OF CHRIST

Devotion to the humanity of Christ was basic to the spirituality of Saint Bernard, whose Cistercian principles seem to have directed him away from visualizing any images in his meditations. Dom Cuthbert Butler points out that Bernard's 'contemplation' involved 'no framing of images of the scenes of the Passion, nor any portrait presented to the mind of Our Lord's human form.'[17] Bernard's regard for the Infancy and Passion of Christ had an immense influence on the spirituality of the period between his own lifetime and the Council of Trent. Though Cistercian monasteries such as those which took root in Yorkshire would not allow the relevant scenes from Christ's life to be shown in their art, elsewhere representations seem strongly affected by the emphasis found in Bernard's spiritual writings. In English wall paintings as early as the thirteenth century, Christ's life is normally presented in two series of paintings, one of which represents the Infancy and the other the Passion.[18] Significantly, the Passion in the later Middle Ages becomes the more important of these series. Indeed, for the late Middle Ages the Passion was itself regarded as the central event of Christ's life; by this period it has supplanted the Resurrection as the crucial occurrence in Christ's life.

The Franciscans, especially through such works as the *Meditations on the Life of Christ,* carried devotion to the Infancy and Passion of Christ one step further: they brought back the images as agents of meditation, and insisted that Christians attempt actively to imagine and visualize the events of the sacred history as if they were present at the very places.[19] For instance, in its account of the Crucifixion, the *Meditations* advise:

Here pay diligent attention to the manner of the Crucifixion. Two ladders are set in place, one behind the right arm, another at the left arm, which the evil doers ascend holding nails and hammers. Another ladder is placed in front, reaching to the place where the feet are to be affixed.[20]

The account continues to describe in minute detail the appearance of the Crucifixion, always with the implicit invitation to the reader to visualize the scene with as much particularity as possible. Christ's right hand is fixed to the cross first, and then the left. Yet, in spite of all the apparent certainty, the *Meditations* admit that Christ may have been crucified another way, with the cross on the ground. 'If this suits you better, think how they take him contemptuously, like the vilest wretch, and furiously cast Him onto the cross on the ground, taking His arms, violently extending them, and most cruelly fixing them to the cross. Similarly, consider his feet, which they dragged down as violently as they could.'[21] This second way of visualizing the Crucifixion (*jacente cruce* instead of *erecto cruce*) suited the writers of the excellent plays in the York and Wakefield cycles, and it is the way in which Christ is placed on the cross in the late fourteenth-century glass formerly in St Saviour's, York and now in the west window of All Saints, Pavement.[22] The visualizing of the scene in devotion and in the visual arts also leaves open possibilities of greater 'realism' in the treatment of the particulars in drama. In the York play, the soldiers discover that the holes are drilled too far apart, so before they can drive the nails they must stretch Christ's body with ropes until it fits the cross. 'It failis a foote and more,' the Third Soldier complains, and the Second Soldier comments: ' Þan muste he bide in bitter bale' (*Crucifixio Cristi*, ll. 107, 110). They try to stretch him, and fail. The First Soldier, responding like a workman with a problem, takes up a rope and suggests a solution: 'Why carpe ȝe so? faste on a corde/ And tugge hym to, by toppe and taile' (ll. 113-14). After some difficulty, the soldiers, who are almost unconscious of their sadism ('It is no force howe felle he feele,' the First Soldier says, l. 136), are able to stretch the body to the point that 'all his synnous go a-soundre' in order to be able to hammer the nails into place. The intense suffering of Christ is underlined in a most graphic and kinetic manner: ' ʒaa, assoundir are both synnous and veynis,/ On ilke a side, so haue we soughte' (ll. 147-48). It is quite clear that the play, which particularly dwells on the human agony of Christ, was intended to bring forth pious tears in the audience among people who felt sympathy for the sufferings of their Saviour.

Yet the rationale for the brutal and realistic nailing of Christ to the cross in the York play is not merely sadistic effect. F. P. Pickering in his book *Literature and Art in the Middle Ages*[23] has forcefully demonstrated that here the medieval writers and visual artists were giving a literal depiction of the symbolism of the Crucifixion as it was prophesied in Psalm 22, which along with Psalm 69 determined the particulars of Christ's death. In the twenty-second psalm, the psalmist writes: 'They have numbered my bones.' The sadistically extended placing of Christ on the cross which is suggested by this passage was new to the West about 1400, and is utilized in the *Speculum humanae salvationis* and in the painting *The Nailing of Christ to the Cross* by Gerard David in the National Gallery, London;[24] in the East this symbolism had existed earlier, for it is given in the *Byzantine Guide to Painting*.[25]

Christ on the cross also has his sinews stretched like the strings of a harp in the York play;[26] after all, he is, as the Flemish music theorist Tinctoris insisted, the 'greatest of musicians' because he brought God and man into harmony.[27] Late medieval spirituality placed very great emphasis upon the act of atonement, the Crucifixion itself; this act was deliberately presented in art in the most sensational ways possible. While early Anglo-Saxon Crucifixions had represented Christ in a more or less formalized manner against the cross, by 1338 when the de Beneston window was painted and installed in York Minster his arms had become stretched out at a painful angle and his suffering had become the emotional focus of the composition. In English wall painting, the middle of the thirteenth century marked the change in the presentation of the crucified Christ; after this time, as Tristram notes, the artists 'stressed the pain and pity of the theme.'[28] In the illumination which shows the Crucifixion in the *Hours of Catherine of Cleves,* [29] Christ's suffering humanity becomes particularly evident, and similar treatment may be observed in other manuscript illuminations. Finally, careful examination of the crucified Christ from the Isenheim Altarpiece by Matthias Grünewald exhibits the beaten and bruised body stretched out with all the sensationalism that a visual artist could utilize.

Good Friday, which commemorates the atonement of Christ for the sins of men and which serves as a reminder that a second Adam has suffered in exchange for the lapse of the first Adam and his companion Eve, became the center of the liturgical year. The victory over sin is achieved here rather than on the Sunday following, which commemorates the Resurrection. Within the Mass itself in the late Middle Ages, the elements of bread and wine were connected very clearly with the events on the cross. In the York rite, the celebrant at the crucial point in the canon of the Mass 'spreadeth his arms after the manner of a cross.' [30] As a manuscript of the *Lay Folks' Mass Book* from the Cistercian monastery at Rievaulx indicates: 'When the preste the eleuacyon has made,/ He wille sprede his armes onbrade. . . .' [31]

THE YORK CYCLE

A great concern with the Passion as a focus for the spiritual life and as a subject for meditative images in art and drama marks the period following the appearance of the Black Death in Europe in 1348-49. Students of the art of the period have almost invariably commented upon the preoccupation with death and mortality, and have commonly identified the age as morbid. Those who have studied the population of medieval England have found themselves surprised to discover that the population had already leveled off around 1300 and that the great decline in population after the plague was not due entirely to disease and pestilence. People, passing through a phase of supreme pessimism, simply did not get married as often,

II. Placing Christ on the cross. Glass formerly in St Saviour's, York, and now in the West Window, All Saints Pavement, York.

nor did they have as many children as they formerly had had; hence in the fifteenth century the population fell to approximately half of what it had been in 1300.[32] The later portion of the Middle Ages in England, from 1349 to the reign of Henry VIII, was also a period of almost frenetic church building. At York, nearly every extant church building was either rebuilt or remodeled during this period. Guilds, especially with regard to their religious functions, thrived.[33] This was the heyday of the Corpus Christi procession, which was under the sponsorship of the prestigious Corpus Christi Guild after 1408. Out of the Corpus Christi celebration and the spirituality prevalent in such cities as York in the late Middle Ages came the cycle (or Corpus Christi) plays which were staged by the towns-people.

The greatest concern of all citizens of the city of York was for the health of the soul after death. On the institutional level, not only the parish churches but also the chantry chapels were of vital interest; Maud Sellers, who edited the *York Memorandum Book A/Y*, was even convinced that 'the real link between municipality and church was the chantry priest; in the chantries the mayor and his brethren had a personal, a vivid interest.'[34] She cites the mayor as declaring 'that all the chantries of this city have been and are founded by the citizens and notabilities of this city; therefore, both the priests of this city and suburbs having chantries, and stipendiary priests not having chantries, are the special officials "oratores" of the citizens, their patrons and masters.'[35] In January 1424, in the third year of the reign of Henry VI, Nicholas Blackburn, Sr., 'alderman of the cytye of Yorke,' founded the chantry chapel of Saint Anne on Foss Bridge. The stated purpose of the chapel was for the use of a priest who would 'syng wythyn the sayd chappell for the sowle of the sayd founder and all Crysten sowles . . . betwene the howers of xj and xij before none, and nowe alteryd [at a later date] by th' advyce of the parochiners there, as well as for ther commodytye as travelynge people, between iiij and v in the mornyng.'[36] In his will, probated in 1432, he left liturgical vestments, a missal, and a chalice to his chantry chapel devoted to Saint Anne on Foss Bridge.[37]

The affluent Nicholas Blackburn, Sr, was also the patron of four other chantry chapels in the city. His portrait, along with that of his wife Margaret, appears in a window which he gave to All Saints, North Street before his death. A leading citizen and alderman who served as mayor twice, Blackburn was concerned with much more than amassing wealth. As a merchant, he moved easily among the ruling oligarchy, which was composed of individuals whom Eileen Power has identified as 'the representatives of capitalism in a pre-capitalistic age.'[38] It is tempting to try to understand such men in terms of modern business men, but clearly Nicholas exemplifies a kind of devoutness not common in our own time. Words at the bottom of the donor panel once asked worshippers to 'pray for the souls of Nicholas Blackburn, *quondam* Mayor of York, and of Margaret his wife, and of all the faithful departed.'[39] On the book held by Margaret Blackburn are written the words from the fifty-first psalm: 'O Lord, open thou my lips; and my mouth [shall show forth thy praise]' (AV).[40] Other donors who appear in windows of the same church are his son Nicholas Blackburn, Jr, and his wife, also named Margaret, and possible members of the Wiloby and Hessle families as well as some others. Such people as these not only rebuilt, remodeled, and decorated churches, but also, as we have seen, provided for the future of their own souls and the souls of others through the endowment of chantry chapels. They were supporters of the ecclesiastical arts and, perhaps even more importantly, they gave staunch backing to the plays which presented the story of the Christian way of salvation on the streets of York every year.

The plays in Middle English at York probably developed out of the series of *tableaux vivants* presented as devotional images on wagons for the Corpus Christi pageant during the last half of the fourteenth century. By 1433, when the Mercers acquired a new pageant,[41] something of a dramatic nature was certainly taking place. In that year, the city fathers were providing a room for themselves to see the plays—something they would not have done if the plays had not been separated from the procession, since they normally themselves took part in the latter.[42] Some speeches must have been used as early as 1415, the date of an *Ordo* which insists that there be 'good players, well arayed and openly spekyng,' who are prepared to begin 'at the mydhowre betwix iiij[th] and v[th] of the cloke in the mornynge, and then all o[th]er pageantz fast followyng ilk one after o[th]er as [th]er course is, without tarieng.'[43] The pageant wagons started thus early in the morning on the feast day of Corpus Christi at the first station, which was at the gates of Holy Trinity Priory near Micklegate, not far from the sheds on Toft Green where the wagons were stored when not in use. They then passed along the street, past the end of North Street and across the Ouse Bridge, then up Low Ousegate, which is today much wider than it was in the fifteenth and sixteenth centuries. Edwin Benson's *Life in a Mediaeval City* aptly describes the streets as 'mere alleys, passages between houses and groups of buildings'; he continues:

They were very narrow and often the sky could hardly be seen from them because of the overhanging upper storeys of the buildings along each side. Goods in the Middle Ages and right down to the nineteenth century were carried in towns by hand. Carriages and waggons and carts were not very numerous and would have no need to proceed beyond the main streets and open squares. . . . [44]

The plays were, according to the orthodox view, produced one after another at a dozen or more stations in all; however, as Robert Davies conjectured in the nine-teenth century, all of the forty-eight plays in the Register could not possibly have been performed in full at all the stations within a single day.[45] Possibly the plays were set forth in truncated form at all the stations except the final one, at the Pavement where the pageant carts could have been lined up and the unabridged plays presented in or-der.[46] It is now known, however, that all the plays in the Register were not necessarily produced every year; in 1535 only thirty-five plays were presented at Corpus Christi.[47]

The whole affair must have had all the trappings of a

major church festival in the Middle Ages. The streets had been especially cleaned and banners had been hung on the route at the various stations where the pageants were to be played.[48] The crowds on this day apparently ranged from a rowdy minority to a majority that found itself edified and deeply affected by the plays. In 1426, a Franciscan, William Melton, argued in a series of sermons for the separation of the Corpus Christi procession and the plays, since attendance at the plays had been leading some people to miss the service at the Cathedral and hence to lose the indulgences promised to them; at the same time he praised the Corpus Christi cycle as 'good in itself and very laudable' in spite of some disorderliness which occasionally took place when it was performed.[49] The Corporation, the sponsor of the plays, was of course extremely concerned that everything be done decently and in good order. In 1476 the Corporation ruled that all the plays to be presented by the various crafts were to be inspected and incompetent actors barred from appearing:

That yerely in the tyme of lentyn there shall be called afore the maire for the tyme beyng iiij of the moste connyng discrete and able players within this Citie, to serche, here, and examen all the plaiers and plaies and pagentes thrughoute all the artificers belonging to Corpus X[ti] Plaie. And all suche as thay shall fynde sufficiant in personne and connyng, to the honour of the Citie and worship of the saide Craftes, for to admitte and able; and all other insufficient personnes, either in connyng, voice, or personne to discharge, ammove, and avoide.[50]

After 1500, the City Clerk was even on hand with the Register at the first station early in the morning to see that things were proceeding properly.[51]

CREATION TO JUDGMENT

The first pageant in the York cycle was the *Creation, and Fall of Lucifer* for which the text was provided by the great York Realist, the master of alliterative verse who also contributed in a major way to the central plays on the Passion. The opening play was the responsibility of the Barkers, who were closely associated with the Tanners. Indeed, in the *Ordo* of 1415 the play is given to the Tanners, though by c. 1422, when another list had been drawn up by the town clerk, the Barkers are listed in connection with it. These guilds had been very important in the life of the city in the early fourteenth century before the wool trade had become dominant,[52] and they managed to retain the opening play in the cycle. Clearly this was a position of honor which dated back to an earlier period when a very prominent trade had been allowed to present the first in a series of *tableaux*, which later developed into plays with speaking parts.

The York cycle continued through the Creation and the fall of Adam and Eve, through certain other Old Testament stories, and through the life of Christ from the Annunciation to the Ascension before concluding at last with a spectacular Doomsday pageant presented by the prestigious Mercers. The pageant and properties for this final pageant are described in an indenture dated 1433 and only recently discovered.[53] Included are puppets representing angels, and a device is even provided for Christ, who wears a gilded mask and 'a Sirke wounded', to come down and sit upon a 'Rainbow' in judgment upon men. The scene must have been not too different from that shown in the restored fifteenth-century wall painting in the Church of St Thomas à Becket, Salisbury. Terror and joy mingle in this tableau, which is far more complex emotionally than any such simple issuing forth into joy as might have been expected if the plays had been primarily dependent upon the Corpus Christi liturgy rather than upon the scenes commonly depicted in art. Here the end of the world comes, bringing home to the viewer a strong element of fear, for who knows how he will fare on that 'dredfull' last day? Significantly, the Last Judgment as set forth in the drama, unlike the Apocalypse scenes in the East Window of York Minster, draws mainly on the account in Matthew 25 rather than on Revelation;[54] Christ, when he turns to saints and sinners who are arrayed at his right and at his left, stresses the corporal acts of mercy—a topic which forms the basis for a window in All Saints, North Street. On the Last Day, all souls will be raised from the grave and will look forward to an eternity of either bliss or torture. Those who have lived wicked lives, even if they had been ecclesiastics of high rank, will be forcibly taken off to hell by demons. An early fifteenth-century English alabaster in the British Museum likewise shows in more stylized form the entry of the damned into the mouth of hell; as another British Museum alabaster shows, however, those who have respected the work of salvation wrought by Christ will receive a much happier reward—everlasting bliss—after being welcomed into Paradise by Saint Peter.

In the fifteenth-century pageant of the York Mercers, nine puppet angels, 'payntid rede to/ renne aboute in þe heuen,[55] apparently so moved around Christ by means of a simple mechanical contrivance that the scene would have borne resemblance to the glass in the West Window at Fairford, where the Judge is encircled by flamelike red angels which we must identify as seraphim. The scene of the Last Judgment is also one that is well represented in a miniature in a York book of hours now in York Minster Library (MS. Add. 2, fol. 208). In the York play, the Judgment ultimately dissolves into music as the Judge announces that 'Nowe is fulfillid all my for-thoght' to indicate that all his work is completed; the angels continue to sing as they cross from place to place.

The Doomsday play is a powerful reminder of the *terminus* of earthly life for the individual man or woman, and it is particularly suited to the emphasis on last things which appears in fifteenth-century art. The painting of the Last Judgment at St Thomas, Salisbury, is over the chancel arch, and hence is immediately noticed by anyone who steps into the nave of the church. Tristram notes that by the fifteenth century the 'normal position' for the Last Judgment 'was above the chancel arch, since it symbolized the division between this world and the next.'[56] The nave itself had come to represent life in this world, beginning from the west, a direction associated with evil and death, and moving toward the east, associated with heavenly bliss. The crossing between the nave and chancel symbolized the entry from earthly life into heaven. The sanctuary, where the sacred rite of the Eucharist was performed daily for the salvation of the living and the dead and where the Sacrament was reserved on the high altar, was set off by the real presence of God. When a citizen or anyone else worshipped in the nave of the parish church, he was conscious that he was within that portion which symbolically represented his current location in the scheme of things; it was appropriate that the upkeep of the nave of the church was normally the responsibility of the parishioners while the upkeep of the chancel was the responsibility of the clergy. When a person stepped forward to the communion rail, he was offered a foretaste of heavenly bliss. The sufferings of Christ, who was *human* as well as divine, were being made real for him within the structure of the rite, and everything was directed toward his ultimate salvation. Because of the rite, he might hope to enter into the final rest of heaven after Judgment Day. But the painting of the Doom over the chancel arch would remind him that the final salvation of heaven could only be reached by passing the ordeal of the Last Judgment.

The Christ who returns in Judgment is, however, not merely a figure to be feared. The tableau which was offered to the viewers of the York play at the end of the cycle was also a dramatized version of an important devotional image. Very prominent in the late medieval representations of the Last Judgment are Christ's wounds, sustained during the Crucifixion when he died for the sins of men, and the symbols of the Passion, which are often held by angels.[57] On the roof bosses of the Choir of Winchester Cathedral are representations of an unusually large number of symbols associated with the Passion, including the ewer and basin which Pilate used when he washed his hands and the lantern dropped by Malchus when Saint Peter cut off his ear. One of these bosses also contains the wounds in Christ's hands, feet, and heart;[58] we see merely the parts of the body afflicted in a sculpture that today might remind us of a work by René Magritte. To a fifteenth-century viewer, however, the design of this boss would have had a devotional purpose which it shared with the representations of the instruments of the Passion. Badges worn by participants in the Pilgrimage of Grace included a similar design.[59] So also the text of the York Mercers' play announces that the people on the final day of history shall 'see þe woundes fyve' suffered by Christ *(The Judgment Day,* 1. 71). The 1433 indenture for the York Mercers' play calls specifically for 'vij grete Aungels halding þe passion of god' and 'iiij smaler Aungels gilted holding þe passion,'[60] The play itself seems to demand a minimum of four signs of the Passion: a crown of thorns, a scourge, a cross, and a spear which 'vnto [Christ's] side was sette' (ll. 253-64).

Elsewhere in painted glass and other art, angels appear separately, holding the spear which pierced his side, the scourge used for the Flagellation, the nails pounded into his hands and feet, the sponge which was put to his mouth, and so forth. All of these are brought together in the arms of Christ, the *Arma Christi,* as in painted glass formerly in St Saviour's, York and on a devotional woodcut now attached to a book of hours from York (York Minster Library MS. XVI.K.6, fol. 44ᵛ).

The emphasis on the Passion even in representations of the Doom is reminiscent of the handling of the Image of Pity, in which Christ appears above the tomb with the object of showing his wounds. The Image of Pity, which was thoroughly discussed by J. W. Robinson in an article in *PMLA* a decade ago,[61] combines the Resurrection theme—Christ rising above the tomb—with the soteriological work which he has accomplished on the cross. The focus of the practice of piety among clergy and citizens alike at York was clearly often these five wounds, each of which might provide a meditative 'place' successively. The number five itself becomes of supreme significance, and Sir Martin Bowes, for example, founded an *Obit* which covered the cost of distributing five penny loaves of bread 'every sonday in the yeare for evermore within the . . . churche' of St Cuthbert, Peasholm Green, 'to v severall poore householders be it men or women of the said paryshe . . . in the honour of the v woundes of our Lord Jesus Chryst. . . .'[62] The wounds of Christ are hence connected not only with the Mass and its commemoration of the Crucifixion, but also with the works of mercy. Good deeds, then, will help to weight the balance against the seven deadly sins at the Last Day, when the Archangel Michael performs the active task of separating the good and bad souls.

GOOD WORKS

In an interesting variant of the Christ showing his wounds and surrounded by the instruments of the Passion, the Christ of the Trades, found only in the West and South of England, connects the work of good deeds with the work actually performed daily by the crafts.[63] An example of a wall painting painted c.1490 at Breage, Cornwall, shows Christ crowned, with the wounds of the scourging. He wears only the loin-cloth that we associate with the Crucifixion so that his bruised body may be shown off to the greatest extent, and he reaches up with his right hand to point out the wound in his side. His other hand is open to show the wound in his left palm. Around him is an aureole-shaped display of the tools of many trades, including a rake, shears, a saw, a trowel, etc. He stands upon a wheel.[64] These instruments of the trades substitute both for the symbols of the Passion and for the aureole which might be expected to surround the body of Christ. Such 'paintings of Christ in the apotheosis of manual work,' writes O. Elfrida Saunders, 'seem to reflect the new social ideas of the time.'[65] But the paintings go much further, for they identify work as the appropriate offering of workmen to a Saviour whose wounds provide a means of salvation and a devotional center for their lives. It is no accident that the York plays seem also to glorify work, with the good workmen pictured as pious craftsmen who understand fully the Christian story; bad workmen, on the other hand, are like the men who nail Christ to the cross: 'What þai wirke wotte þai noght,' Jesus says (*Crucifixio Cristi,* l. 261).[66]

Also important in this regard was the identification of the craftsmen of York with the Infancy story, which was, along with the Passion, the part of the life of Christ most commonly illustrated in the visual arts. Joseph was, after all, a carpenter, whose status in life might cause Satan to

sneer in the *Harrowing of Hell* (Play XXXVII)—'Thy fadir
. . . was a write his mette to wynne' (ll. 229-30)—but whose
occupation was one whose practitioners were responsible
for staging the very next play in the cycle, the *Resurrection*
(Play XXXVIII). The first announcement of the birth of the
Saviour had also been to the humblest of men, shepherds
watching their sheep on the hillside. In the York *Angels
and Shepherds,* the shepherds, who were traditionally
musicians who played instruments and sang as they tended
their flocks, begin immediately after seeing the angel to attempt to imitate the angelic song (ll. 60-64; *s.d.* at l. 64).
Then they offer gifts, which are no less in value because
they are humble than the gifts that will be presented to the
Child by the Magi. The offerings of the crafts themselves
must not be less worthy than the gifts of the greatest men in
the realm. What emerges here is a civic piety that is
democratic even within the dominance of the more important citizens, normally the Mercers who controlled the
city council.

ICONOGRAPHY

The society of such a city as York in the late Middle
Ages must also have been conservative, resisting change often at the price of declining as a commercial force in the
nation. In Queen Elizabeth's reign the citizens tended to
cling to the old spirituality, which included the presentation of the cycle plays during the summer. Archbishop
Edmond Grindal, who played a role in the suppression of
the plays, complained shortly after his arrival in the North
in 1570:

For the little experience I have of this people, methinks I see in them
three evil qualities; which are, great ignorance, much dulness to conceive
better instruction, and great stiffness to retain their wonted errors. I will
labour as much as I can to cure every of these, committing the success to
God.[67]

Ideas which seemed alien and aliens themselves were never
very welcome in York, and among aliens were numbered

men from other parts of England. In 1579, the Minstrel's Guild, which in the twilight of the civic plays had been assigned 'the pageant of herod' formerly 'broughte forth by the late masons of the said citie,' drew up ordinances that absolutely forbid any 'manner of forryner' from 'singing or plainge upon annie instrument within annie parishe within this citie. . . .'[68] But the conservatism of York did not mean that her citizens did not change their taste in art or in civic spirituality. In the *Ordo* prepared by the town clerk, Roger Burton, in 1415, the Nativity play included midwives—a fact which points to the older way of presenting the events of Christ's birth, i.e., in the manner shown in the liturgical dramas such as the *Officium Pastorum* from Rouen.[69] Excellent fourteenth-century glass in York Minster shows the scene after the birth of the Child, with Joseph on the right and the Virgin reclining in bed, with the Infant in a manger overhead. But the text of the Nativity play in the Register demands something quite different, with the need for the midwives totally eliminated and with the scene entirely changed.

The York play exemplifies a radically altered treatment of the iconography of the Nativity. The source of this new way of visualizing the Nativity is a book, the influential *Revelations* of Saint Bridget of Sweden who, during a visit to Jerusalem near the end of the third quarter of the fourteenth century, had a vision in which she saw Christ's birth. Her description of the event is as follows:

And when all was prepared, the Virgin knelt down with great veneration in an attitude of prayer. . . . Thus, with her hands extended and her eyes fixed on the sky, she was rapt as in ecstasy, lost in contemplation, in a rapture of divine sweetness. And while she was thus engaged in prayer, I saw the child in her womb move, and suddenly in a moment she gave birth to her son, from whom radiated such an ineffable light and splendor that the sun was not comparable to it. . . . [A]ll of a sudden I saw the glorious infant lying on the ground naked and shining. . . . Then I heard also the singing of the angels, which was of miraculous sweetness and great beauty.[70]

In the Fairford and Great Malvern glass, the Child, who is shivering with cold, extends 'His hands in expectation of

III. Arma Christi. Glass formerly in St. Saviour's, York, and now in
the West Window, All Saints Pavement, York.

being clasped to His mother's breast,'[71] and in the York play the Virgin takes up the Child and prepares to dress him in whatever clothing happens to be available. Thereupon the York play reintroduces Joseph, who, as in a portion of the Fairford window, returns on this cold evening with a candle and is struck by the greater light radiating from the Child. In this new way of setting forth the Nativity, the scene has been specifically devoid of 'cloth' and 'bedde' in the York play, a detail which underlines the poverty of the place of Christ's birth—a theme which had been much emphasized in such Franciscan works as the *Meditations on the Life of Christ.* Joseph must be gone on an errand when Mary kneels to pray for grace, experiences 'grete ioie' in her soul, and recognizes that she has painlessly given birth to a Son who is at once God and man. It is characteristic of this new representation of the Nativity that the Child should miraculously appear on the ground before the Virgin; in drama at York he must have been represented by a doll placed in the center of a radiant mandorla.

The York *Birth of Jesus* simply carries one step further the devotional attitude which was normally directed at sacred images, both those imagined and those present in art or drama. Mary must react to her divine child in a way consistent with Northern spirituality, in which men and women were expected to respond emotionally to the event depicted. The scene takes on a life of its own as the action is generated by the image of the Infant Christ on the ground. The play is dependent upon not only the iconography found first in the visual arts, but also upon the emotional aesthetic of religious art which arose in the Low Countries and spread to York and other parts of England. The stage is simply not innovative with regard to iconographic details. Hence we may not believe the theory set forth by Emile Mâle, Otto Pächt, M. D. Anderson, W. L. Hildburgh, and so many others[72] that the stage influenced the painting of scenes, the carving of alabasters, even the production of illuminations in manuscripts. Instead, the presentations on pageant wagons and on fixed stages in York and elsewhere in England in the fifteenth and sixteenth centuries were, rather, dependent upon the forms present in the visual arts. In the instance of the new form of the Nativity, the influence of Saint Bridget must first have found its way to the artists working with the visual arts, and then to the plays.

Lawrence J. Ross has suggested that 'Instead of looking for records of the stage in art,' the attention of those primarily concerned with drama should instead be 'directed to what we might find in art which might help us better to comprehend the drama.'[73] The range of what can be learned from the visual arts is very large indeed, and a great portion of this information involves matters which hardly concern the art historian at all. As I hope I have been able to demonstrate, the 'reciprocal illumination' (and here I am using Pickering's terminology) through which drama and art can elucidate each other can also throw new light on the spirituality of a late medieval city such as York.

Actually such areas of scholarly concern as *drama, art,* and *spirituality* cannot be properly understood if they are artificially cut off from each other. No expert in chess can understand a chess game well under way if he knows only the moves that have been made by a single piece on the chess-board.[74] In other words, diachronic studies which single out one area can never provide the kind of enlightenment that places events both aesthetic and historic in perspective. The spirituality of the citizens of York is capable of being understood, but only if we are able to engage in the kind of synchronic and cross-disciplinary study that I have been advocating.

The purpose of my paper has been broader than to look merely for 'evidences of spirituality' in the drama and art of the late Middle Ages. Instead I have tried to piece together as much as possible within the space available the very structure of that spirituality. I trust that I have demonstrated that the images of art and drama were essential to this spirituality.

Clifford Davidson

Western Michigan University

MARTIN LUTHER: LANGUAGE
AND DEVOTIONAL CONSCIOUNESS

Martin Luther (1483-1546), a Saxon miner's son, began his studies in the law faculty of the University of Erfurt. Impelled by a conversion experience to enter an Augustinian monastery, he continued his work in Scripture. Ordained in 1507, he began lecturing the next year at the newly founded University of Wittenburg. A trip to Rome a few years later seems to have disillusioned the devout German monk. The worldliness of prelates and ecclesiastical politics, coupled with a profound anxiety over human sin and the spectre of damnation, led him to seek some assurance of salvation. In studying the Epistle to the Romans, he found St Paul's assurance that 'the just are saved by faith.' In 1517 he posted the Ninety-Five Theses, an attack on pious beliefs and practices frenetically pursued by his contemporaries as a means of guaranteeing their salvation. The Theses sparked a 'nation-wide' reaction and precipitated the Protestant Reformation.

A gifted writer, Luther took full advantage of the recently-invented printing press in disseminating his reform ideas. In addition to writing theological and palemical works, he translated the Bible into German and composed numerous hymns for congregational worship.

Luther recorded in his familiar autobiographical fragment of 1545, that the origin of his reform thought was intimately related to his experience as an Augustinian monk and to the encounter with the language and traditions of monastic life.[1] It is surprising therefore how little scholarly attention has been devoted to the immediate life-situation of the young Luther—the day-to-day routine of a late medieval cloister. Only recently, Heiko A. Oberman could remark, on the occasion of the Fourth International Luther Congress, that the spiritual life which Luther met in the Augustinian cloister at Erfurt remains poorly understood and difficult to reconstruct.[2] That being so, the significance of Luther's early thought has yet to be

152

established within that context which Luther himself identified as the most relevant: late medieval monasticism.

The difficulties of attempting this are several. Most importantly, the sources essential to a reconstruction of the Augustinian heritage in the Late Middle Ages have not been available, and only recently has work on the relevant texts begun.[3] The paucity of sources aside, the interpretation of late medieval monasticism has frequently reflected the confessional biases of historians. Protestant historians have been concerned to contrast a 'decadent' monasticism and the reform movement, while Catholic historians have been equally concerned to portray late medieval monasticism in positive terms and so to absolve it from responsibility for the reform movement.[4] The study of monastic life has suffered as well from an academic tendency to superimpose upon the language of devotion categories drawn either from scholasticism or from Reformation theology, rendering that language an extension—and very often a corruption—of scholasticism or the antithesis of Protestant theology.[5] The relevance of the monastic tradition to Luther's reform thought can only be assessed if that tradition is reconstructed in its historical integrity, and if its idiom is understood not under the categories of the schoolmen, but in terms of its own pattern and usage.

This point touches on a larger problem, one which has plagued Reformation analysis much beyond the study of Luther. The problem is methodological: how may religious language and religious consciousness be understood historically without being either isolated from the complex fabric of late medieval society, as though religious ideas and language constitute some self-enclosed realm, or reduced to an extra-linguistic, material force.[6] The tendency to ignore the monastic context of Luther's development is related to this methodological difficulty, because monastic religious consciousness seems to defy the normally theological categories by which the Reformation is understood. It therefore poses the problem of interpretation most sharply. It has proven relatively easy to set up contrasts between Luther and individuals and schools of thought in the Middle Ages by adopting the definitions of the reformers and schoolmen as themselves adequate for historical analysis. It is another matter, however, to write about the monastic heritage without either imposing alien definitions or disrupting its internal coherence. Until that is done, both for monasticism and popular religiosity, the problem of Luther and the origins of the reform movement will remain incompletely understood.

A solution to these problems must begin with a reconstruction of the historical context in which Luther encountered the devotional idiom and with a careful analysis of the interplay between monastic devotion and the communities for which this idiom was the dominant mode of expression. The historical study of ideas, then, begins with the study of language—language understood as a dynamic element in such specific social structures and functions as the form and exercise of authority, the need for social cohesion and continuity over time, and the socialization of individual members. Only against this kind of recovery, by which the specifically historical character of a particular idiom is identified, can the significance of intellectual innovation be assessed.[7] The thought of individuals—like Luther—may then be set within the patterns of language usage so defined, and the meaning of their thought interpreted in relation to traditional patterns and usages.

The intent of this paper is to explore the application of this kind of analysis to the monastic context of Luther's early thought. Such an orientation begins with the notion that the monastic tradition is a 'context' of some complexity: going beyond the recent attempts to outline an Augustinian monastic theology, we focus rather upon traditional patterns of monastic devotional idiom in the late Middle Ages, and on the usage of these patterns in specific settings and structures. More precisely, our task is to identify and characterize the linguistic tradition Luther encountered daily in the Augustinian cloister at Erfurt and Wittenberg, to understand this language as the idiom of a specific setting, rooted in the conditions and structures of the cloister, and finally, to attempt to relate Luther's early thought to the use of language in this setting.

The first step in the attempt to reconstruct Luther's encounter with religious language is a recognition of the existence of a distinctive and identifiable monastic style among late medieval religious idioms. Recent studies in medieval religious history have established this, studies covering the range of exegetical, speculative and devotional literature, and challenging the notion that scholasticism—in whatever version—governed the cultural life of medieval monasticism.[8] These studies clarify outlines of a theological tradition which was, if not unique, at least common among writers and teachers of the Augustinian Order—a tradition which Adolar Zumkeller has characterized as a kind of 'affective meditation,' and which was known to Luther through such authors as Simon Fidati of Cascia, Jacob Perez, John Paltz, and John Staupitz.[9]

A second point is that this monastic style is highly traditional; it has a structure and a set of meanings which persisted over a long period of time, and it maintained its essential features of usage and custom. It appears, therefore, in the late Middle Ages as a long-standing cultural structure whose internal parts and relationships have been remarkably stable and consistent, and whose uniformity, in devotional emphasis and literature, transcends the institutional divisions of the major orders.[10] Jean Leclercq has demonstrated that large elements of the monastic vocabulary and experience had been set down as early as Gregory the Great and given distinctive medieval shape by scholars of the Carolingian revival. [11] The monastic style flowered in the work of the spiritual writers of the twelfth century, and in a recent study Giles Constable has demonstrated the widespread appeal of these twelfth-century authors to the fourteenth and fifteenth centuries on the evidence of the numbers of manuscript versions of earlier works.[12] The Augustinians were no exception; the masters of the spiritual life are the writers of the early Middle Ages, and the late Middle Ages saw a movement among the Augustinians to reject scholastic speculation in favor of a more precisely historical cultivation of the sources of the Order.[13]

As to the forms of the monastic tradition, Jean Leclercq has described the wide range of literature produced by the monks. Our interest in the active day-to-day traditions, however, draws attention to the primary routine of the medieval cloister—the *opus dei* and *lectio divina*—and to the literature suited to liturgical services and prayers and serving as an extension of the sacred readings and meditations.[14] The devotional literature which sprang from liturgical usage shares what Huizinga has called the tendency of medieval thought to crystallize into visual images in which spiritual attitudes and practical concerns are represented by the exemplary behavior and gestures of heroic figures. The gospel narratives themselves provided the framework for much of this devotional tradition; what emerged within the cloister, for use in chapters and readings, were meditative narratives centering upon the lives of Jesus and his followers. Versions of these devotional lives of Christ may be found as early as the ninth century, but the best known and most popular are the large 'Lives of Christ' of the thirteenth and fourteenth centuries put together by such authors as Ludoph of Saxony, Jordanus of Quedlingberg, and Simon Fidati of Cascia, whose *De gestis Domini Salvatoris* was to be found in the library of the Augustinian cloister at Wittenberg.[15]

The popularity and influence of this devotional literature has long been recognized in all areas of medieval culture; less obvious is its historical significance within the monastic context from which it arose. In this regard, it is useful to identify this literature as a form of heroic epic and seek to understand monastic meditation and devotional experience in relation to the form of epic literature.[16] The lives of Christ are heroic in that they center upon the exemplary deeds and actions of primary figures, and epic in that they are structurally organized into separate and distinct scenes, which became standardized and arranged into fixed patterns. The language of the narrative is direct and simple, designed more to involve the hearer in the dramatization of the action than to explain its meaning. Towards the end of the Middle Ages meditations became more systematic and regularized, and increasingly fixed upon the scene of the Passion: countless sermons, treatises and artistic representations were based upon the monastic depiction of this scene and upon the terms in which it was to be experienced.[17]

Devotional writings of Luther's Augustinian contemporaries drew directly upon this meditative tradition. John Paltz, for example, who was responsible for the *studium generale* in the Erfurt cloister up to 1505, refers to Simon Fidati as the most profound of the medieval spiritual teachers, and he bases large parts of his sermonic and devotional writings upon *De gestis Domini Salvatoris*.[18] His best-known work, *Die himmlische Fundgrube,* is primarily an exercise in meditation upon the imagery of the suffering Christ designed to fix the imagery in the consciousness of the hearer.[19] Paltz opens his meditation with the familiar counsel of Bernard: 'Nothing is more useful or more powerful for healing the wounds of sin than meditation on the wounds of Christ.' This meditative tradition received fuller articulation in the works of John Staupitz; from there it had a direct impact on Luther. The late medieval focus upon the figure of *Passio Christi* as the paradigm of christian experience is documented in Staupitz's treatise from 1515, *Ein Buchlein von der nachfolgung des willingen sterbens Christi,* where the whole of religious experience is cast as an effective imitation of the suffering Christ.[20]

Telling the christological tale has a didactic and devotional purpose; it is a heroic paradigm, offering dramatic representations of exemplary behavior and attitudes. It entails the staging of typical figures, teaching appropriate modes of behavior and attitude by word and example. Staupitz puts it as follows:

On the hill of Calvary he has shown us a model (*vorbilde*) of all sanctity .
. . . He is a model given by God, according to which I would work, suffer,
and die. He is the only model which man can follow, in which every good
in life, suffering and death is usefully modeled. Therefore, no one can do
right, suffer correctly, or die rightly, unless it happens in conformity
(*gleichformig*) with the life, suffering and death of Christ.[21]

Cultivators of this tradition, to a man, warn against using it
as the basis of theological speculation; the tradition itself is
damaged by the attempt to abstract a meaning. This
feature of monastic traditions has been obscured by a tendency in modern scholarship to force an artificial
separation between the contemplative and active elements
of monastic culture; the core of the monastic tradition,
even in its contemplative aspects, remains a behavioral, affective tradition.[22]

An essential part of this literature is a clearly prescribed
set of responses in its hearers and readers. The basic rubric
here is *imitatio,* an imitative—or better,
mimetic —response, further specified in two ways: *imitatio
effectus operis*—an external imitation of the deeds and
gestures of the narrative, and *imitatio affectus mentis*—the
internalization of appropriate attitudes, emotions and self-
awareness.[23] The two modes of imitation are inter-related;
external gestures both represent and shape internal attitudes. The appropriate responses are clearly and extensively spelled out: obedience, self-denial, humility, con-
trition, and self-contempt. What is significant is that this
catalogue of virtues, as it appears in devotional literature,
is not an isolated ethical code but an integral part of the
public performance, the *lectio,* of the christological epic,
and it receives elaboration as the appropriate response of
its hearers to its telling.

At its center, therefore, the monastic devotional
tradition prescribes an identity or fusion of the knower and
the known. The content cannot—and must not—be
separated from the mechanics of its reception in the
behavior and self-consciousness of the hearer. This fusion
cuts across the wide range of monastic literature and is an
essential mark of the monastic style, evident in theological
meditation, styles of mysticism, and an exegetical emphasis

upon the tropological or moral sense of the Biblical text—always for monastic commentators the dominant level of meaning.[24] The sense of monastic language is in the telling—in the dynamics of active performance and mimetic response—prior to the thematic content. Much of this tradition of language, therefore, relates to its traditionality, to a concern for the mechanisms by which it was used and maintained within monastic groups over a long period of time.[25]

DEVOTION AND THE ORDERING OF MONASTIC COMMUNITIES

If this is a fair description of the core of a tradition alive in monastic communities in the late Middle Ages and available to Luther in the devotional writings of such Augustinians as John Paltz and John Staupitz, it remains to locate this language more precisely in its historical setting and to seek to identify the conditions of medieval monastic life which govern and explain the pattern and usage of devotional language.

The first point here is that medieval monastic communities were, in a unique sense, language-based communities, heavily dependent upon the authority and reception of language for internal cohesion and survival in time. The encounter with monasticism was the encounter with its language. The structure of the community was identified by a reading of the rule and continually reinforced by daily readings at meals and chapters.[26] The main task of the monk, the task which shaped his identity and his culture, was the *opus dei,* the performance and cultivation of sacred language in the daily offices.[27] The detailed concern in the monastic rules for the discipline of silence suggests in turn the awareness that cohesion and stability in the community depended upon the control of language.[28]

The primary contact between monks and their tradition was, moreover, an aural contact; the monastic tradition, in both its constitutional and liturgical forms, was socially available in oral performances. Most monastic devotional literature was composed not for a private reading, but for an audience.[29] The *vita Christi* tradition bears clear marks

of this language transmission: there are repeated references
to hearers and listeners: the scenes are described in vivid
language, as if to recreate the stage for the audience; and
the narrative employs the repetition of key words and
phrases designed precisely to fix the figures of the narrative
in the minds of the audience. This concern dominates, for
example, the devotional treatise of John Paltz, who took
care to present the imagery of the Passion in such a way as
to captivate the memory of the hearer.[30] And, as Jean
Leclercq has pointed out, devotional reading, whether
private or public, entailed an aural experience; the *lectio
divina* was an 'acoustical reading,' an activity which fully
engaged emotional and intellectual sensibilities.[31]

This essentially oral condition of language-preservation
and transmission means that the fundamental elements of
the society—its rules, structure, and practical
knowledge—must be so cast as to be effectively communicated in a public setting and easily remembered and
responded to by its hearers. The form of a linguistic
tradition, in this situation, is intimately related to the maintenance of social cohesion. From this, it is readily apparent
why the *vita Christi* epic, with its dramatic and exemplary
figures and its demand for mimetic response, arises as the
dominant linguistic pattern in monastic culture. The epic
idiom embodies the social ethos—the elements of cultural
coherence—and its recitation is an exercise in social identity essential for the survival of the community.

A similar correspondence between devotional language
and its social setting may be observed in the authority
structures outlined in monastic rules. Both the Benedictine
and Augustinian rules articulate clearly drawn lines of
authority and give clear directions to the modes of the exercise of authority. The rules themselves reveal that the order
is carried less by the letter of the rules than by the personal
authority of the abbot or prior.[32] The constitutional
authority of the abbot is most pronounced, of course, in the
rule of Benedict, where the cloister is pictured as a school of
servants (*scola servitii*) under the direction and discipline of
a master. In his constitutional function, the abbot merges
with the divine figure of Christ: 'Because the abbot is

esteemed to be in the place of Christ, he shall be called Lord and Abbot.'[33] The Augustinian rule shows a similar regard for the personal authority of the prior: 'You should faithfully obey your father, honoring him next to God, and give esteem to the prior as befits a saint.'[34] The mode of authority exercised by the abbot is two-fold—word and example:

When anyone takes upon him the office of abbot, he is to instruct his disciples in two ways. That is: he is to lay before them what is good and holy, more by example than by words, to teach the law of the Lord by word of mouth to such as are of quicker comprehension, and by example to those of harder hearts and meaner capacities.[35]

Above all else, the prior should be an example of good works for everyone.[36]

Language and example are the media for exercising power and maintaining social order. There is a correlation, then, between the mode by which social order is maintained and the modes of the devotional idiom: both entail the dramatic and exemplary behavior of primary figures, carried by the medium of word and example and dependent, for their effect, upon the receptivity of the hearer to paradigmatic gestures.

There were, moreover, within monastic constitutional history developments which worked to intensify the interdependence of social order and devotional exercises. With the reform movements of the tenth and eleventh centuries, and continuing into the observant constitutions of the twelfth century, the shape of the social order came to be embodied less in the personal rule of an abbot than in liturgical uses and customs. David Knowles describes the changes as follows:

When the community became very large and wealthy, and the abbot a territorial magnate on the fringe of political life, the constant daily interpenetration of abbatial government, regular observance, and personal spiritual direction ceased. The void was filled, if at all, by liturgical elaboration and by detailed uses and customs. The direct and personal guidance and governance of the abbot was replaced by the impersonal impact of an exacting round of observance, the *districtio ordinis.*[37]

Such developments had the effect of reinforcing the dependence of political and constitutional order upon liturgical and devotional routines; the core of common observance and discipline was devout attention to the christological paradigm.

The rules are clear, finally, about what may be called a code of behavior. The code breaks into two parts: external actions and gestures—obedience, silence, service; and inner attitudes—humility, self-denial, hatred of self and love of others. Moreover, this two-part code is based upon the capacity of persons to respond to the language and example of public models of authority, to imitate them in attitude and deed.[38] This interplay between christological imagery and monastic order is evident in an early sermon by John Staupitz:

In the first place, we should follow the life of Christ, which is our instruction; if we have the example of the apostles and other saints, this [the life of Christ] ought to be examined most carefully . . . . Christ, the living son of God, is foremost among the brothers and therefore he is the rule and norm of the brothers.[39]

The condition for social cohesion and order is a kind of linguistic sensibility—the person's capacity to identify with and imitate words and gestures—precisely the same linguistic sensibility which governs the performance and reception of monastic devotional literature.

What emerges from these considerations is the striking identity of devotional literature and the constituted order and social structure of monastic groups. Devotional and constitutional literature share a common vocabulary, because the use of religious language is embedded in the structure of monastic communities and in the conditions for social cohesion. These conditions dictate that the cultural traditions be cast in the forms of heroic narratives and received by way of mimetic identification and imitation. At stake in the telling of tales and in the maintenance of the mimetic spell of their reception, is the very cohesion of the community.

Luther And Monastic Devotion

We turn to the relevance of these observations for understanding Luther's early development. Luther's encounter with the traditions of the late Middle Ages was a complex process, and our focus upon the devotional idiom cannot reduce this complexity to a simple explanation for the shape of his reform thought. What it may achieve, however, is some clarity about the way in which elements of Luther's early thought are related to his encounter with the devotional idiom in its actual usage in the cloister. We may then recover some sense of the historical dynamic by which Reformation ideas crystallized.

The pattern which seems to emerge from this analysis is two-fold: it corresponds closely to Luther's external relations with his monastic affiliation; and it highlights the significance of the transformations which historians have identified as taking place in his thought after 1518.[40] The indications are that, at least until his appearance before the Augustinians in Heidelberg in 1518, Luther fully embraced the monastic life, and played an active role in his order as teacher, preacher, and administrator.[41] The monastic devotional style is fully present in Luther's work of this period, and informs his early sermons as well as his academic lectures. The real crisis in Luther's relation with his order came in 1518; only then did Gerhard Hecker, the Augustinian provincial in Saxony, brand Luther 'a man in rebellion against his religion' (*hominem suae religionis rebellem*).[42] Setting Luther's thought from this phase (1518-1521) in the context of monastic devotional usage seems only to underscore Hecker's judgment and suggests that the emerging Reformation ideas involved an assault upon the monastic usage and reception of language, and hence upon the mechanics of monastic cultural survival.

First, the themes of Luther's earliest sermons and lectures correspond to patterns of monastic spirituality. The recurrent theme in these works is the Divine Word (*verbum dei*), its meaning, its authority, and its impact upon religious consciousness. As was true in the monastic tradition, the Word in these works is the medium of the sacred; just as the structures of history are called into being by the sacred word, so human experience and con- sciousness are ordered in the encounter with sacred language.[43] Furthermore, that encounter was primarily for young Luther an internal process. In a sermon from 1514, Luther explains:

> The word is two-fold. The primary word is internal, which is the only genuine word ... if it is spoken in your heart, then it is the word, and the perfect word, because you know by experience. The spoken external word is incomparably inferior and weak.[44]

The Christological form of the word is an emphasis in Luther which has long been recognized, but has less often been identified as entirely consistent with the monastic devotional and exegetical tradition. Gerhard Ebeling has demonstrated the degree to which Luther, in his psalms commentary (1513-1515) make Christ the speaker of the psalms, thereby integrating the core of the liturgical offices into the structure of the christological epic.[45] This christological emphasis corresponds exactly with the monastic devotional practice of fixing the image of *passio Christi* in the memory and consciousness of the hearer in the context of public liturgical exercises. Luther repeatedly refers to the figure of the suffering Christ as the 'brief word' (*verbum brevum*), or the summation of the sacred word (*verbum abbreviatum et consummatum*), themes and phrases which abound in the *vita Christi* literature and which document the tendency of the monastic tradition to crystallize into christological imagery.

The young Luther, in his sermons and lectures, required his hearers to relate to the sacred images in didac- tic and devotional ways. The images are models to be imitated in external actions and inner attitudes and self- awareness. In his lectures on Romans (1515-1516), he writes:

> Whatever is written about Christ is written for our learning, that we might imitate him. Hence we should not accept what is said about Christ in a speculative way, but as an example for us ... all of Christ'. !eeds

are our instruction . . . therefore the narrative or history of these deeds is always intended for our learning, because this image contains everything.[46]

The Christian life is an imitation, one which conforms to the christological model both in external behavior and in interior attitudes and self-consciousness. The core of the imitation is self-awareness, cultivated by identification with the suffering Christ, and issuing in attitudes and behavior essential for the maintenance of social order:

What Christ displays to us in his passion is that he gives us self-understanding and displays what we are internally before God . . . . When such knowledge of self is established in us, and a sense of weakness prevails, then it is easy for us to be gentle, patient, lowly, compassionate, hating the world, imitating the example of the suffering Christ.[47]

Finally, Luther is clear that necessary religious sensibilities depend upon a capacity for psychic participation in the tale of *gesta Christi,* in the capacity to pattern one's own existence by re-enacting the christological epic.[48] And precisely these concerns about the mechanics of interior identification with *passio Christi* provide the basis for Luther's attack upon the sale of indulgences. Luther opens the Ninety-Five Theses with a definition of the christian life as an interior and exterior imitation of the suffering Christ, and he directs his critique against the harmful impact of indulgences on the intensity and permanence of the identification process.[49]

In the period 1518-1521, new themes were increasingly evident in Luther's thought and were highlighted by the clarification of the Word-Faith dialectic in the treatises of 1520. The significance of these reformulations is a subject of considerable controversy among Luther's scholars. When examined in the context of monastic usage, they appear to have been designed precisely to disrupt that usage and intended as an assault upon the delicate structure and cultural mechanisms of the monastic tradition. At points Luther used the very content of devotional language against its traditional usage. Three themes from this period of reformulation work together to undermine the linguistic sensibilities fundamental to monastic culture.

First, the Word becomes for Luther primarily an external word, its sense clear and precise, a word which 'means' independently from the processes of its reception and internalization. This turn is evident in his sharpening focus upon the Word as Promise, and by Luther's rejection, after 1518, of the four-fold levels of biblical commentary with its concern for allegorical and tropological meanings, in favor of the text in its literal and historical meaning.[50] The significant encounter becomes now the encounter with the content of a text, identified by its literal or grammatical sense, and with its meaning as promise, a meaning with clear and unambiguous historical and contextual references. The monastic art of *meditatio* has become the critic's *explicatio,* and the word of interior experience has been replaced by the word of external promise.[51]

The tale of the suffering Christ has correspondingly lost its primarily didactic and devotional point and has acquired a theological meaning, one which can be abstracted from the narrative and its imagery. The christological drama has been relocated in history and its meaning defined not in terms of the modes of its reception, but in terms of a statement, a testimony, about divine intentionality. In his treatise on Christian liberty from 1520, Luther rejects the paradigmatic use of the devotional epic and its impact upon emotional sensibilities; he calls rather for a response of faith, a perception into the meaning of the narrative abstracted from its form:

. . . It is not enough or in any sense Christian to preach the works, life, and words of Christ as historical facts, as if the knowledge of these would suffice for the conduct of life; yet this is the fashion among those who must today be regarded as our best preachers . . . . Now there are not a few who preach Christ and read about him that they may move men's affections to sympathy with Christ, to anger against the Jews, and such effeminate nonsense. Rather ought Christ to be preached to the end that faith in him may be established . . . . Such faith is produced and preserved in us by preaching why Christ came, what he brought and bestowed, what benefit it is to us to accept him.[52]

To reject both the epic form and affective response of *gesta Christi,* as Luther here prescribes, is to undermine the very purpose of its telling in monastic usage and to render it powerless as an instrument of social cohesion.

Thirdly, there emerges a concept of 'faith' defined not as the process of internalization and receptivity to language, but as the perception of meanings and the capacity to disengage experience from perception. The meaning of Christological imagery is distinguished from the traditional pattern of affective responses, from the processes of internalization. In his record of the 1518 meeting with Cajetan, Luther employs a notion of 'faith' which excludes interior responses:

For faith born of this word will bring peace of conscience, for it is according to this word that the priest shall loose. Whoever seeks peace in another way, for example, inwardly through experience, certainly seems to tempt God and desires to have peace in fact, rather than in faith. For you will have peace only as long as you believe in the word of that one who promised, 'whatever you loose,' etc. Christ is our peace, but only through faith . . . . Whoever believes this confidently has truly obtained the peace and remission of God . . ., not by the certainty of the process but by the certainty of faith, according to the infallible word of the one who has mercifully promised.[53]

With the assertion of this notion of faith, the monastic fusion of knower and known, believer and believed—the foundation of the spirituality of *imitatio Christi*—has been broken and the workings of monastic culture short-circuited, transformed into an ideology. The central motif of the ideology is the dialectic of Word and faith, a dialectic which breaks any psychic identification with *passio Christi* and which works the alienation of language and its meaning from the experience of its reception and usage.

CONCLUSION

This paper has sought to establish two points: first, that an essential feature of the monastic tradition in the late Middle Ages was the interplay between devotional styles and social structure, between christological imagery and monastic discipline; second, that the historical significance of Luther's thought, particularly after 1518, is clarified by a recognition of this interplay. The problem of Luther's development is thereby cast as a problem in the play of language and consciousness, the key to which is an identification of the institutional context of language and language usage, and an understanding of how institutional processes—the maintenance of inner coherence and continuity over time, socialization and the internalization of codes of attitude and behavior—employ the medium of language and determine its style and meaning. The history of thought may then be viewed as conceptualizations about these processes, conceptualizations which are not without significance for the workings of the tradition upon which they are based.

Luther himself remarked, in his 1521 treatise on monastic vows, that he was held in the monastery for sixteen years by being '. . . led astray, seduced, by the various usages of words' *(seductus variis verborum consuetudinibus).*[54] In the context of monastic usages, Luther's thought from 1518 appears as an attempt to break these usages, working changes in the linguistic tradition whereby the dramatic figures and deeds of the Christological epics were frozen into theological meanings, and so divested of their prescriptive character. Taken more broadly, the choices Luther made in 1518, and the theological formulations emerging from these choices, mark a crisis in the historical workings of an institution and its linguistic tradition, a moment of disruption in the transmission of a cultural tradition. Such an analysis suggests that the Reformation crisis, as a historical phenomenon, involves a crisis in the mechanisms of cultural coherence and continuity, and that the significance of Reformation thought lies in its articulation of changed conceptualizations about these mechanisms and their linguistic modes.

Darrell R. Reinke

Rhode Island College

JOHN CALVIN:
INGRAFTING IN CHRIST

John Calvin (1509-1564) was born in Picardy. After reading theology at the University of Paris, he settled on a career in law and studied at Orleans and Bourges. As a result of contacts with early Protestants and a personal conversion experience, he became persuaded that he had the mission of restoring the church to its original purity. His first attempts led to persecution and, fleeing to Switzerland, he settled first in Basel and then in Geneva. His intentions of embracing a quiet studious life were interrupted by calls to teach Scripture and to preach the word of God. A statesman and moralist, he was instrumental in establishing theocratic rule in Geneva. His Institutes of the Christian Religion, *several times revised, established the doctrinal and ethical standards of non-Lutheran Protestantism.*

'It must never be forgotten . . . that the true man—the spiritual man—is not given, is not the result of a natural process. He is "made" in accordance with the models revealed by the Divine Beings and preserved in the myths.'[1]

Mircea Eliade

The general topic of these lectures, *The Spirituality of Western Christendom,* would seem to imply that there exists a genus 'spirituality' among the various species of which we may count Western Christendom, which species, in turn, includes families such as the Pauline, Johannine, Augustinian, Bernardine, and Franciscan as well as assorted mutations: Lutheran, Calvinist, and Anabaptist. It is all the more surprising, therefore, to discover that while the word spirituality is used freely and with the ease that comes from close familiarity, none of the preceding authors except one seems to have felt the necessity of defining it. I recall the remark of one of the lecturers that he was quite certain that he knew what spirituality is but was at a loss when asked to articulate and define the meaning, a remark which

I find revealing. That answer in itself discloses something of the essence of spirituality: it is a mode of being religious, a mode of participation, of engagement, which makes definition of the act as well as of the object of participation irrelevant, unnecessary, if not impossible.

But then, what we are engaged in here is not spirituality, but the study of spirituality; and we cannot very well study something without some general idea of what it is we are studying. So I propose to preface my discussion of Christian Spirituality according to John Calvin with some brief observations regarding the idea of spirituality and *homo religiosus.*

What constitutes the religious man is, according to Mircea Eliade, an experience of or encounter with 'the Sacred.'[2] Man becomes aware of the Sacred because it manifests or shows itself as something wholly other than the Profane. Hence Eliade defines the Sacred as the opposite of the Profane. In his encounters with the Sacred, man experiences a reality that does not belong to our world and yet is encountered in and through objects or events that are part of the world. Thus the world becomes translucent, it opens up and ceases to be simply natural by revealing its 'true' dimension, its cosmic sacrality. The Sacred is perceived as equivalent to reality, as the 'really real,' as saturated with being and hence with meaning. Religious man, therefore, assumes a mode of existence in the world which in its totality is characterized by an orientation toward the Sacred.

What is significant is that 'despite the great number of religious forms this characteristic mode is always recognizable. Whatever the historical context in which he is placed, religious man always believes that there is an absolute reality, the Sacred, which transcends this world but manifests itself in this world, thereby sanctifying it and making it real. He further believes that life has a sacred origin and that human existence realizes all of its potentialities in proportion as it is religious—that is, participates in reality.'[3]

Spirituality, then, may be defined as that specific mode of existence characteristic of *homo religiosus* by which he participates in the Sacred and conforms himself to it. Such participation takes place through imitation or better, through the personal appropriation of exemplary, authoritative models which are disclosed in sacred narrative (myths) and enacted in sacred rites.

To the extent that *homo Christianus* is also *homo religiosus* the characteristic mode of existence described above as spirituality can be expected to be recognizable in Christianity. Christian spirituality is thus to be approached as a specific instance of spirituality, understood as the characteristic mode of being religious. Already in the eighth chapter of the apostle Paul's letter to the Romans there emerges what may be called the quintessence not only of Pauline spirituality but of the spirituality of Western Christendom.

For God has done what the law, weakened by the flesh, could not do: sending his own son in the likeness of sinful flesh and for sin, he condemned sin in the flesh, in order that the just requirement of the law might be fulfilled in us, who walk not according to the flesh but according to the Spirit. For those who live according to the flesh set their minds on the things of the flesh, but those who live according to the Spirit set their minds on the things of the Spirit. To set the mind on the flesh is death, but to set the mind on the Spirit is life and peace. . . . But you are not in the flesh, you are in the Spirit, if the Spirit of God really dwells in you. . . . If the Spirit of him who raised Jesus from the dead dwells in you, he who raised Christ Jesus from the dead will give life to your mortal bodies also through his Spirit which dwells in you. . . . When we cry, 'Abba! Father!' it is the Spirit himself bearing witness with our spirit that we are children of God, and if children, then heirs, heirs of God and fellow heirs with Christ, provided we suffer with him in order that we may also be glorified with him. . . . We know that in everything God works for good with those who love him, who are called according to his purpose. For those whom he foreknew he also predestined to be conformed to the image of his Son, in order that he might be the first-born among many brethren. And those whom he predestined he also called; and those whom he called he also justified; and those whom he justified he also glorified.[4]

The basic structure of Christian spirituality that emerges here is expressed in the formula: *kata pneuma—kata sarka;* life according to the spirit as opposed to life according to the flesh. The spiritual life is described, furthermore, as a life conformed to the image of Christ through participation in his death and resurrection, his suffering and glorification. In other words, life *kata pneuma* is *imitatio Christi,* life informed by and conformed to Christ the exemplar. Finally, being conformed to the image of Christ is seen as a process which, initiated by divine purpose and calling, begins with justification and ends in glorification.

There can be little doubt that, morphologically, Christian spirituality exhibits a structure which is characteristic of *homo Christianus* as *homo religiosus.* This basic structure remains recognizable in all the historical forms which it produced. The spiritualities of a St Francis, Augustine, Bernard, and Calvin, are different historical expressions and forms of a Christian spirituality which exemplifies a mode of existence recognized as a universal religious form.

CHRISTIAN SPIRITUALITY ACCORDING TO CALVIN

From the preceding brief analysis of spirituality as a religious form it appears that spirituality includes an epistemological as well as an ontological dimension; it involves a certain mode of knowing and a corresponding mode of being. It is under these two aspects that we now turn to the spirituality of Calvin.

The Knowledge of God and its Source

'True and substantial wisdom principally consists of two parts, the knowledge of God, and the knowledge of ourselves.'[5]

This famous opening statement of Calvin's *Institutes* indicates, at the very outset of his major systematic work, the fundamental importance of the category of knowledge in Calvin's spirituality. The immediate result of true knowledge of God and of ourselves is 'piety' (*pietas*), the dominant category in which Calvin's spirituality is given expression. In fact, the very purpose of the *Institutes* was, ac-

cording to the dedication to King Francis I of France, 'to
lay down some elementary principles, by which inquirers on
the subject of religion might be instructed in the nature of
true piety.'⁶ True piety is, according to Calvin, 'a reverence
and love of God arising from a knowledge of his benefits.'⁷
While Calvin agrees with Cicero that all men have some innate sense of deity, such knowledge does not result in piety.
Despite the fact that the marvellous powers of the human
mind, of memory, imagination and invention, seem to give
proof of man's divine origin, man's sin has left him incapable of rendering the proper response of obedience and
service to God. And since we are incapable of responding
properly to the manifestation of God in creation, he has
mercifully chosen to reveal himself in his Word as it is
found in Scripture. There is no source of true piety other
than the Word of God, and the content and nature of what
God reveals in his Word become the authoritative basis of
Christian spirituality according to Calvin. In order to understand the category of knowledge in Calvin's spirituality
it is therefore necessary to examine the problem of the
authority of Scripture in Calvin's teaching, as well as the
nature of the proper response to that authority.

Calvin's view of biblical authority is in essential
agreement with the traditional teaching of the church. That
God is the author of Scripture was never questioned by any
Christian writer. What is distinctive, however, is Calvin's
insistence upon the exclusive authority of the Bible as the
source and norm of all true knowledge of God. Even more
distinctive is the way in which Calvin relates the objective
authority of Scripture to the believer's subjective appropriation of that authority through faith, and it is within
this context that the basic structure of Calvin's spirituality
begins to emerge. That structure is, from the outset,
characterized by the dialectical tension between the self-
authenticity of the Scriptures and the authenticating witness of the Holy Spirit within the believer. There can be little doubt that Calvin not only believed in but actually
taught a literal inspiration of the Scripture. He calls the
biblical writers 'organs' of the Holy Spirit, and he refers to
the Law and the Prophets as doctrine dictated by the Holy

Spirit (*dictante Spiritu sancto*).[8] Calvin's statements with reference to the literal inspiration of the biblical writings are meant to express the objective validity of the Bible as the Word of God. This objective validity and authenticity of Scripture is the result of inspiration, of the activity of the Holy Spirit in the men to whom God had spoken and revealed himself. 'The Bible is not invested with validity by the believer or by the inner testimony of the Holy Spirit within the believer, but by special works of the Spirit in the chosen men to whom the divine oracles were originally given.'[9] Thus Calvin can insist that Scripture is self-authenticating, and 'of itself commands our reverence by its own majesty.'[10]

If it is true that the Bible has inherent validity, this does not yet constitute its authority for the believer, however. For Calvin the divine inspiration of Scripture is not a source of the believer's knowledge. The knowledge and certainty that God speaks in the Bible derives solely from the inner witness of God himself through the Spirit. It is by this witness alone that the intrinsic validity of Scripture is recognized and confirmed. God alone is the proper witness for his own Word, which will never find faith in human hearts unless it is sealed by the inner testimony of the Spirit. The same Spirit who spoke through the mouth of the Prophets must penetrate our hearts in order to convince us that they delivered faithfully what was divinely given.[11] In clear contrast to later orthodox thought, Calvin bases the certainty of the Bible's authority not upon a theory of verbal inspiration but upon the present witness of the same Spirit that inspired the Prophets—yet not in such a way as to circumvent, but rather as to confirm and to accredit, that inspiration. It remains true that the Bible has intrinsic validity, 'is self-authenticating and not subject to demonstrations and arguments.'[12] But only the inner testimony of the Spirit can enable us to perceive the Bible's authentication and thus create within our hearts the certainty that the Scripture comes from the very mouth of God.[13] Calvin himself sums up his view on the relationship between Word and Spirit:

The Word itself has not much certainty for us unless it is confirmed by the testimony of the Spirit. For the Lord has joined together by a kind of mutual connection the certainty of his Word and Spirit: so that a genuine reverence for the Word possesses our minds when the Spirit shines upon it, enabling us there to behold the face of God; and that, on the other hand, we embrace the Spirit without fear of illusion when we recognize him in his image, that is, in the Word.[14]

The term 'mutual connection' expresses the very heart of Calvin's doctrine. Word and Spirit form a correlation the two elements of which cannot be separated. Both are connected in an inviolable union (*inviolabili nexu*).[15] Calvin's entire doctrine of the authority of Scripture is based on that correlation. On the one hand, the divinely inspired Scripture is identified as such only by the inner witness of the Spirit within the believer. No theory of inspiration can therefore become an independent source for the authority of Scripture apart from the Spirit's witness. On the other hand, the Spirit today reveals nothing else than what he revealed once through the Prophets and Apostles. Therefore, 'we are not to expect the Holy Spirit from any other side than from the testimony of the Bible.'[16] We might say that the Spirit identifies himself through the Word of Scripture or—in the language of the Westminster Confession—speaks to us 'by and with the Word.'[17]

Faith and Illuminatio

Given the dialectic tension between the objective authority of the Bible and the believer's subjective acknowledgment of that authority through the inner witness of the Holy Spirit, it is not surprising that faith, for Calvin, is not mere intellectual assent to the divine truths proposed by Scripture. It is true that Calvin defines faith, first of all, as the 'knowledge of the divine will toward us received from his Word. And the foundation of it is a previous persuasion of the truth of God.'[18] Faith can never be separated from the Word: 'Take away the Word, and no faith will remain.'[19] 'Faith has a constant relation to the Word and can no more be separated from it than the rays from the sun.'[20] Calvin can define the veracity of God, that is, his truth and trustworthiness, as the general object of faith.[21] Complete trust in God's truth or veracity is the very foundation of faith.[22]

But this is merely a preliminary definition of faith's object. Scripture is not the exact object of faith. In a sense, only part of Scripture can be called the proper object of faith:

Since the heart of man is not aroused to faith by every utterance (*vocem*) of God, we must now inquire what it is in the word that faith properly respects . . . what faith finds in God's word upon which to lean and rest.[23]

Although Calvin does not deny that faith 'subscribes to the veracity of God whenever, wherever and in whatever manner he speaks,'[24] he declares the gratuitous promise, the promise of mercy (*gratuita promissio, misericordiae promissio*) the real foundation of faith. Faith properly begins with the promise of mercy, although it holds that God is true in whatever he says. Nothing can really establish faith except the Gospel, the 'Word of faith,' the 'free embassy, by which God reconciles the world to himself.'[25] The foundation and proper object of faith is the Gospel, not the precepts and promises of the law.[26] Faith and Gospel are correlatives.[27] To point to the Gospel as object of faith, however, is to point to Christ.

It is Christ alone on whom faith properly must look.[28]

Thus Christ proposes himself as the object to which our faith should be directed. . . .[29]

Everything which faith should contemplate is exhibited to us in Christ. . . .[30]

The Gospel is called the 'doctrine of faith' (*doctrina fidei*) by the apostle Paul because it manifests Christ more fully than did Moses and the prophets.[31] For if the same apostle calls the advent of faith the end of the law, he means to convey a new *genus* of teaching, by which the Father's mercy is exhibited far better, and our salvation is given a more certain witness where Christ is the teacher.[32]

Calvin calls this narrowing down of faith's object from Scripture as a whole to God's promise of mercy in the Gospel a descent from 'genus to species.'[33]

Calvin clearly distinguishes between the whole Scripture as a general object of faith, and the gratuitous promise of God in Christ as the proper object of faith. Although faith believes every word of Scripture, it cannot be identified with the acceptance of whatever God says, but has as its specific and proper object the promise of God's mercy in Jesus Christ.[34]

Faith, inasmuch as it is directly related to God's revelation in his Word, is a certain and explicit knowledge for Calvin. But faith is not sufficiently described in terms of its object, not even if that object is Christ and God's promise of grace. For Calvin the knowledge of faith is in no way a natural perception of God's revelation; it is rather the work of the Holy Spirit.

It is here, in his doctrine of faith, that Calvin introduces the term 'illumination' to describe the inner working of the Holy Spirit. Although faith, as knowledge of God's will toward us, is received from the Word,[35] 'the Word accomplishes nothing without the illumination by the Holy Spirit.'[36] This illumination is described in various ways by Calvin. It is the renewal of the mind[37] to hear and understand the preaching of Christ,[38] the 'interior'[39] and 'effectual'[40] call, by which the 'word preached,' the 'universal call' is caused 'to sink into the hearts.'[41] Illumination is the inward gift of the Spirit enabling the elect to accept and receive the external manifestation of revelation through Scripture and preaching. Through illumination the Spirit overcomes our sinfulness which makes our minds 'wholly blind and stupid' toward divine things.[42] All these statements refer to the noetic aspect of faith, to man's knowledge of God's revelation as brought about through the illumination of the mind by the Holy Spirit. But for Calvin faith is more than mere knowledge of God's promise in Christ, more than a simple assent to the objective truth and abstract certainty of revelation, as the Scholastics had falsely held.[43] Rather than in the certainty of knowledge, the real nature of faith's certainty for Calvin lay in man's

personal appropriation of God's promise,[44] that is, in the
personal assurance of salvation. Faith is the 'assistance
and trust *(fiducia)* of the heart' in God's mercy.[45]

This is the chief axis on which faith turns, that we should not think of
God's promises of mercy to be true apart from us and not in us, but
rather make them ours by embracing them inwardly. From this arises
that trust *(fiducia)* which the same [apostle] in another place calls
peace.[46]

That is the very heart of Calvin's doctrine of faith. Faith is a
firm and certain conviction of one's own personal salvation
in Christ.

In short, no one is truly a believer, unless he is firmly persuaded that
God is a propitious and benevolent Father to him and promises him all
things from his goodness; unless he depends on the promise of divine
benevolence toward himself and feels an undoubting expectation of
salvation.[47]

These two elements, knowledge and personal assurance
of God's gratuitous promise in Christ, describe the nature
of faith as Calvin sees it. Both are the work of the Holy
Spirit. Thus Calvin gives his formal definition of faith:

Now we shall have a right definition of faith, if we say that it is a firm
and certain knowledge *(cognitionem)* of the divine benevolence toward
us which, founded upon the truth of the gratuitous promise in Christ, is
both revealed to our minds and sealed in our hearts by the Holy Spirit.[48]

It is, indeed, the personal relationship between the
believer and Christ which for Calvin also guarantees the
continuity of faith within the believer. For, by faith, we are
indissolubly connected with the body of Christ,[49] who dwells
within us,[50] in whose body we have been ingrafted[51] through
the secret working of the Holy Spirit. 'Through the grace
and power of that same Spirit we are made his members, so
that he keeps us under him and we, in turn, possess him.'[52]

It is in terms of this intimate, living relationship between the believer and Christ, this 'sacred marriage,'[53] that

Calvin understands the object, nature, and perpetuity of faith.

Returning to the problem of knowledge, we recall that for Calvin the certainty of faith is truly knowledge—although the aspect of knowledge does not exhaust the meaning of faith. This knowledge (*notitia*), however, is not the natural intellect or reason, but rather a supernatural knowledge which depends entirely upon the work and revelation of the Spirit. It is the Holy Spirit who raises the human mind above itself and gives it a super-natural certainty rather than comprehension.[54] The mind attaining to this knowledge does not 'comprehend what it perceives, but being persuaded of that which it cannot com-prehend, it understands more by the certainty of this per-suasion, than it would comprehend of any human object by the exercise of its natural capacity.'[55] 'For . . . what our mind apprehends by faith is absolutely infinite' and therefore 'this kind of knowledge far exceeds all un-derstanding. Yet, because God has revealed to his saints the secret of his will . . . therefore faith is in Scripture justly called . . . knowledge.'[56] Faith is indeed a certain knowledge, but one that is not 'taught by any demon-stration of reason.'[57]

For Calvin, then, natural reason contributes nothing to what faith knows. The natural man cannot understand the things of God, and our understanding is wholly blind and stupid; we are despoiled of any faculty for spiritual un-derstanding.[58] Indeed, human reason is so despoiled, so confused and defective that the first step toward ad-vancement in the school of God is to abandon reason altogether.[59] Not only the finiteness but also the sinfulness of man's reason stands in the way of any knowledge of God.

There is no other way in which men can be prepared for receiving the doctrine of the Gospel . . . than by withdrawing all their senses from the world and turning to God alone, and seriously considering that it is with God that they have to do.[60]

Knowledge of God for Calvin begins with revelation. It is nothing but the knowledge of what God has revealed.

Although it is man's *mind* that knows, his mind is able to know only through the work of the Holy Spirit who raises the mind above its natural state to a supernatural knowledge and certainty.

THE SPIRITUAL LIFE

We recall that spirituality involves a certain mode of knowing as well as a corresponding mode of being and that, according to Calvin, the mode of knowing appropriate to Christian spirituality is faith. Faith is a spiritual mode of knowing precisely because, in all its aspects, it is not taught by any demonstration of reason but by the Holy Spirit. In a sense, God is both the object and the subject of faith's knowledge. This indissoluble, intimate union between object and subject, between revealer and knower points beyond the noetic aspect of faith to a corresponding spiritual mode of being. Faith is more than mere knowledge of God's revelation in Christ; it involves the believer's personal appropriation of Christ in becoming, through faith, one substance with Christ.[61] The same Spirit which is the source of faith is also the source of the fruits of faith: the regeneration and sanctification of life.

Lucien J. Richard, in his recent study on Calvin's spirituality,[62] has rightly stressed the central importance of the distinction introduced by Calvin between justification and sanctification,[63] a distinction which Luther had never made clear. Calvin's view of justification agrees with that of Luther in that both see justification as a forensic act on the part of God by which the righteousness of Christ is communicated to man by imputation.

We see that our righteousness is not in ourselves, but in Christ; and that all our title to it rests solely on our being partakers of Christ; for in possessing him, we possess all his riches with him.[64]

Justification, for Calvin, is 'an acquittal from guilt of him who was accused, as though his innocence had been proved. Since God, therefore, justifies us through the mediation of Christ, he acquits us not by an admission of our personal innocence, but by an imputation of righteousness; so that we, who are unrighteous in ourselves, are considered as righteous in Christ.'[65]

Over and over again Calvin emphasizes that 'we are received into the favor of God through his mere mercy; that it is accomplished by the mediation of Christ; that it is apprehended by faith; and that the end of all is, that the glory of the divine goodness may be fully displayed.'[66] What is of utmost importance to Calvin is that justification by faith does not mean that faith itself produces righteousness in man, but that 'by faith we apprehend the righteousness of Christ, which is the only medium of our reconciliation to God.'[67]

While Calvin regards justification as the 'necessary prerequisite'[68] for salvation, he insists that it is not granted once and for all, but continually extends into sanctification:

When God, by the imputation of the righteousness of Christ, reconciles us to himself and . . . esteems us as righteous persons, he adds to this mercy also another blessing; for he dwells in us by his Holy Spirit, by whose power our carnal desires are daily more and more mortified, and we are sanctified. . . .[69]

Although justification and sanctification must be distinguished, they are perpetually and indissolubly connected:

This [the righteousness of Christ] you cannot attain, without at the same time attaining to sanctification; for he is 'made unto us wisdom and righteousness, and sanctification and redemption.' Christ therefore justifies no one whom he does not also sanctify. For these benefits are perpetually and indissolubly connected, so that whom . . . he justifies, he sanctifies. . . . We may distinguish between them, but Christ contains both inseparably in himself. Do you wish, then, to obtain righteousness in Christ? You must first possess Christ; but you cannot possess him without becoming a partaker of his sanctification; for he cannot be divided. Since, then, the Lord affords us the enjoyment of these blessings only in the bestowment of himself, he gives them both together, and never one without the other. Thus we see how true it is that we are justified, not without works, yet not by works; since union with Christ, by which we are justified, contains sanctification as well as righteousness.[70]

Once again, as in the case of the knowledge of God, objective truth and the subjective appropriation of it are seen by Calvin in terms of a correlation that cannot be dissolved: Justification is an objective event, the juridical act by which we are accepted by God on account of Christ's righteousness. Sanctification is a subjective event effecting the inner renewal of man. 'Justification is based on what Christ has done for us; sanctification is based on what he does within us,'[71] and the 'indissoluble connection' between the two implies an on-going process for the Christian, as well as progress which continues throughout life.

This view of sanctification as a life-long regenerative process by which man is being re-made in the image of Christ brings us to the very heart of Calvin's spirituality. Calvin devoted five chapters of his *Institutes* to a treatise on the Christian life.[72] In them all the essential aspects of Christian spirituality are present. The purpose of the treatise is to present the method by which a pious man may be taught to regulate his life properly, a method for which he finds the outline in Scripture:

This Scripture plan . . . consists chiefly in these two things: the first, that a love of righteousness, to which we have otherwise no natural propensity, be instilled and introduced into our hearts; the second, that a rule be prescribed to us to prevent our taking any devious steps in the race of righteousness . . . with what better foundation can it begin than when it admonishes us that we ought to be holy because our God is holy?[73]

In this 'race of righteousness' Christ is the authentic model and exemplar:

As God the Father has reconciled us to himself in Christ, so he has exhibited to us in him a pattern to which it is his will that we should be conformed . . . Christ, by whom we have been reconciled to God, is proposed to us as an example, whose character we should exhibit in our lives. What can be required more efficacious than this one consideration? Indeed, what can be required besides? For if the Lord has adopted us as his sons on this condition—that we exhibit in our life an imitation of Christ, the bond of our adoption—unless we addict and devote ourselves to righteousness, we not only most perfidiously revolt from our Creator but also abjure him as our Savior.[74]

Since Christ has united us to his body, we 'should use our utmost exertions that the glory of God may be displayed by us.'[75] Imitation of Christ is thus not a matter of doctrine; it is a union or communion with Christ which Calvin described in the strongest possible terms. Union with Christ means to become 'one substance' with him,[76] it is a 'mystical union' of the highest rank,[77] a 'sacred marriage, by which we become bone of his bone, and flesh of his flesh.'[78]

All knowledge and doctrine of the gospel will only then be profitable and authentic when it is 'transfused into our breast, pervades our marrow, and thus transforms us into itself.'[79] Sanctification is not 'a doctrine of the tongue but of life; and it is not apprehended merely with the understanding and memory, like other sciences, but it is only then received when it possesses the whole soul and finds a seat and residence in the inmost affection of the heart.'[80]

Since this 'doctrine of life' cannot be apprehended conceptually like other sciences, a different agent is necessary and, once again, Calvin points to the Holy Spirit as the agency through which we become united with Christ in 'sacred marriage.'

The Lord by his Spirit bestows upon us the blessings of being one with him in soul and body and spirit. The bond of that connection therefore is the Spirit of Christ who unites us to him, and is a kind of channel by which everything that Christ has and is, is given to us.[81]

The goal of the spiritual life is the perfection of goodness, the full display of the image of Christ in the life of the Christian. But this goal, the complete and perfect communion with God, is not attainable in this life, although it must be constantly aimed at. In fact, if perfection were to be the prerequisite for being a Christian, 'then all would be excluded from the church, since no man can be found who is not still at a great distance from it, and many have hitherto made but a very small progress.'[82] The Christian life is, therefore, a life of progress, of spiritual growth toward final and complete communion with God.[83]

. . . The beginning of a life of uprightness is spiritual, when the internal affection of the mind is unfeignedly devoted to God in the cultivation of holiness and righteousness. But since no man in this terrestrial and corporeal prison has strength sufficient to press forward in his course with a due degree of alacrity, and the majority are oppressed with such great debility that they stagger and halt and even creep on the ground, and so make very inconsiderable advances—let us everyone proceed according to our small ability and prosecute the journey we have begun. No man will be so unhappy but that he may every day make some progress, however small. Therefore let us not cease to strive, that we may be incessantly advancing in the way of the Lord; nor let us despair on account of the smallness of our success, for however our success may not correspond to our wishes, yet our labor is not lost when this day surpasses the preceding one; provided that, with sincere simplicity, we keep our end in view, and press forward to the goal . . . till we shall have arrived at a perfection of goodness which, indeed, we seek and pursue as long as we live, and shall then attain, when, divested of all corporeal infirmity, we shall be admitted by God into complete communion with him.[84]

The remainder of Calvin's treatise on the Christian pilgrimage toward full communion with God describes this journey as one of self-denial for our neighbor's sake, as the bearing of the cross after the example of Christ, and in patient hope and lively anticipation of the life to come. Hence the Christian life is *meditatio futurae vitae* preceded by a *contemptus mundi:*

We therefore truly derive advantage from the discipline of the cross only when we learn that this life, considered in itself, is unquiet, turbulent, miserable in numberless instances, and in no respect altogether happy . . .; and in consequence of this at once conclude that nothing can be sought or expected on earth but conflict, and that when we think of a crown we must raise our eyes toward heaven. For it must be admitted that the mind is never seriously excited to desire and meditate on the future life without having previously imbibed a contempt of the present.[85]

Although Calvin expresses the *contemptus mundi* in vigorous and traditional terms, he insists that this contempt should not lead to hatred of the present life. Since the present life is a pilgrimage toward the celestial kingdom, and 'we are only to pass through the earth, we ought undoubtedly to make such a use of its blessings as will assist rather than retard us in our journey'[86] in such a way as to avoid the extremes of indulgence and human austerity.[87] In contrast to monastic spirituality, Calvin's view of the *contemptus mundi* is based solely on the comparison of the present with the future life, as he emphasizes over and over again.[88] Hence 'contempt' of the world leads not to withdrawal from it, according to Calvin, but to a life of service to God and neighbor within the world, and Christian spirituality is, therefore, apostolic in nature.[89] In the final section of his treatise on the Christian life Calvin expresses the apostolic nature of spirituality in terms of the Christian's vocation.

. . . The Lord commands every one of us, in all the actions of life, to regard his vocation . . . Every individual's line of life, therefore, is, as it were, a post assigned to him by the Lord, that he may not wander about in uncertainty all his days. . . It is sufficient if we know that the principle and foundation of right conduct in every case is the vocation of the Lord . . . Our life, therefore, will then be best regulated when it is directed to this work, since no one will be impelled by his own temerity to attempt more than is compatible with his calling . . . The magistrate will execute his office with greater pleasure, the father of a family will confine himself to his duty with more satisfaction, and all, in their respective spheres of life, will bear and surmount the inconveniences, cares, disappointments, and anxieties which befall them, when they shall be persuaded that every individual has his burden laid upon him by God. Hence also will arise peculiar consolation, since there will be no employment so mean and sordid (provided we follow our vocation) as not to appear truly respectable and be deemed highly important in the sight of God.[90]

The social implications of this aspect of Calvin's view of spirituality are obviously far-reaching and, equally obviously, open to misinterpretation when taken out of the total context of his theology, as has been the case time and again.[91] Since it has not been my purpose here to explore the social and political consequences of Calvin's spirituality, however, I shall forego a critical examination of those various interpretations, and confine myself to a brief summary of the stated purpose of this paper and the conclusions we have reached.

SUMMARY AND CONCLUSION

We started with the thesis that spirituality, defined as the characteristic mode of being religious, exhibits a distinctive structure which is always recognizable, regardless of the different historical and cultural contexts in which it assumes its various forms. We may therefore expect to recognize that structure in Christianity as a whole (inasmuch as it is a religion), as well as in the varying historical expressions of Western Christendom. More specifically, the spirituality of Western Christendom may be expected to demonstrate that the spiritual man regards himself not as one given by nature, but as one who has been re-made, as it were, 'in accordance with the exemplary models revealed by Divine Beings and preserved in the myths.'

That this is, indeed, the case throughout the history of Western Christendom can hardly be denied. St Paul intoned the main theme of Christian spirituality: God has destined us to be conformed to the image of his Son, in order that he might be the first-born among many brethren. The development of this theme and its many variations only testify to the power and potentiality inherent in the theme itself. It seemed to call for augmentation as well as diminution, and invited splendid harmonies as well as highly complex counterpoint to accompany it. It went through dazzling modulations and could yet be heard as a simple, sweet folk-melody. While the degree of complexity and length, the style and language of those variations depend on the experience, skill, perception and taste of their respective composers, in the final analysis it is the structure of the theme itself, its inherent potentiality as well as its restrictions, that determines and limits its development. No one, I think, was more aware of this than Calvin. One is almost tempted to regard Calvin's spirituality as simply a re-statement of the theme in its original Pauline intonation, as some of his less perceptive students have insisted. But this would not be correct nor would it be fair to the originality of Calvin. While he—more scrupulously perhaps than most of his predecessors—observed, and felt bound by, the givenness of the theme and its components, his own treatment of it clearly reveals that he had listened to and learned from the efforts of such predecessors as Augustine and Bernard, not to mention the *Devotio Moderna* and Martin Luther. We have observed the consistency with which he links the epistemological and ontological dimensions of spirituality, re-uniting thereby theology and piety. We have noted, furthermore, Calvin's sensitivity to the distinction between the objective givenness of his theme and its subjective appropriation while refusing to separate the two. Word and Spirit, justification and sanctification, thus remain indissolubly correlated in dialectical tension. But never is there the slightest uncertainty as to the identity and centrality of the theme itself, which is the Christian's relationship with Christ. Christ is the thrust of God's revelation, Christ is, therefore, the true object of faith. It is the righteousness of Christ imputed by God that justifies the sinner; and it is the Christian's growth in the likeness of Christ that sanctifies and transforms his life.

If, as has often been pointed out, Calvin's theology is strongly christocentric, this is so because the very nature of Christian spirituality, as Calvin understands it, demands that this be so. *Homo Christianus* is he who, being conformed to the image and exemplar of Christ, lives not according to the flesh but according to the Spirit. And 'it is the Spirit himself bearing witness with our spirit that we are children of God and fellow heirs with Christ—provided we suffer with him in order that we also be glorified with him.'

Otto Gründler

Western Michigan University

Notes

Abbreviations used generally

CCh   Corpus Christianorum series. Turnhout, Belgium.
CSEL   Corpus Scriptorum Ecclesiasticorum Latinorum. Vienna,
       1886-
Ep(p) Letter(s)
Op. S.
Bern. *Sancti Bernard Opera,* edd. J. Leclercq, H. M. Rochais,
       & C. H. Talbot. Rome: Editiones Cistercienses, 1957-
PG   J.-P. Migne, *Patrologia Graeca.* Paris, 1857-66.
PL   J.-P. Migne, *Patrologia Latina.* Paris, 1844-64.
RB   *The Rule of St Benedict*
SCh   Sources chrétiennes series. Paris: Editions du Cerf.

General Works on Spirituality
Bouyer, Louis, Jean Leclercq, François Vandenbroucke, Louis Cognet,
       A History of Christian Spirituality, 4 vols.
       I. *The Spirituality of the New Testament and the Fathers.*
       London: Burns & Oates; New York: Desclee, 1963.
       II. *The Spirituality of the Middle Ages.* London: Burns &
       Oates, 1968.
Squire, Aelred. *Asking the Fathers.* London: SPCK, 1963.

AUGUSTINE OF HIPPO:
THE APPROACH OF THE SOUL TO GOD
BIBLIOGRAPHY

Works of Saint Augustine
Latin

PL 32-47
CSEL 25, 33-4, 41-4, 51, 60, 63, 74
CCh 29, 32-50

Translations in the series:
Ancient Christian Writers, 9 volumes. Westminster, Md., 1946-
Fathers of the Church, 21 volumes. Washington, D.C. 1948-
Library of Christian Classics, 3 volumes. Philadelphia, 1955-
Nicene and Post-Nicene Fathers, 8 volumes. Edinburgh, 1887-92; rpt. Grand Rapids, Mich.
Bourke, Vernon J. *The Essential Augustine.* New York: New American Library, 1964.
Oates, W. J., *Basic Writings of St. Augustine.* 2 vols. 1948.
Przywara, Erich, *An Augustine Synthesis.* 1945.

Studies

The bibliography of Augustine studies is enormous. Among the introductory works are:
Battenhouse, Roy et al. *A Companion to the Study of St. Augustine.* New York, 1954.
Brown, Peter. *Augustine of Hippo: A Biography.* London: Faber, 1967.
Marrou, Henri. *Saint Augustine.* New York, 1957.

NOTES

[1] *Retractationes* 1, prologo: 'Inveniet enim fortasse, quomodo scribendo profecerim, quisquis opuscula mea ordine quo scripta sunt legerit.'
[2] For the terminology of Augustine's spiritual teaching, see W. A. Schumacher, *Spiritus and Spiritual* (Chicago: Mundelein, 1957). Except for one article by Fulbert Cayré, the symposium edited by Agostino Trapé, *Sanctus Augustinus Vitae Spiritualis Magister* (Rome: Analecta Augustiniana, 1956) is of no great scholarly value.
[3] *De musica* 6, 5, 13: 'Oportet enim anima et regi a superiore, et regere inferiorem. Superior illa solus Deus est, inferius illa solum corpus, si ad omnem et totam animam intendas.' Earlier in the same book (6, 1, 1) he had spoken of the one God, 'qui humanis mentibus nulla natura interposita praesidet. . . .' For more texts on this three-level ontology, see my *Augustine's View of Reality* (Villanova, PA: University Press, 1964).
[4] *De Trinitate* 10, 11, 18. This 'trinitarian' analysis of psychic activity runs throughout Books IX to XV.
[5] *De quantitate animae* 27, 53. In this passage *ratio* is kept quite distinct from discursive reasoning, which Augustine calls *ratiocinatio.*
[6] *De quantitate animae* 33, 70-76.
[7] *De Genesi contra Manichaeos* 1, 25, 43.
[8] *De vera religione* 30, 54; 31, 57; 32, 59; 39, 72; 42, 79; 55, 108; and 55, 113.
[9] *Retractationes* 1, 6: 'per corporalia cupiens ad incorporalia . . . ducere.'

[10] See M. F. Sciacca, *Sant' Agostino* (Brescia: Morcelliana, 1949) pp. 298-300.

[11] *De sermone Domini in monte* 1, 1, 3; 2, 4; 2, 5; 2, 6; 2, 7; 2, 8; 2, 9.

[12] Thus he speaks in the last text (*De sermone* 2, 9) of 'omnes animi sui motus . . . componentes et subjicientes rationi, id est menti et spiritui.'

[13] *De doctrina Christiana* 2, 7, 9-11.

[14] E. Gilson, *Introduction à l'étude de saint Augustin* (Paris: Vrin, 1949) p. 160, note 1, suggests that these seven grades in *De doct. Christ.* parallel the last four steps in *De quantitate animae* 33, 70-76. i.e. *virtus, tranquillitas, ingressio* and *contemplatio.*

[15] *Confessiones* 7, 10, 16: 'Et inde admonitus redire ad memetipsum intravi in intima mea duce te . . . et vidi . . . supra mentem meam lucem incommutabilem.'

[16] *Conf.* 7, 17, 23: 'Atque ita gradatim a corporibus ad sentientem per corpus animam atque inde ad eius interiorem vim, cui sensus corporis exteriora nuntiaret . . . atque inde rursus ad ratiocinantem potentiam . . . quae se quoque in me comperiens mutabilem erexit se ad intelligentiam suam . . . unde nosset ipsum incommutabile . . . et pervenit ad id quod est, in ictu trepidantis aspectus.'

[17] *Conf.* 9, 10, 24: 'Nam fuisse et futurum esse non est aeternum. Et dum loquirmur et inhiamus illi, attingimus eam modice, toto ictu cordis.'

[18] *Western Mysticism,* 2nd ed. (London: Constable, 1926) p. 46.

[19] *St. Augustine of Hippo* (Philadelphia: Westminster Press, 1963) p. 83, says that what is described in *Conf.* 7 might 'be regarded as a mystical experience.'

[20] *Augustins Verhältnis zur Mystik* (Wurzberg 1936) p. 176.

[21] See J. M. LeBlond, *Les Conversions de saint Augustin* (Paris 1960) who stresses throughout the theme of *conversio ad Deum* in the *Confessions.*

[22] *Ep.* 147, *De videndo Deo.*

[23] *Ep.* 147, 1, 3.

[24] *Ep.* 147, 6, 19: 'Beati mundo corde: ipsi enim Deum videbunt,' and 'Deum nemo vidit umquam.'

[25] Ibid., the key sentence is: 'Illi autem ideo viderunt, quicumque Deum viderunt, quia cui vuluerit, sicut voluerit, apparet ea specie, quam voluntas elegerit, etiam latente natura.'

[26] Ambrose, *Super Lucam* 1, 1, 11; cited in *Ep.* 147, 6, 17-18.

[27] See Gilson, *Introduction,* pp. 150-245. In English this book is entitled *The Christian Philosophy of St. Augustine,* translated by Larry Lynch (New York: Random House, 1960).

[28] *De Genesi ad litteram* 12, 6, 15. My *Essential Augustine* (Indianapolis: Hackett, 1974) prints an English version by John H. Taylor of this passage, pp. 93-95; the *Commentary* is not yet fully translated but Father Taylor is working on it.

[29] *De Trinitate* 15, 6; for the Latin see the critical edition by W. J. Mountain, in CCh 50 and 50a (1968).

[30] *De Trin.* 8, 3; CCh, vol. I: 271-272.
[31] *De gratia Christi et peccato originali* 1, 43, 46; 1, 43, 47; and 1, 46, 51.
[32] *Enchiridion de fide, spe et caritate* 30.
[33] Ibid. chapters 31-32 and 107.
[34] *De civitate Dei* 22, 24.
[35] Ibid. 'Ipse itaque (1) animae humanae (2) mentem dedit, ubi ratio et intellegentia in infante sopita est quodam modo . . . excitanda scilicet atque exserenda aetatis accessu, qua fit scientiae capax atque doctrinae, et habilis (3) perceptioni veritatis et (4) amoris boni: qua capacitate haurit (5) sapientiam (6) virtutibusque praedita, quibus prudenter, fortiter, temperanter, et juste, adversus errores et cetera ingenerata vitia dimicet, eaque nullius rei (7) desiderio nisi boni illius summi atque immutabilis vincat.' (Parenthetical numbers added.)
[36] *De gratia et libero arbitrio* 43.
[37] Ibid. 46; see Jm 1:17 and 3:17.
[38] *De praedestinatione sanctorum* 2, 5.
[39] Ibid. 3, 7.
[40] *De civitate Dei* 22, 24, 5.

DIONYSIUS THE PSEUDO-AREOPAGITE: THE GNOSTIC MYTH

BIBLIOGRAPHY

Works of Dionysius

Editions

Denys l'Aréopagite: La hiérarche céleste, ed. G. Heil, R. Roques, M. de Gandillac. SCh 58. Paris, 1970.

Latin Translations

PG 3-4.

Dionysica, 2 vols., ed. P. Chevalier. Paris, 1937 and 1950.

PL 122: 1023-1194 (Eriugena's translation)

English translations

The Works of Dionysius the Areopagite, 2 vols., tr. J. Parker. London-Oxford, 1897, 1899.

Dionysius the Areopagite on the Divine Names and the Mystical Theology, tr. C. E. Holt. London, 1920.

NOTES

[1] *De captivitate Babylonica;* WA 6:562.
[2] *Mystical Theology* I, *Divine Names* I, 5.

[3] DN I, 1.

[4] DN II, 2.

[5] DN III, 2. Note the technical terms borrowed from mystery religions.

[6] DN, I, 1.

[7] DN III, 4.

[8] DN V, 1-131.

[9] DN IV, 1.

[10] DN I, 5 & IV, 19.

[11] DN IV, 7.

[12] DN V, 3.

[13] DN II, 11 & *Celestial Hierarchy* III, 1.

[14] DN V, 8.

[15] DN III, 1.

[16] DN III, 2.

[17] DN I, 5.

[18] Cf. DN IV, 12.

[19] DN IV, 20.

[20] DN V, 5.

[21] DN VIII, 7.

[22] DN I, 5.

[23] DN I, 7.

[24] DN I, 5.

[25] DN I, 7.

[26] DN IV, 10.

[27] DN IV, 17.

[28] DN III, 1.

[29] *Ibid.*

[30] DN IV, 13.

[31] DN IV, 2.

[32] DN IV, 4.

[33] DN II, 1.

[34] DN VIII, 5.

[35] *Ibid.*

[36] DN IX, 6.

[37] CH III, 7.

[38] DN II, 7.

[39] MT II.

[40] MT III.

[41] MT I.

[42] DN V, 1 & XIII, 3.

[43] DN I, 4 f.

[44] DN IV, 11.

[45] Etienne Gilson, *History of Christian Philosophy in the Middle Ages* (New York: Random House, 1955) 82.

[46] DN I, 7 & II, 4.

[47] Cf. DN IV, 3.

[48] DN I, 1.
[49] MT I.
[50] MT III.
[51] MT I.
[52] DN I, 5. Cf. II, 9.
[53] MT I.
[54] MT II.
[55] οὐ μόνον μαϑὼν καὶ παϑὼντ ιὰ ϑειᾶ (DN II, 9).
[56] *Assertio omnium articulorum M. Lutheri . . . (1520); WA 7:97.*
[57] *Apologeticum* 17:6; ed. E. Dekkers, CCh I :117.
[58] DN VIII, 9.
[59] DN V, 4.
[60] *De reductione artium ad theologiam,* 5.

EARLY PRAEMONSTRATENSIAN ESCHATOLOGY:
THE APOCALYPTIC MYTH

NOTES

[1] See above, p. 34.
[2] When we compare the two book titles of John Eriugena and Augustine, *De divisione naturae* and *De civitate Dei,* the difference becomes almost palpable.
[3] See the brilliant analysis of this symbolism in Jean Daniélou, *The Theology of Jewish Christendom* (London: Darton, Longman, Todd, & Chicago. Regnery, 1964)
[4] X: 32 and XI: 1.
[5] For example, Marjory Reeves' brilliant tracing the *The Influence of Prophecy in the Later Middle Ages.* (Oxford: Clarendon, 1969).
[6] Such as K. Löwith, *Meaning in History ,* (Chicago, 1949, 1957).
[7] PL 170: 477-538.
[8] PL 170:535 f.
[9] PL 182:676-80.
[10] *Op. S. Bern.* 2:102-111.
[11] CCh 36:90-100.
[12] Eucharius († 449). Gallo-roman bishop and writer. His works are in PL 50: 686-1214.
[13] The identity of this Haimo is still uncertain. See *Dictionnaire de théologie catholique* 6/2:2068-9. Works in PL 117-118.
[14] PL 169:805-26.
[15] Ed. G. Salet, SCh 118:68-118.
[16] PL 170:490 ff.
[17] PL 182:162-3.
[18] PL 167.
[19] PL 25:491-584.

[20] Ed. Rhaban Haacke (Weimar, 1970).

[21] PL 170:536.

[22] We should not leave this analysis of Eberwin's critique of Rupert's work without at least calling attention to a problem. The *Song of Anno,* a curious literary product in the vernacular representing what might be called the genre of epic hagiography and having been composed shortly after either 1080 or 1105, uses the four-empire motif of Daniel as its basic structure. It is highly likely, and significant, that the *Song of Anno* originated at Siegburg—the very place where Rupert studied and wrote—and we must assume that Rupert knew it and was, perhaps, even inspired by it when using the Daniel motif to structure his own *De victoria verbi dei.* But did Eberwin know the *Song of Anno,* and is it possible that he derived from it his curious exegesis? We cannot be certain at this time, but I should think not because Eberwin seems to have refrained deliberately from making use of what, after all, is one of the main points of the song's interpretation of the four-empire motif: the identification of the Roman and German empires. Obviously, this problem requires further attention and careful study.

[23] Walter Schmithals, *The Apocalyptic Movement.* Tr. John E. Steely (Nashville: Abingdon Press, 1975), p. 248.

BERNARD OF CLAIRVAUX:
THE MYSTIC AND SOCIETY

BIBLIOGRAPHY

Works of Bernard of Clairvaux

PL 182-183

Sancti Bernardi Opera, edd. J. Leclercq, H. M. Rochais, and C. H. Talbot. Rome, 1957-

Translations

All the works of Bernard will appear in the Cistercian Fathers Series (1969-   ). To date have appeared:

Apologia to Abbot William of St. Thierry / On Precept and Dispensation (CF 1: *Treatises* I, 1970).

Sermons on the Song of Songs I (CF 4: 1971).

The Steps of Humility and Pride & On Loving God (CF 13: *Treatises* II, 1974).

Five Books on Consideration (CF 37: 1976).

Studies

Bouyer, Louis. *The Cistercian Heritage.* London, 1958.

Gilson, Etienne. *The Mystical Theology of Saint Bernard,* 2nd ed. London, New York, 1955.

Leclercq, Jean. *Saint Bernard and the Cistercian Spirit.* Kalamazoo, 1976.

Abbreviations

Csi   *De consideratione libri v ad Eugeniam papam (Five Books on Consideration)*

Div   *Sermones de diversis*

IV HM   *Sermo in feria IV hebdomadae sanctae (Sermon for the fourth feria in Holy Week)*

Hum   *De gradibus superbiae et humilitatis (The Steps of Humility and Pride)*

SC   *Sermones 86 in Cantica canticorum (Sermons on the Song of Songs)*

NOTES

[1] Arnold of Bonneval, *Sancti Bernardi abbatis Clarae-Vallensis vita et res gestae (Vita prima), Liber secundus,* I, 3; PL 185:270.

[2] Bernard's preaching of the Crusade on his trip down the Rhine was accompanied by the working of many miracles according to a large number of eye witnesses. See *Sancti Bernardi abbatis Clarae-Vallensis vita et res gestae, Liber sextus seu miracula a sancto Bernardo per Germaniam, Belgium Galliamque patrata, anno 1146, passim.;* PL 185:373-416. The validity of Bernard's miracles is not a question with which an historian can deal. However, the fact that Bernard's contemporaries regarded him as a miracle-worker doubtlessly increased his authority in his society and thus the effectiveness of his appeals.

[3] *Epistola ad dominum papam Eugenium, pro Remensi archiepiscopo,* 2; PL 182:447.

[4] SC 23, 11 and 16; Op. S. Bern., 1:145, 149-50; PL 183:890 and 893.

[5] Csi, II, ii, 5; Op. S. Bern., 3:414; PL 182:972.

[6] SC 80, 2; Op. S. Bern., 2:277-78; PL 183:1166-67.

[7] SC 23, 11; Op. S. Bern., 1:145-46; PL 183:890.

[8] SC 23, 12 and 14; Op. S. Bern., 1:146-47; PL 183:890-91.

[9] See above, p. 75.

[10] SC 23, 15; Op. S. Bern., 1:148-49; PL 183:892-93.

[11] Div 22, 2; Op. S. Bern., 6/1:171; PL 183:596.

[12] SC 52, 5; Op. S. Bern., 2:92-93; PL 183:1031.

[13] SC 1, 11; Op. S. Bern., 1:7-8; PL 183:789.

[14] SC 22, 2; Op. S. Bern., 1:130; PL 183:878.

[15] SC 74, 5-6; Op. S. Bern., 2:242-43; PL 183:1141.

[16] See the intellectual nature of contemplation in Thomas Aquinas' *Summa theologiae,* IIae IIa, q. 180, a. 3.

[17] SC 8, 6; Op. S. Bern., 1:39-40; PL 183:812-13.

[18] Div 29, 1; Op. S. Bern., 6/1:210; PL 183:620. Italics mine. It should be said that this statement did not refer only to mystical love and knowledge.

[19] SC 52, 4; Op. S. Bern., 2:92; PL 183:1031.

[20] SC 1, 12; Op. S. Bern., 1:8; PL 183:789.

[21] See SC 34, 1; Op. S. Bern., 1:246; PL 183:960.

[22] Hum, I, 2; Op. S. Bern., 3:17; PL 182:942.

[23] Ep 142, 3; PL 182:297-98. See also IV HM, 3; Op. S. Bern., 5:58; PL 183:264.

[24] Hum, VII, 21; Op. S. Bern., 3:32; PL 182:953.

[25] Div 40, 3, Op. S. Bern., 6/1:236-7; PL 183:648.

[26] *Ibid.*

[27] Hum, IV, 15; Op. S. Bern., 3:27; PL 182:949-50.

[28] See my 'The Social Theory of Bernard of Clairvaux,' in *Studies in Medieval Cistercian History,* CS 13 (Spencer, Mass., 1971) 35-48 (esp. 42-6).

[29] Hum, III, 6; Op. S. Bern., 3:20; PL 182:944.

[30] SC 27, 10-11; Op. S. Bern., 1:189-90; PL 183:919-20.

[31] Hum, VII, 21; Op. S. Bern., 3:32; PL 182:953.

WILLIAM OF ST THIERRY:
RATIONAL AND AFFECTIVE SPIRITUALITY

BIBLIOGRAPHY

Works of William of St Thierry
Editions

PL 180 & 184.

M.-M. Davy, *Meditative orationes.* Paris: Vrin, 1934.

        Deux traités de l'amour de Dieu. Paris, 1953.

        Deux traités sur la foi. Paris, 1959.

        Un traité sur la vie solitaire. Paris, 1940.

J.-M. Déchanet, *Le miroir de la foi.* Bruges: Ch. Beyaert, 1946.

Translations

Cistercian Fathers Series. To date have appeared:

On Contemplating God, Prayer, and *Meditations* (CF 3, 1971)

Exposition on the Song of Songs (CF 6, 1970)

The Enigma of Faith (CF 9, 1974)

The Golden Epistle (CF 12, 1971)

The Nature and Dignity of Love, tr. A. Webb and G. Walker, London, 1956.

The Mirror of Faith, tr. Webb and Walker, London, 1959.

Studies

J. M. Déchanet, *William of St Thierry: The Man and His Works.* CS 10 (Cistercian Publications, 1972)

Abbreviations

Aenig   *Aenigma Fidei (The Enigma of Faith)*

Contempl *De contemplando deo (On Contemplating God).*

Ep frat   *Epistola ad fratres de Monte Dei (The Golden Epistle).*

Nat am   *De natura et dignitate amoris (On the Nature and Dignity of Love).*

Nat corp   *De natura corporis et animae (On the Nature of the Body and the Soul).*

Spec fid   *Speculum fidei (The Mirror of Faith)*

NOTES

[1] Nat corp; PL 180:719B.
[2] 719D.
[3] 722B: 'Haec omnia anima intellectu conscipiens. . . .'
[4] 720B.
[5] 702AB.
[6] 711C.
[7] 713C.
[8] 711.
[9] 711C.
[10] 716C.
[11] 716C.
[12] 717A.
[13] 719B.
[14] 718B.
[15] 718C.
[16] 718C.
[17] 718CD.
[18] Citing Jn 1:19.
[19] Nat corp 721B.
[20] 714B.
[21] 721D.
[22] Because the Nat am presents a well-ordered and apparently

unimpeded ascent to the vision of God, this work would seem to have been written before the Contempl, which begins the same ascent only to falter at an early step. The difficulties which William encountered in the Contempl continue and are intensified in the subsequent Med orat.

[23] Nat am 33; Davy edn p. 110; PL 180:397C.

[24] Nat am 4; p. 74; 382A.

[25] *Affect* has been used throughout this paper to translate the Latin work *affectus*. William usually meant by it an inner disposition of love which results from the person's having been touched, affected, by God.

[26] Nat am 54; p. 136; 408B.

[27] 5; p. 76; 382B.

[28] 1; p. 70; 379C. Cf. Augustine, *Conf.* 13, 9, 10.

[29] Nat am 25; pp. 100-102; 393C.

[30] 25; p. 102; 393C.

[31] 25; pp. 100-102; 393B.

[32] 17; p. 92; 389A. Cf. Contempl 8; p. 42; 370C. 'Enjoying' translates *fruitio:* fruition, enjoyment, fulfillment.

[33] Nat am 15; p. 88; 387D.

[34] 18; p. 94; 390B.

[35] 27; p. 104; 394B.

[36] 12; p. 92; 389A. Cf. 1 Cor 13:12.

[37] William indisputably had read Abelard's *Theologia 'scholarium'* (*Introductio ad theologiam*), which he quotes. The second book has not been identified but seems to have been a compilation by one of Abelard's students rather than a work of Abelard himself. See D. E. Luscombe, *The School of Peter Abelard* (Cambridge, 1969) 106-107, and Ludwig Ott, *Untersuchung zur theologischen Briefliteratur der Frühscholastik* (Münster im W., 1937) 173.

[38] *Disputatio adversus Abaelardum* 7; PL 180:270CD.

[39] *Sic et Non.* Prol.; PL 178:349B.

[40] Bernard, Ep.190.

[41] Ibid.

[42] See J. Leclercq, 'Les lettres de Guillaume de Saint-Thierry à saint Bernard,' *Revue Bénédictine* 79 (1969) 381: 'Ainsi de plus en plus se confirme l'impression que Bernard n'a connu Abélard qu'à travers Guillaume.'

[43] Aenig 40, Davy edn p. 126; PL 180:414BC.

[44] 41; p. 128; 414CD.

[45] Spec fid 27; p. 48; 376D (citing Heb 11:6).

[46] 1; p. 24; 365C.

[47] 9; p. 32; 369B.

[48] Bernard had written his *Liber de gratia et libero arbitrio* at William's behest. (*Praef., Op. S. Bern.* 3:165).

[49] *Meditativae Orationes* I; Davy edn p. 48; PL 180:208A.

[50] Spec fid 44; p. 62; 383B.

[51] 12; pp. 34-36; 370D.

[52] 53; p. 68; 387A (citing Mark 16:16).

[53] 48; p. 64; 385AB.

[54] See William's criticism of Abelard's teaching on the Trinity and the Incarnation-Redemption in *Dispitatio* II, VII, VII: PL 180:250-54, 269-80.

[55] Spec fid 17; p. 40; 373B.

[56] 20; p. 42; 374AB.

[57] 35; p. 54; 379C.

[58] Aenig 48; pp. 132-34; 417C.

[59] 44; p. 130; 415D-16A.

[60] Spec fid 24; p. 46; 375D.

[61] 31; p. 50; 378B. Cf. 25; p. 46; 375D.

[62] 31; p. 50; 378B. Cf. 24; p. 46; 375D.

[63] 21; p. 42; 374C.

[64] 31; p. 50; 378B.

[65] 24; p. 46; 375C.

[66] 38; p. 56; 380D.

[67] 63-64; p. 76; 390D-91A. Cf. Nat corp; PL 180:705D.

[68] Spec fid 2; p. 26; 365-66C. Cf. Augustine, *De libero arbitrio* 2. 6. 13; PL 32:1248), and Ep 148. 2. 9; PL 33:626B.

[69] 2 Cor 3:18.

[70] Spec fid 62; p. 76; 390CD.

[71] Aenig 62-63; p. 146; 414BC.

[72] Spec fid 43; p. 60; 382C. Cf. 2 Peter 1:4.

[73] Spec fid 66; p. 78; 391D.

[74] 68; p. 80; 392D. Cf. John 17:3.

[75] On the diffusion of William's works, especially *The Golden Epistle,* see the dissertation of Volker Honemann, 'Lateinische Uberlieferung und mittelalterliche Ubersetzungen der *Epistola ad fratres de Monte Dei* des Wilhelm von Saint-Thierry,' Würzburg, 1973.

[76] Ep frat I. v. 12; PL 184:315C. Cf. 1 Cor 15:41.

[77] I. v. 12; 315D-16A.

[78] I. xiv. 42; 335CD.

[79] I. xiv. 43; 335D-36A.

[80] I. v. 12; 316B.

[81] 316A.

[82] E. g. *Scito te ipsum,* ed. D. E. Luscombe, *Peter Abelard's Ethics* (Oxford: Clarendon, 1971) p. 2.

[83] Ep frat II. ii. 4; 340BC. Cf. Augustine, *De quantitate animae* 13. 22; PL 32:1048. In Nat corp (PL 180:717D) William had equated *anima* and *animus.*

[84] Ep frat II. ii. 4; 340C.

[85] II.ii. 5; 341C.

[86] II. ii. 4; 340 C: 'ob imaginem conditoris et capacitatem rationis.'

[87] 340CD. Cf. Abelard, *Commentaria in epistolam Pauli ad Romanos,* ed. E. M. Buytaert, CCh 11 (1969) p. 166. Both are drawing on Boethius, *In Periermenias;* PL 64:492-3, but William does not cite Boethius by name.

[88] Ep frat II. ii. 4; 344D-45A.

[89] 340D.

[90] 341A.

[91] 341A. The liberation of which William is speaking can only occur, he says, when the will becomes love: when the will 'tends upwards,
as fire to its own place, that is when it is joined to truth and moves upward toward yet higher things.' (345A) This, while important, is an aside
from the main thrust of his ascent pattern in the Ep frat. See below, n.
99.

[92] Ep frat II. ii. 4; 341C.

[93] 341B. Cf. Augustine, *De quantitate animae* 6. 10; 1026. See
above, 'Augustine of Hippo', note 5.

[94] 352A.

[95] 341C.

[96] 341D-42A.

[97] 347A.

[98] II, iii, 23; 353A.

[99] 14; 347A.

[100] 15; 348AB.

[101] 25; 354A.

[102] 18; 350B.

[103] 21; 351CD.

[104] *Conscientia,* shared knowledge, the knowledge of participation.

[105] 351B.

[106] 30; 352BC. Cf. 348C.

[107] 16; 348C: 'Perfectum autem nolle esse deliquere est.'

[108] 32; 340A.

[109] 6; 343B-D.

[110] 13; 346C-D.

GUIGO II: THE THEOLOGY OF THE
CONTEMPLATIVE LIFE

BIBLIOGRAPHY

The Works of Guigo II

Editions

*Guigues II Le Chartreux, Lettre sur la Vie Contemplative (L'échelle
des moines), Douze Méditationes.* Edd. with introduction by Edmund Colledge and James Walsh. SCh 163. Paris, 1970.

PL 40: 997-1004 (Under the name of St Augustine)

PL 184: 475-484 (under the name of St Bernard)

Translations

A Ladder of Four Rungs of Guy II, a translation of the Middle English version. Stanbrook Abbey, 1953.

See note 1.

Studies on the Carthusian Life

Merton, Thomas. *The Silent Life.* New York, 1957.

C. M. Boutrais, *The History of the Great Chartreuse,* tr. E. Hassid. London, 1934.

NOTES

[1] Thanks to Edmund Colledge OSA and James Walsh SJ there has been since 1970 a critical edition of the *Scala claustralium* and an extremely valuable introduction. Guigues II Le Chartreux, *Lettre sur la Vie Contemplative (L'échelle des moines), Douze Méditations.* Introduction et Texte Critique par E. Colledge et J. Walsh; traductions par Un Chartreux. SCh 163. (Paris: Cerf, 1970.) Edmund Colledge has informed me that a translation of the *Scala* and *Meditations* will appear in English probably in 1977 published by Anthony Clarke Books, England.

[2] Ch. I, XV, pp. 82, 120-2

[3] Ch. I, p. 82.

[4] *The Solitary Life, A Letter of Guigo.* Introduction and translation by Thomas Merton. Worcester, Stanbrook Abbey Press, 1963, pp. 1-4.

[5] Ch. I, p. 82.

[6] Ch. II, p. 84.

[7] Giles Constable, 'Twelfth-Century Spirituality and the Late Middle Ages,' *Medieval and Renaissance Studies.* Edited by O. B. Hardison. (Chapel Hill: The University of North Carolina Press, 1971) pp. 31, 48; Giles Constable, 'The Popularity of Twelfth-Century Spiritual Writers in the Late Middle Ages,' *Renaissance Studies in Honor of Hans Baron.* Edited by A. Molho and J. Tedeschi (DeKalb, Ill.: Northern Illinois University Press, 1971) pp. 5, 6, 9, 12, 14, 22, 23, 28.

[8] *Meditations of Guigo, Prior of the Charterhouse.* Translated by J. Jolin (Milwaukee: Marquette University Press, 1951) p. 64.

[9] On Neo-Platonism and Symbols see M.-D. Chenu, *La Théologie au Douzième Siècle* (Paris: Vrin, 1957) Chapters V, VII, VIII.

[10] Ch. II, p. 84: 'Si quis diligenter inspiciat.'

[11] *The Collected Works of St. John of the Cross.* Translated by K. Kavanaugh and O. Rodriquez (Washington, D.C.: Institute of Carmelite Studies, 1973) *Maxims and Counsels,* p. 680.

[12] *Ibid., The Dark Night,* Bk. II, Ch. 18. Translation used in the paper is by E. A. Peers: *Dark Night of the Soul (New York: Image Books, 1959) p. 165.*

[13] See T. S. Eliot, *Four Quartets* (New York: Harcourt, Brace & World, 1971) p. 10, and *passim*.

[14] *The Cloud of Unknowing*, translated by Clifton Wolters (Baltimore: Penguin Books, 1961) p. 94.

[15] Ch. II, p. 84.

[16] Ch. III, pp. 84 ff.

[17] Chenu, p. 191.

[18] Colledge and Walsh, *Introduction*.

[19] Paul Philippe, 'Mental Prayer in the Catholic Tradition,' *Mental Prayer and Modern Life*, translated by F. C. Lehner (New York: P. J. Kenedy, 1950, pp. 20-3.

[20] Jean Leclercq, *The Love of Learning and the Desire for God*. 2nd revised ed., translated by C. Misrahi (New York: Fordham University Press, 1974). See especially chapter IX.

[21] *Sermo 16 in cantica*; Op. S. Bern. 1:89.

[22] Ch. III, p. 84 ff.

[23] *Ibid.*

[24] Ch. II, p. 84.

[25] Chenu, pp. 116-7.

[26] Ch. V, p. 92.

[27] Ch. XIV, p. 116.

[28] Chenu, Chapter VIII.

[29] Ch. VIII, p. 100.

[30] Colledge and Walsh, *op. cit.*, p. 202.

[31] Mt 5:8.

[32] Ch. IV, p. 86.

[33] Cf. E. Bertaud et A. Rayez, 'Echelle Spirituelle,' *Dictionnaire de Spiritualité* 4 (1960) 62-86.

[34] Ch. VII, p. 96.

[35] Ch. III, pp. 84-6.

[36] Ch. XII,pp. 106-8.

[37] Ch. XIV, p. 112.

[38] Ch. XIV, p. 116.

[39] Ch. XV, pp. 120-2.

FRANCIS OF ASSISI: AN APPROACH
TO FRANCISCAN SPIRITUALITY

BIBLIOGRAPHY

Works of Saint Francis

Editions

Opuscula S. Francisci. Quaracchi, 1904.

Works of Thomas of Celano

Editions

Vita Prima S. Francisci Assisiensis. Quaracchi, 1926.

Vita Secunda S. Francisci Assisiensis. Quaracchi, 1927.

Vita Prima S. Francisci in *Analecta Franciscana* 10, pp. 1-117.

Translations

St. Francis of Assisi: Writings and Early Biographies. English Omnibus for the Life of St. Francis, ed. Marion A. Habig. Chicago: Franciscan Herald Press, 1972.

Studies

J. R. H. Moorman, *Saint Francis of Assisi.* London: SPCK, 1963.

——————————— , *The Sources for the Life of S. Francis of Assisi.* Manchester, 1940.

Abbreviations

1 Celano   *Vita prima s. Francisci, Analecta Franciscana* edition.

Omnibus   *St. Francis of Assisi: Writings and Early Biographies,* ed. Habig.

NOTES

[1] St Francis of Assisi is, of course, by no means unique in this regard. One might well say the same thing about St Paul, St Augustine, Blaise Pascal, the Buddha, Muhammad, and many others.

[2] Since the last third of the thirteenth century, Celano's lives of St Francis have been overshadowed by the *Legenda major* of St Bonaventure. In the last part of the nineteenth century, however, modern critical research 'rediscovered' these *legendae* of Celano; today they, together with the writings of St Francis, are prized as reliable sources for the early history of the Franciscan Order. For a critical appraisal concerning the historical value of Celano's *legendae,* see Engelbert Grau, *Thomas von Celano. Leben und Wunder des hl. Franziskus von Assisi,* 2nd ed. (Werl, Westf.: Dietrich-Coelde-Verlag, 1964) pp. 27ff.

[3] The critical edition of the *Vita prima s. Francisci* is found in *Analecta Franciscana,* 10, 1-117. The English translation used in the present study is taken from *St Francis of Assisi: Writings and Early Biographies. English Omnibus of the Sources for the Life of St Francis,* ed. Marion A. Habig (Chicago: Franciscan Herald Press, 1972) pp. 227-355.

[4] For an excellent study concerning the theology of conversion in the *legendae* of Thomas of Celano, see F. de Beer, *La conversion de saint*

François selon Thomas de Celano. Etude comparative des textes relatifs à la conversion en Vita I et Vita II (Paris, 1963).

[5] Concerning the 'sinfulness' of the young Francis as presented in the early biographies, see Sophronius Clasen, 'Franziskus, der Gottes Absicht noch nicht erkannte,' *Wissenschaft und Weisheit* 27 (1964) 117-128.

[6] 1 Celano, 2 (*Omnibus*, p. 230).

[7] *Ibid.* (*Omnibus*, p. 231).

[8] See 1 Celano, 3 and 6.

[9] 1 Celano, 3 (*Omnibus*, p. 231).

[10] *Ibid.*

[11] 1 Celano, 4 (*Omnibus*, p. 232).

[12] For an excellent study concerning spiritual awakening, viewed within a psychological framework, see Roberto Assagioli, *Psychosynthesis: A Manual of Principles and Techniques* (1965; rpt. New York: Viking Press, 1971) pp. 35-59.

[13] 1 Celano, 4 (*Omnibus*, p. 232).

[14] 1 Celano, 5 (*Omnibus*, p. 233).

[15] 1 Celano, 71 (*Omnibus*, p. 288).

[16] *Ibid.*

[17] 1 Celano, 6 (*Omnibus*, p. 235).

[18] *Ibid.* (*Omnibus*, p. 234).

[19] 1 Celano, 15 (*Omnibus*, p. 241). The process of undergoing the *transitus Christi* continued throughout Francis' life. In the *Vita secunda s. Francisci,* 217, Thomas of Celano describes Francis' 'passing' to the Father in these words: 'The hour therefore came, and all the mysteries of Christ being fulfilled in him, he winged his way happily to God.' See *Omnibus*, p. 536.

[20] 1 Celano, 22 (*Omnibus*, pp. 246-247).

[21] *Ibid.*

[22] *Ibid.*

[23] *Ibid.*

[24] 1 Celano, 35 (*Omnibus*, p. 257).

[25] 1 Celano, 26 (*Omnibus*, p. 249). See also 1 Celano, 5 and 8.

[26] See 1 Celano, 7.

[27] See 1 Celano, 16.

[28] See 1 Celano, 26 (*Omnibus*, p. 250).

[29] See *The Testament of St Francis* (*Omnibus*, pp. 67 ff.).

[30] See Duane V. Lapsanski, 'The Meaning of Fraternity in the Writings of Saint Francis of Assisi,' *The Cord* 25 (1975) 316-319.

[31] See Duane V. Lapsanski, 'Poverty and Minority in the Early Sources of the Franciscan Order,' *The Cord* 25 (1975) 288-292.

[32] See Duane V. Lapsanski, 'Obedience/Authority in Francis' Writings,' *The Cord* 25 (1975) 251-255.

[33] *The Rule of 1221,* ch. 23 (*Omnibus*, pp. 51-52).

NORTHERN SPIRITUALITY AND THE
LATE MEDIEVAL DRAMA IN YORK

NOTES

[1] In particular, see O.B. Hardison, Jr, *Christian Rite and Christian Drama in the Middle Ages* (Baltimore: Johns Hopkins Press, 1965) pp.1-34; Thomas Munro, *Evolution in the Arts and Other Theories of Culture History* (Cleveland: Cleveland Museum of Art, 1963).

[2] George Benson, *Later Medieval York* (York, 1919) p. 128; *The Fabric Rolls of York Minster,* ed. James Raine, Jr, Surtees Soc. 35 (Durham, 1859) p. 218.

[3] Ibid.

[4] John A. Knowles, *The York School of Glass-Painting* (London: SPCK, 1936) p. 42.

[5] See ibid., pp. 215-21; E. A. Gee, 'The Painted Glass of All Saints' Church, York,' *Archaeologia* 102 (1969) 190.

[6] See Clifford Davidson, 'The Realism of the York Realist and the York Passion,' *Speculum* 50 (1975) 270-83.

[7] *The Hours of Catherine of Cleves,* Guennol Collection, fol. 60^v; ed. John Plummer (New York: Braziller, n.d.), Pl. 22.

[8] Quoted by Johan Huizinga, *The Waning of the Middle Ages* (1949; rpt. Garden City, NY: Doubleday, 1954) p. 265.

[9] On my own 'pilgrimage' to the Basilica of the Holy Blood in Bruges on Friday, 22 July 1975, I saw no tears; nevertheless, it was clear that those in attendance at Mass when the Holy Blood was displayed were deeply affected by the presence of the relic.

[10] *Altenglische Sprachproben,* ed. Eduard Mätzner (Berlin, 1869) Vol. I, pt. 2, p. 229.

[11] With regard to drama, see especially Sandro Sticca, 'Drama and Spirituality in the Middle Ages,' *Medievalia et Humanistica* n.s. 4 (1973) 69-87.

[12] William L. Smoldon, 'The Melodies of the Medieval Church-Dramas and Their Significance,' *Comparative Drama* 2 (1968) 185-93. For an explanation of the early development of the *Quem queritis* trope and play, see C. Clifford Flanigan, 'The Roman Rite and the Origins of the Liturgical Drama,' *University of Toronto Quarterly* 43 (1974) 263-84.

[13] Contained in *The Play of Herod,* ed. Noah Greenberg and William L. Smoldon (New York: Oxford Univ. Press, 1965).

[14] Quoted by Rosemary Woolf, *The English Mystery Plays* (Berkeley and Los Angeles: Univ. of California Press, 1972) p. 202; see also David Staines, 'To Out-Herod Herod: The Development of a Dramatic Character,' *Comparative Drama* 10 (1976) 29-53.

[15] See W. O. Hassall, ed., *The Holkham Bible Picture Book* (London: Dropmore Press, 1954) p. 101; Henry Martin, 'Les enseignements des

miniatures: attitude royale,' *Gazette des Beaux-Arts,* 4th ser., 9 (1913) 173-88.

[16] *The Digby Plays,* ed. F. J. Furnivall, EETS, extra ser. 70 (1896) pp. 6-15.

[17] Cuthbert Butler, *Western Mysticism* (1922; rpt. New York: Harper and Row, 1966) p. 119.

[18] E. W. Tristram, *English Medieval Wall Painting: The Thirteenth Century* (London: Oxford Univ. Press, 1950) 1:47. On the utilization of similar matter in the dramas, see Patrick J. Collins, 'Narrative Bible Cycles in Medieval Art and Drama,' *Comparative Drama* 9 (1975) 125-46.

[19] *Meditations on the Life of Christ,* trans. Isa Ragusa (Princeton: Princeton Univ. Press, 1961) p. 333. See also David L. Jeffrey, *The Early English Lyric and Franciscan Spirituality* (Lincoln: Univ. of Nebraska Press, 1975) *passim.*

[20] *Meditations,* p. 333.

[21] Ibid., p. 334.

[22] On this window, see Knowles, p. 211.

[23] Coral Gables: Univ. of Miami Press, 1970, pp. 238-41.

[24] See Gordon McN. Rushforth, *Medieval Christian Imagery* (Oxford: Clarendon Press, 1936) p. 72; Max Friedländer, *Die Altniederländsche Malerei* (Leiden: Sijthoff, 1934) 6:Pl. LXIX.

[25] Adolphe N. Didron (and Margaret Stokes), *Christian Iconography,* trans. E. J. Millington (1851; rpt. New York: Ungar, 1965) 2:317.

[26] Pickering, pp. 285-301.

[27] Joannes Tinctoris, *Proportionale musicae,* in *Source Readings in Music History,* ed. Oliver Strunk (New York: Norton, 1950) p. 194.

[28] E. W. Tristram, *English Wall Painting of the Fourteenth Century* (London: Routledge and Kegan Paul, 1955) pp. 21-2.

[29] *Hours of Catherine of Cleves,* Guennol Collection, fol. 66^v; ed. Plummer, Pl. 26.

[30] *The Lay Folks Mass Book,* ed. Thomas Frederick Simmons, EETS, orig. ser. 71 (1879) p. 109.

[31] Ibid., p. 42.

[32] J. D. Chambers, *Population, Economy, and Society in Pre-Industrial England* (Oxford: Oxford Univ. Press, 1972) p. 19.

[33] See H. F. Westlake, *The Parish Guilds of Mediaeval England* (London: SPCK, 1919) 26 ff.

[34] Maud Sellers, ed., *York Memorandum Book A/Y,* Pt. II, Surtees Soc. 125 (Durham, 1915) p. lxiii.

[35] Ibid., p. lxiv; translation from p. 19.

[36] *Chantry Surveys,* Pt. I, Surtees Soc. 91 (Durham, 1894), p. 61. See also the discussion in Clifford Davidson, 'Civic Concern and Iconography in the York Passion,' *Annuale Mediaevale* 15 (1974) 126-8.

[37] *Testamenta Eboracensia,* Pt. II, Surtees Soc. 30 (Durham, 1855) p. 21. The Blackburn chantry in Saint Anne's Chapel on Foss Bridge continued to be maintained by the city Corporation in the sixteenth century

even after others had been dissolved; see A. G. Dickens, 'A Municipal Dissolution of Chantries at York, 1536,' *Yorkshire Archaeological Journal* 36 (1947) 164-72.

[38] Eileen Power, *The Wool Trade in English Medieval History* (London: Oxford Univ. Press, 1941) pp. 104-5. On the Blackburn window, see Gee, pp. 153-7.

[39] Gee, p. 156; translation of Latin text.

[40] Ibid.

[41] Alexandra F. Johnston and Margaret Dorrell, 'The Doomsday Pageant of the York Mercers, 1433,' *Leeds Studies in English* n.s. 5 1971) 29-30.

[42] For a theory of indoor production before the Mayor and Council *et al.,* see Alan H. Nelson, *The Medieval English Stage* (Chicago: Univ. of Chicago Press, 1974) 38-81. The conventional view of the plays as performed on wagons along the pageant route is defended by Alexandra Johnston in her review of Professor Nelson's book (*University of Toronto Quarterly* 44 [1975] 238-48).

[43] E. K. Chambers, *The Mediaeval Stage* (Oxford: Clarendon Press, 1903) 2:400.

[44] Edwin Benson, *Life in a Mediaeval City* (London: SPCK, 1920) p. 10.

[45] Robert Davies, *Extracts from the Municipal Records of the City of York* (London, 1843) 236; cf. Nelson, pp. 15-37.

[46] Martin Stevens, 'The York Cycle: From Procession to Play,' *Leeds Studies in English* n.s. 6 (1972) 37-61.

[47] Johnston, citing the work of Margaret Dorrell, in her review of Nelson, *Medieval English Stage* (p. 239).

[48] See *Memorandum Book A/Y,* Pt. II, p. 64.

[49] Ibid., pp. 156-7; trans. in Davies, p. 243; see also Davidson, 'The Realism of the York Realist and the York Passion,' p. 282.

[50] Chambers 2:401.

[51] Johnston, review of Nelson, *Medieval English Stage* (pp. 245-6).

[52] Benson, *Later Medieval York,* p. 41.

[53] Johnston and Dorrell, 'The Doomsday Pageant,' pp. 29-30.

[54] See Emile Mâle, *Gothic Image,* trans. Dora Nussey (1913; rpt. New York: Harper and Row, 1961) 365.

[55] Johnston and Dorrell, 'The Doomsday Pageant,' p. 30.

[56] Tristram, *Fourteenth Century,* p. 19.

[57] Mâle, pp. 355-89.

[58] C. J. P. Cave, 'The Bosses on the Vault of the Quire of Winchester Cathedral,' *Archaeologia* 76 (1927) Pl. XXVIII, fig. 3.

[59] 'A Relic of the Pilgrimage of Grace,' *Yorkshire Archaeological Journal* 21 (1910-11) 108-9.

[60] Johnston and Dorrell, 'The Doomsday Pageant,' p. 30.

[61] J. W. Robinson, 'The Late Medieval Cult of Jesus,' *PMLA* 80 (1965) 508-14.

[62] *York Civic Records,* ed. Angelo Raine (York, 1946) 5:173.

[63] O. Elfrida Saunders, *A History of English Art in the Middle Ages* (Oxford: Clarendon Press, 1932) 131.

[64] Ibid., fig. 59; E. W. Tristram, ' "Piers Plowman" in English Wall Painting,' *Burlington Magazine* 31 (1917) 140. Tristram's association of the Christ of the Trades at Breage, Cornwall, with Piers Plowman is repeated in Tancred Borenius and E. W. Tristram, *English Mediaeval Painting* (Paris: Pegasus Press, 1927), but is refuted by Ruth Ryan in *Art Bulletin* 11 (1929) 302-3.

[65] Saunders, p. 131.

[66] The extensive references to work in the York cycle have been catalogued by Francis Sheehan in a paper entitled 'The Work Ethic and the York Cycle,' which he read at the Tenth Conference on Medieval Studies sponsored by the Medieval Institute at Western Michigan University in May 1975.

[67] Quoted by Davies, p. 270.

[68] Quoted by Maud Sellers, 'The City of York in the Sixteenth Century,' *English Historical Review* 9 (1894) 285.

[69] See Karl Young, *The Drama of the Medieval Church* (Oxford: Clarendon Press, 1933) 2:14-15.

[70] Hendrik Cornell, *The Iconography of the Nativity of Christ*, Uppsala Universitets Årsskrift (Uppsala, 1924) 12-13.

[71] Oscar G. Farmer, *Fairford Church and Its Stained Glass Windows*, 8th ed. (1968) 9.

[72] See especially M. D. Anderson, *Drama and Imagery in English Churches* (Cambridge: Cambridge Univ. Press, 1963) and W. L. Hildburgh, 'English Alabaster Carvings as Records of the Medieval Religious Drama,' *Archaeologia* 93 (1955) 51-101.

[73] Lawrence J. Ross, 'Art and the Study of Early English Drama,' *Research Opportunities in Renaissance Drama* 6 (1963) 35-46.

[74] This analogy is derived from Ferdinand de Saussure's comparison of language and a chess game as summarized in Susan Wittig, 'The Historical Development of Structuralism,' *Soundings* 58 (1975) 146-7.

MARTIN LUTHER: LANGUAGE AND
DEVOTIONAL CONSCIOUSNESS

BIBLIOGRAPHY

Works of Martin Luther

Editions

D. Martin Luther's Werke (Weimarer Ausgabe), edd. J. C. F. Knaabe et al. Weimar, 1883-

Translations

Luther's Works, 54 vols., ed. Jaroslav Pelikan. Philadelphia, 1952-
Library of Christian Classics, vols. 15-18.
Selected Writings of Martin Luther, 4 vols., ed. T. G. Tappert. 1967.

Studies

R. L. Bainton, *Here I Stand: A Life of Martin Luther.* 1950.

Abbreviations

LW   *Luther's Works,* ed. Pelikan.

RAP   *Regula Sancti Augustini Prima.*

RAS   *Regula Sancti Augustini Secunda,* ed. R. Arbesmann-Humptner
      in *Liber Vitasfratrum.* New York, 1943.

WA   Weimarer Ausgabe

NOTES

[1] LW 43:336f.

[2] Heiko A. Oberman, 'Headwaters of the Reformation,' *Luther and
the Dawn of the Modern Era* (Leiden, 1974) 74f. The most extensive
work remains that of Theodor Kolde, *Das religiose Leben in Erfurt beim
Ausgange des Mittelalters* (Halle, 1898), and idem, *Die deutsche
Augustiner-Congregation und Johann von Staupitz* (Gotha, 1879). See
also Ernst Wolf, *Stauptiz und Luther* (Leipzig, 1927); Robert Fischer,
'Paltz und Luther,' *Luther-Jahrbuch* 37 (1970), 9-36; Martin Elze, 'Das
Verständnis der Passion Jesu im ausgehenden Mittelalter und bei
Luther,' *Geist und Geschichte der Reformation* (Berlin, 1966) 127-151;
idem, 'Züge spätmittelalterlicher Frommigkeit in Luther's Theologie,'
Zeitschrift für Theologie und Kirche 62 (1965), 381-402; and the review
article by David Steinmetz, 'Luther and the Late Medieval
Augustinians: Another Look,' *Concordia Theological Monthly* (1973),
245-260.

[3] Much of this work is being done at the Institut für Spätmittelalter
und Reformationgeschichte in Tübingen, West Germany, under the
direction of Heiko A. Oberman. The manuscript sources have been identified by Adolar Zumkeller, *Manuskripte von Werken der Autoren des
Augustiner-Eremitenordens in mitteleuropaischen Bibliotheken* (Würzburg, 1966).

[4] A case in point is the portrait of monastic decline in the late Middle Ages sketched by G. G. Coulton, *Five Centuries of Religion* (Cambridge, 1929). See the historiographical discussion by Giles Constable,
'The Study of Monastic History Today,' *Essays on the Reconstruction of
Medieval History,* ed. by Vaclav Mudroch and G. S. Couse (Montreal,
1974) 21-51.

[5] See, for example, Wolf, *Stauptiz und Luther,* and the portrait of a disjointed Catholicism in the late Middle Ages by Joseph Lortz, *The Reformation in Germany,* 2 Vols. (New York, 1968).

[6] See the comments of Natalie Zemon Davis, 'Missed Connections: Religion and Regime,' *The Journal of Interdisciplinary History,* 1 (1971) 384f, and Bernd Moeller, 'Problems of Reformation Research,' *Imperial Cities and the Reformation* (Philadelphia, 1972) 3-16.

[7] These comments draw upon the methodological essays by J. G. A. Pocock, *Politics, Language and Time: Essays on Political Thought and History* (New York, 1973). See also Nancy Struever, 'The Study of Language and the Study of History,' *Journal of Interdisciplinary History* 4 (1974) 401-415.

[8] See especially Jean Leclercq, *The Love of Learning and the Desire for God* (New York, 1961); Amédée Hallier, *The Monastic Theology of Aelred of Rievaulx* (Spencer, Mass., 1969); M-D. Chenu, *Nature, Man and Society in the Twelfth Century* (Chicago, 1968).

[9] See Adolar Zumkeller, 'Die Augustinerschule des Mittelalters: Vertreter und Philosophisch-Theologische Lehre,' *Analecta Augustiniana* 27 (1964) 167-262, and idem, 'Die Lehrer des Geistlichen Lebens unter den deutschen Augustinern vom Dreizehnten Jahrhundert bis zum Konzil von Trent,' *Sanctus Augustinus: vitae spiritualis magister,* Vol. 2 (Rome, 1961) 239-338.

[10] See Giles Constable, 'Twelfth Century Spirituality and the Late Middle Ages,' *Medieval and Renaissance Studies* 5 (1971) 27-60, and the survey by F. Vandenbroucke in *The Spirituality of the Middle Ages, A History of Christian Spirituality,* Vol. 2 (London, 1968) 223-543.

[11] Leclercq, *The Love of Learning,* 33-56, and idem, 'From St Gregory to St Bernard,' *The Spirituality of the Middle Ages,* Vol. 2 (London, 1968) 5-28.

[12] Giles Constable, 'The Popularity of Twelfth Century Spiritual Writers in the Late Middle Ages,' *Renaissance Studies in Honor of Hans Baron* (DeKalb, Ill., 1971) 5-28.

[13] See Damasus Trapp, 'Augustinian Theology of the Fourteenth Century,' *Augustiniana* 6 (1956) 146-274.

[14] On the context of this literature, David Knowles makes the following comment: 'It is clear beyond all doubt that the monastic life was primarily a liturgical one: a life of the service of God by vocal prayer, chant and ceremony. . . . Too few, it may be, of those who endeavour to reconstruct the mentality of the monks of this period make adequate allowance for the influence of the monuments and treasures of spiritual doctrines which were present in the round of every day's life.' *The Monastic Order in England* (Cambridge, 1963) 452.

[15] The literature upon which the following is based includes: Candidus, 'De Passione Domini,' PL 106, 59-102; Aelred of Rievaulx, 'De Institutione Inclusarum,' and ''De Jesu Puero Duodenni,' in *Aelredi Rievalensis Opera Ascetica* Corpus Christianorum. (Turnholt, 1971); Jordon of Quedlinburg, *Meditationes De Passione Domini* (Basel, 1492);

Ludolphus of Saxony, *Vita Christi* (Antwerp, 1637); Simon Fidati of Cascia, *De Gestis Domini Salvatoris* (Basel, 1517); Pseudo-Bonaventura, *Meditationes vitae Christi,* English translation by Isa Raguse, *Meditations on the Life of Christ* (Princeton, 1961). A more detailed analysis of these works and their significance for late medieval monasticism may be found in my dissertation, 'Luther, The Cloister, and the Language of Monastic Devotion,' (Dissertation, Washington University, 1972) 93-169. For surveys of this literature, see René Aigrain, 'Quelques "Vies de Jesus," ' *Le Christ: Encyclopédie populaire des connaissances Christologiques* (Paris, 1952) 1119-1149; Barbara Kiefer Lewalski, *Milton's Brief Epic* (Providence, 1966) 37-67; Hans Rupprich, *Die Deutsche Literatur vom späten Mittelalter bis zum Barock,* Vol. 1 (Munich, 1970) 88-106, 239-272.

[16] For a definition of epic literature in these terms, see Erik Havelock, *Preface to Plato* (Cambridge, 1963), and the comments on the 'historico-political function' of the medieval epic by Erich Auerbach, *Mimesis: The Representation of Reality in Western Literature* (New York, 1953) 83-107.

[17] See especially Joseph Jungmann's discussion of late medieval piety in *Pastoral Liturgy* (New York, 1962) 1-101.

[18] Johannes Paltz, *Celifodina* (Erfurt, 1502). See Fischer, *Paltz und Luther,* and Zumkeller, 'Die Lehrer,' 317f.

[19] Johannes Paltz, *Die himmlische Fundgrube* (Augsburg, [b]501).

[20] *Johannis Staupitii Opera,* Vol. 1, ed. by I. Knaake (Potsdam, 1867) 52-88.

[21] Ibid., 62.

[22] Simon Fidate of Cascia, *De Gestis Domini:* 'Post Christi doctrinem quae in eius deificis moribus et supernaturali vita et gestibus nobis monstrata est . . . ad simplicem et verbalem (verbis humanis nostris non gestis ipsius Christi configuratam) doctrinam humili studio veniamus. Et tantum verba tractantes quae manifeste vitam moralem atque christianam informant et expressam et imitabilem veritatem ostendunt.' 427v. Ludolphus of Saxony, *Vita Christi:* 'Sic etiam ipsam vita Christi legat, ut mores eius pro posse imitari studeat. Parum enim prodest si legerit: nisi et imitatus fuerit.' 1.

[23] The following passage is typical: 'Inspice exemplar dominicae passionis, ipsam tibi per imtimam compassionem visceraliter incorporando, et fac secundum illud exemplar, ipsum efficaciter imitando.' *Vita Christi,* 570r. Simon Fidate states his purpose as follows: 'Cum principaliter nostrae intentionis existat, primo interiorem hominem in Christiana vita et doctrina perficere: secundo exteriorem in Christianicis agibilibus coaptare, in quibus praestante altissimo, intermissus servabitur ordo.' *De Gestis Domino,* 1.

[24] See Henri de Lubac, *The Sources of Revelation* (New York, 1968) 1-84; James Walsh, 'William of Saint Thierry and Spiritual Meanings,' *Revue d'ascétique et de mystique* 35 (1959) 27-42; and my 'From

Allegory to Metaphor: More Notes on Luther's Hermeneutical Shift,'
Harvard Theological Review 66 (1973) 386-395.

[25] The notion of 'mechanisms of traditionality' is drawn from Edward Shils, 'Tradition,' *Comparative Studies in Society and History* 13 (1971) 122-159.

[26] The Augustinian rule closes as follows: 'Ut autem vos in hoc libello tamquam in speculo possitis inspicere, ne per oblivionem aliquid negligatis, semel in septimana vobis legatur.' The text of the Augustinian rules may be found in *Liber Vitasfratrum*, ed. R. Arbesmann-Humptner (New York, 1943) 491-504.

[27] For a discussion of the ceremonial in late medieval Augustinian cloisters, see Kolde, *Die deutsche Augustiner-Congregation.* See also Jean Leclercq, 'The Poem of the Liturgy,' *The Love of Learning,* 232-249.

[28] *RAP,* 9: 'Otiosum verbum apud illos non sit. A mane ad opera sua sedeant, post orationes tertiae eant similiter ad opera sua; non stantes fabulas contexant, nisi forte aliquid sit pro animae utilitate, Sedentes ad opera taceant, nisi forte necessitas operis exegerit, ut loquatur quis.'

[29] This is clearly indicated, for example, in the Prologue to *Meditations on the Life of Christ:* 'I shall attempt to overcome my inadequacy and speak to you in a familiar manner, in a rough and unpolished sermon, so that you may better understand what is said, not that the ear may be pleased but that the mind may seek to be filled. For one should be diligent not in ornate sermons but in the contemplation of our Lord Jesus. . . . However, you must not believe that all things said and done by Him on which we may meditate are known to us in writing. For the sake of greater impressiveness I shall tell them to you as they occurred or as they might have occurred according to the devout belief of the imagination and the varying interpretation of the mind. . . . And if you wish to profit you must be present at the same things that it is related that Christ did and said, joyfully and rightly, leaving behind all other cares and anxieties.' For broader discussions of this point, see H. Chaytor, *From Script to Print: An Introduction to Medieval Literature* (Cambridge, 1945); Richard Scholes and Richard Kellogg, *The Nature of Narrative* (New York, 1968) 3-56; Jan Vansina, *Oral Tradition* (Chicago, 1965); Michael Curschman, 'Oral Poetry in Medieval English, French, and German Literature: Some Notes on Recent Research,' *Speculum* 42 (1967) 36-52.

[30] Paltz, *Die himmlische Fundgrube,* 4f.

[31] Leclercq, *The Love of Learning,* 23. 'What does this [*lectio divina*] consist of? How is this reading done? . . . in the Middle Ages, as in antiquity, they read usually, not as today, principally with the eyes, but with the lips, pronouncing what they say, and with the ears, listening to the words pronounced, hearing what is called the "voices of the pages." It is a real acoustical reading; *legere* means at the same time *audire*; one understands only what one hears . . . when *legere* and *lectio* are used without further explanation, they mean an activity which, like chant and

writing, requires the participation of the whole body and the whole mind.'

[32] See Adalbert de Vogüé, *La communauté et l'abbé dans la regle de saint Benoît* (Paris, 1960); M. Thiel, 'Der Ordnungsgedanke in der Règel des hl. Benedikt,' *Studia Benediktina* (Rome, 1947).

[33] RB 43, 13.

[34] RAP 6.

[35] RB 2, 11-12.

[36] RAS 11.

[37] David Knowles, *From Pachomius to Ignatius. A Study in the Constitutional History of the Religious Orders* (Oxford, 1966) 76.

[38] Note, for example, the parallel of social order and *imitatio Christi* piety in the advice of Bernard: 'Are you unaware that obedience is better than sacrifice? Have you not read in your rule that what is done without the permission of the spiritual father shall be ascribed to presumption and vainglory and not reckoned meritorious? Have you not read in the Gospel the example of obedience given by the boy Jesus as a way to holiness?' *On the Song of Songs,* Sermon *The Works of Bernard of Clairvaux,* Vol. 2 (Spencer, Mass., 1971) 145.

[39] Translated from David Curtis Steinmetz, *Misericordia Dei. The Theology of Johannes von Staupitz in its Late Medieval Setting* (Leiden, 1968) 139.

[40] For a discussion of the transformation in Luther's thought of 1518, see especially Ernst Bizer, *Fides ex auditu. Eine Untersuchung über die Entdeckung der Gerechtigkeit Gottes durch Martin Luther* (Neukirchen, 1966); Oswald Bayer, *Promissio: Geschichte der reformatorischen Wende in Luthers Theologie* (Göttingen, 1971); Edward F. Cranz, *An Essay on the Development of Luther's Thought on Justice, Law, and Society* (Cambridge, Mass., 1959). A critique of Bizer's presentation may be found by Heinrich Bornkamm, 'Zur Frage der *Iustitia Dei* beim jungen Luther,' *Archive for Reformation History* 52 (1961) 16ff. and 53 (1962) 1ff.

[41] The language and concerns of the Augustinian rule are reflected, for example, in the letter Luther wrote in 1516 to the Augustinian cloister in Neustadt: 'You live without peace and unity. You live in one house, but you are not of one mind, and you are not of one heart and one soul in the Lord, as required by the rule (. . . sit vobis anima una et cor unum in Deo. *RAS* I).' *LW* 31, 20.

[42] Hecker's letter about Luther is printed in *Zeitschrift für Kirchengeschichte* 2 (1879) 476-478; see also Wilhelm Borth, *Die Luthersache, 1517-1524: Die Anfänge der Reformation als Frage von Politik und Recht* (Hamburg, 1970) 39f., and Walter Delius, 'Der Augustiner Eremitenorden im Prozess Luthers,' *Archive for Reformation History* 63 (1972) 22-42.

[43] See especially Luther's sermon in 1514: *In Natali Christi,* WA 1:20-29.

[44] WA 1:23.

[45] In the preface to his early psalms lectures, Luther wrote: 'Omnis prophetia et omnis propheta de Christo domino debet intelligi, nisi ubi manifestis verbis appareat de alio loqui. . . . Quiequid de domino Ihesu Christo in persona sua ad literam dicitur, hoc ipsum allegorice: de adiutorio sibi simili et ecclesia sibi in omnibus conformi debet intelligi. Idemque simil tropologice debet intelligi, de quolibet spirituali et interiori homine: contra suam carnem et exteriorem hominem.' *WA* 55, I. 1. 6f. See Gerhard Ebeling, 'Luthers Psalterdruck von Jahre 1513,' *Zeitschrift für Theologie und Kirche* 50 (1953) 43-99.

[46] *WA* 56: 137f. Compare this passage from Ludolphus of Saxony: 'Toto itaque vita eius in terris . . . disciplina morum fuit . . . omnis Christi actio, est nostra instructio. Item abibi habemus de passione Domini, exemplum enim dedi vobus ut ita faciatis.' *Vita Christi,* 4.

[47] *WA* 1:337.

[48] *WA* 1:336.20: 'If Christ dwells in a man, how can he not weep when Christ weeps (*complorare*), not feel pain when he feels pain (*condolere*), not fear when he fears (*contremere*), not suffer when he suffers (*compati*). A spiritual man should rejoice with the happy and weep with the grieving, be in prison with the imprisoned and wounded with the wounded, suffer with the suffering; he should feel every human emotion as his own; and where else should one learn these things . . . than beside the cross of Jesus.'

[49] *WA* 1:233: 'Dominus et magister noster Iesus Christus dicendo "Penitentiam agite," etc., omnem vitam fidelium penitentiam esse voluit. . . . Non tamen solam intendit interiorem, immo interior nulla est, nisi foris operetur varias carnis mortificationes.'

[50] Luther opens his psalms commentary from 1519 with this: 'Sed primo grammatica videamus, verum ea theologica,' and goes on to distinguish his new method from the traditional allegory: 'Non autem allegoricum dico more recentiorum, quasi alius sensus historialis sub eo sit quaerendus, quam qui dictus est, sed quod verum et proprium sensum figurate locutione expresserit.' *WA* 5:27.8 and 51.36. See F. Beisser, *Claritas Scripturae bei Martin Luther* (Göttingen, 1966).

[51] See the discussion of the *promissio* theme in Luther by James S. Preus, *From Shadow to Promise. Old Testament Interpretation from Augustine to the Young Luther* (Cambridge, Mass., 1969), and Oswald Bayer, *Promissio.*

[52] *LW* 31:357.

[53] *LW* 31:98f.

[54] *WA BR* 8:571.31.

JOHN CALVIN: INGRAFTING IN CHRIST

BIBLIOGRAPHY

Works of John Calvin

Editions

Ioannis Calvini Opera quae supersunt omnia, edd. G. Baum, E. Cunitz, E. Reuss,et al., 59 vols., Corpus Reformatorum vols. 29-77. Braunschweig, 1963-1900.

Supplementa Calviana, ed. E. Muhlhaupt. 1961-

Translations

Institutes of the Christian Religion, tr. John Allen, 8th American ed., rev. and corr., 2 vols. Grand Rapids, 1949.

The Institutes of the Christian Religion, ed. J. T. McNeill, tr. F. L. Battles. 1960.

The Library of Christian Classics, vols. 20-21: *Institutes,* vols. 22-23: *Theological Treatises and Commentaries.*

John Calvin, Selections from his Writings, ed. John Dillenberger, 4 vols. 1971.

Studies

Dowey, Edward A., Jr. *The Knowledge of God in Calvin's Theology.* New York, 1952.

Richard, Lucien J., *The Spirituality of John Calvin.* Atlanta: John Knox Press, 1974.

Abbreviations

CO   *Ioannis Calvini Opera quae supersunt omnia.*

Inst.   *Institutes of the Christian Religion,* cited from the Allen edition.

NOTES

[1] Mircea Eliade, *Rites and Symbols of Initiation,* New York, 1965, p. 132.

[2] M. Eliade, *The Sacred and the Profane,* New York, 1961, pp. 10 f.

[3] Ibid., p. 202.

[4] Rm 8:3-6, 9, 11, 16-17, 28-30.

[5] Inst. I, 1, 1.

[6] Dedication of Calvin's Institutes to King Francis of France, *Institutes of the Christian Religion,* transl. John Allen, 2 vols., Eighth rev. edition, Grand Rapids, 1949, p. 20.

[7] Inst. I, 2, 1.

[8] Comm. II Tim. 3:16; CO 52:383.

[9] Edward A. Dowey, Jr., *The Knowledge of God in Calvin's Theology* (New York, 1952) p. 91.

[10] Inst. I, 7, 5.

[11] Inst. I, 7, 4.

[12] Inst. I, 7, 5.
[13] Ibid.
[14] Inst. I, 9, 3.
[15] Inst. I, 9, 1.
[16] W. Niesel, *Die Theologie Calvins* (München, 1957) p. 38.
[17] *The Westminster Confession of Faith,* chapter I, art. 5, quoted in Ph. Schaff, *The Creeds of Christendom,* 4th ed. (New York, 1931) 3:603.
[18] Inst. III, 2, 6.
[19] Ibid.
[20] Ibid.
[21] Inst. III, 2, 30.
[22] Inst. III, 2, 6.
[23] Inst. III, 2, 7.
[24] Ibid.
[25] Inst III, 2, 29.
[26] Ibid.
[27] Ibid.
[28] Comm. John 3:16; CO 47,64.
[29] Comm. John 14:1; CO 47.321, 322.
[30] Comm. Eph. 3:12; CO 51.183.
[31] Inst. III, 2, 6.
[32] Ibid.
[33] Ibid.
[34] Cf. Dowey, p. 159.
[35] Inst. III, 2, 6.
[36] Inst. III, 2, 33.
[37] Inst. II, 2, 20.
[38] Ibid.
[39] Inst. III, 24, 2.
[40] Inst. III, 24, 1.
[41] Inst. III, 24, 8.
[42] Inst. II, 2, 19.
[43] Inst. III, 2, 33.
[44] Cf. Dowey, p. 181.
[45] Inst. III, 2, 33.
[46] Inst. III, 2, 16.
[47] Ibid.
[48] Inst. III, 2, 7.
[49] Inst. III, 2, 24.
[50] Ibid.
[51] Inst. III, 2, 30.
[52] Inst. III, 1, 3.
[53] Ibid.
[54] Inst. III, 2, 14.
[55] Ibid.
[56] Ibid.
[57] Ibid.

[58] Inst. II, 2, 19.
[59] Inst. III, 2, 34.
[60] Comm. Joh. 6:44; CO 47.12.
[61] Inst. III, 2, 24.
[62] Lucien J. Richard, *The Spirituality of John Calvin* (Atlanta, Ga., John Knox Press, 1974).
[63] Ibid., p. 106.
[64] Inst. III, 11, 23.
[65] Inst. III, 11, 3.
[66] Inst. III, 14, 17.
[67] Inst. III, 16, 1.
[68] Inst. III, 14, 8.
[69] Inst. III, 14, 9.
[70] Inst. III, 16, 1.
[71] Richard, p. 106.
[72] Inst. III, 6-10.
[73] Inst. III, 6, 2.
[74] Inst. III, 6, 3.
[75] Ibid.
[76] Inst. III, 2, 24.
[77] Inst. III, 11, 10.
[78] Inst. III, 1, 3.
[79] Inst. III, 6, 4.
[80] Ibid.
[81] Inst. IV, 17, 12.
[82] Inst. III, 6, 5.
[83] Ibid.
[84] Ibid.
[85] Inst. III, 9, 1.
[86] Inst. III, 10, 1.
[87] Inst. III, 10, 3.
[88] Inst. III, 9, 3 and 4.
[89] Apart from Thomas à Kempis' *Imitation of Christ,* this is also true of the *Devotio Moderna* it seems to me—contrary to the view of Lucien Richard, p. 125. Gerhard Groote, the founder of the Modern Devotion, left his Carthusian monastery to devote his life to the service of God in the apostolate.
[90] Inst. III, 10, 6.
[91] See the two best known social interpretations of Calvin: Max Weber, *The Protestant Ethic and the Spirit of Calvinism* (London, 1930), and Ernst Troeltsch, *The Social Teaching of the Christian Churches,* 2 vols. (London, 1949).